MASTER VIRTUE, MASTER SELLING

MASTER VIRTUE, MASTER SELLING

AN INNOVATIVE AND AUTHORITATIVE COMPANION TO THE **LEAD** PERSONALITY PROFILE PROGRAM FOR SELLING

BILL WILSON

Copyright © 2022 by Bill Wilson. All rights reserved.

This book, or parts thereof, may not be produced in any form without permission from the publisher; exceptions are made for excerpts used in printed reviews and other media-related materials as long as proper attribution is made.

ISBN 978-0-578-33951-1 (hardcover)

ISBN 978-0-578-33952-8 (ebook)

Printed in the United States of America

First Printing

10 9 8 7 6 5 4 3 2 1

Contents

Foreword ix
Acknowledgments xi
Introduction ix

CHAPTER 1

Red Personalities   1

Red: A Nonstarter 1
About *Not for OCS* 5
The *Preparer* Candidate 10
If You Were Profiled as a *Preparer* 19

CHAPTER 2

Orange Personalities   21

The *Sensitive* Candidate 24
If You Were Profiled as a *Sensitive* 27
Questions for Someone with a *Sensitive* Personality 28
The Six Global Interview Questions 28
The Interview Questions Specific to a *Sensitive* Personality 31
A Manager's 30-Day Assessment of the *Sensitive* Personality 33
The Candidate with *Inconsistencies* 37
Understanding True Fulfillment 41

Repurpose Honest Inconsistencies into Productive Change	46
If You Were Profiled with *Inconsistencies*	47
Questions for Someone Who Profiled with *Inconsistencies*	48
The *Soloist* Candidate	51
If You Were Profiled as a *Soloist*	53
Questions for Someone with a *Soloist* Personality	54
The *Professional* Candidate	57
If You Were Profiled as a *Professional*	60
Questions for Someone with a *Professional* Personality	61

CHAPTER 3

Yellow Personalities 63

The *Willful* Candidate	68
Comparing the Yellow Willful and the Green Persistent (Stage 5)	72
How a Willful Person Can Become Persistent	73
If You Were Profiled as *Willful*	81
Questions for Someone with a *Willful* Personality	82
The *Respectful* Candidate	85
If You Were Profiled as *Respectful*	94
Questions for Someone with a *Respectful* Personality	95
The *Instinctive* Candidate	99
If You Were Profiled as *Instinctive*	102
Questions for Someone with an *Instinctive* Personality	102
If You Were Profiled as a *Potential*	107
Questions for Someone Who Profiled as a *Potential*	108
The *Activist* Candidate	111
If You Were Profiled as an *Activist*	116
Questions for Someone with an *Activist* Personality	117
The *Novice* Candidate	119
If You Were Profiled as a *Novice*	131
Questions for Someone Who Profiled as a *Novice*	132
The *Idealist* Candidate	135

If You Were Profiled as an *Idealist*	137
Questions for Someone with an *Idealist* Personality	138

Green Personalities: Introduction to the Five Stages 139

Awareness Comes First	140
The Destruction of Good Company Culture	140
In the Big Picture, Virtue and Process Will Beat Instinct	142
The Five Green Personality Profiles: A Road Map	144
The Five Stages of Green	146

CHAPTER 4

Green Personalities: Stages 1 and 2 149

GREEN STAGE 1	149
The *Demonstrative* Candidate	151
If You Were Profiled as *Demonstrative*	168
Questions for Someone with a *Demonstrative* Personality	168
GREEN STAGE 2	169
The *Advantageous* Candidate	171
If You Were Profiled as *Advantageous*	188
Questions for Someone with an *Advantageous* Personality	189

CHAPTER 5

Green Personalities: Stage 3 191

GREEN STAGE 3	191
The *Serious* (Selling Maturity) Candidate	194
Part 1: Developing Self-Determination and Self-Governance	196
Part 2: Developing Sound Judgment Based on Core-Belief Thinking	218
Part 3: Growing with an Open Mindset and Transferable Practices	250

Online Interview	279
If You Were Profiled as *Serious*	286
Questions for Someone with a *Serious* Personality	287

CHAPTER 6

Green Personalities: Stages 4 and 5 289

GREEN STAGE 4	289
The *Influencer* Candidate	292
If You Were Profiled as an *Influencer*	300
Questions for Someone with an *Influencer* Personality	301
GREEN STAGE 5	302
The *Persistent* Candidate	305
If You Were Profiled as *Persistent*	317
Questions for Someone with a *Persistent* Personality	318
Final Thoughts	318
Index	321

Foreword

I've known Bill Wilson for more than 30 years, and I feel blessed to have him as a friend. I was excited when he told me that he had plans to write a book, and equally excited to get a chance to read it myself. In every respect, Bill is a master of the art of sales and not just from personal experience, although he has plenty of that. He possesses a deep understanding of how to read people, spot the champions, and motivate them to become superstars.

Like myself, Bill came from a humble upbringing raised by a single parent. When we first met, we were in the music business, and like Bill I was an aspiring entrepreneur with an interest in acquiring the skills necessary for success. When we talked, we would talk for hours.

Bill built a company called Peoples Products, and many years ago, when I visited his office, he invited me to go with him on a sales call. As I watched him talking with his prospective customer, I thought, "This guy is great, and if I just shut up and pay attention, I could learn something." Since then, my respect for Bill Wilson has grown exponentially.

He has become not only a great friend but also a person who understands how to create a sales force to grow a business. And he does it all with the most positive outlook one can imagine.

When Bill sent me his first manuscript, there was a problem. Bill is too smart! He included so much, and it was so sophisticated, I was afraid the reader would get overwhelmed. Thus, I made some suggestions, and Bill ran with them. The result is the book you hold in your hands, and it really is a gem.

Bill has honed and quantified his extensive years of experience and distilled the key traits to becoming a super seller, a champion in sales, and a champion in team building. Like most great books, this is one you will likely read several times. *Master Virtue, Master Selling* is a deep dive and powerful.

If you want to understand selling in the most comprehensive and useful way, this is your book, and Bill is your man.

Enjoy, learn, and prosper.

Mark Minervini
Four-time international best-selling author

Acknowledgments

First and foremost, I want to thank my family for their support in this and in every other endeavor in which I've chosen to involve myself. It's not always easy to be around someone needing to be hyperfocused on something, such as writing this book, but, man, it is appreciated! Thanks to my wife, Jane; daughters Sydney and Haley; sons Bill and Dylan; and son-in-law, Shariq Dean. They are all amazing people who've shown me love and inspired my life.

Trying to acknowledge everyone who deserves to be mentioned is impossible. There are so many wonderful friends, family, and coworkers who mean the world to me, I simply cannot name them all. I would, however, like to acknowledge a few people who inspired me in the writing of this book. They are, in no particular order, Jeff Batter, Tom Morris, Greg Dardick, Tom Dardick, Jay Escudero, Mike Galante, Wayne Jones, Rob Fried, Brad Bishop, Tony Hoty, Michael Keiser, Maria Visci Keiser, Neil Imbimbo, Mike Bryce, Jeff Pitchell, John Anglis, Darrin McGuire, Chuck Wetmore, Mark Curry, Sue Laydon, Kristal Murren, Mark Deluzio, and Robert Quillen.

I would like to offer a very special thank-you to my friend Mark Minervini, a successful best-selling author in his own right, without whom this book might not have seen the light of day. His encouragement to push through and keep going (especially when it seemed it would never be completed) was tremendously helpful in keeping me focused and diligent in this effort.

To my editor, Kathleen Becker Blease, thank you! Your focus and your talent were immeasurable. You are amazing.

A very Special thanks to Patricia Wallenburg, Judy Duguid, David Johnstone, and WordCo Indexing Services for all the great work and care they put into copy editing, proofreading, and indexing. It was a great pleasure to have worked with you all.

I would like to thank the many people who agreed to be profiled for the LEAD Personality Profile Program research. Studying behavior is a deep dive, and those who helped bring it through the beta version and onto the final presentation of the profile (available at myleadprofile.com) provided an invaluable service and benefit to this work.

Finally, I would like to thank the many people who have been encouraging to me personally—from my family to my friends, and personal and professional relationships. When people believe in you, you are immediately uplifted by their support. I can count on more people than I'm sure I deserve who do that for me. I thank you more than you can know!

Bill Wilson

Introduction

Honesty sells. Trust sells. And to sell is to serve.

If you think that hard-core overpromising and pushy selling are the marks of a seasoned salesperson, think again. Times have changed, and so have consumers. More than ever, the world resides in every phone, making instantly accessible to even the most ordinary prospective customer a tally of product and service features and price comparisons . . . along with in-depth personal reviews and a ton of social media opinions. It's very much like living in a small town again. Everyone knows, in one way or another, everyone else and what each of us is doing. It's hard to ignore that with today's technology and culture, honesty, trust, and transparency are quickly coming back in style—thank goodness!

Today, being truly you is the most effective way to work with a purpose and to live a fulfilling life and career.

Thus, this book isn't just about selling, in and of itself. Front and center, the message of *Master Virtue, Master Selling* is about people—the people in sales. Simply put, it's about you—a genuine you selling, and selling well. Think of this: If your company has the best product, or the best service, and offers the best value, who wins? The customer who invests in it wins. Wouldn't you like to serve and honor more people by bringing them the best product that's clearly presented by the best you?

Maybe you're a hiring manager who is charged with finding talent and developing a strong sales force. Maybe you're a sales trainer who is tired and discouraged by a high employee turnover. Or maybe you're the salesperson who, like your supervisors, wonders if there's a better way to succeed in what we can call the "selling industry." Indeed, I'm here to share with you a better path that's designed for both the manager at the office and the salesperson who's out in the field, for both the novice and the seasoned professional.

And by the way, quite frankly, wherever you are in the experience factor, the learning should never stop. Every good thing is forever a work in progress, and the salespeople who have the most successful sales record—and the longevity—are lifelong learners. They are also trustworthy, considerate and kind, and conversational, and they have consciously developed the heart of a servant.

Yet, interestingly, with everything that master salespeople have in common, they also come in different packages, different personalities. Some are soloists and professional in nature, while others are demonstrative and people-oriented. They can be willful or sensitive, idealists or instinctive, or anywhere in between. But at the apex of their selling profession, they all have one thing in common: Step by step, they've learned how to tame their excesses (we'll get into those in later pages) and dial into their personal virtues (which is what this book is all about). Then, they present sales presentations as themselves—their truest selves—and honorably serve their client by selling.

Virtues—we all have them. Yet they often go unnurtured, and most of us can sense that something's missing. Enter *Master Virtue, Master Selling.* Coupled with the LEAD Personality Profile Program, this book is designed to take you step by step into the core of virtuous master selling. And what's at the core? A chemistry. It's a unique relationship between your personality type and your mindset. Behaving in virtue or not, it's in your mindset where your personality traits have found traction over the years and have taken you to where you are now. They will also take you to where you will go . . . and how far.

In the past few years, I've studied the behavior of salespeople who are all across the personality spectrum. And the outcome is interesting. Some persons looked impressive by conventional standards and seemed like shoo-ins for sales positions, but failed. Others had great challenges and looked far from what you might consider winning sales personalities, yet made it. I've learned that, ultimately, if hiring managers are using their gut feelings to predict who stands the best chance at succeeding, they're rolling the dice. And just how effective can that be? If you're the hiring manager, how much of your energy and investment come up a loss as different personalities walk in and out the door? And if you're the salesperson, how is your company connecting with you, understanding what you personally need in order to rise to the challenge of making quality sales that stick and building a lucrative career?

Consider this: Companies spend obscene amounts of time and money trying to attract the right sales candidates. According to CloserIQ, depending on the recruitment process, a single hire might cost $25,000 or more to train. And the *Harvard Business Review* stated that U.S. companies spend more than $70 billion annually on training, at an average of $1,459 per salesperson. Those using a proven hiring and training strategy do the best.

Of course, others get lucky once in a while, but it's hard to repeat that luck often enough to gain the traction that's necessary for growth and development. And a good many companies are stuck where they are because of a hole in their structure, which usually looks like one or more (or all!) of these:

- Not understanding how to hire the right salespeople with an efficient and revealing process. According to a 2018 study from the Sales Management Association, "Sixty-two percent of companies consider themselves ineffective at onboarding new sales hires."
- Suffering the syndrome of about-facing through the lack of a highly structured process, turning excited sales interviewees into lazy hires. By sending the wrong messages to new

employees by not showing them what to do, or how and when, companies decrease those employees' drive without even knowing it.
- Wrangling between the management and sales force, a common company culture issue.
- Companies not developing strong enough core-belief thinking in the minds of their salespeople, i.e., about the good their product or service brings to the prospect, should they become a customer.
- Not reviewing important selling metrics on a consistent basis. This leads to creating big chasms between what's expected and what's actualized and defaulting to bottom-line results, which are unreliable. And when tracking such information, it leads to not seeing the story that the numbers tell.
- Regularly falling short of stated selling goals. It's bad for growing a career or a business. The lack of a planning strategy defaults to an unpredictable reality. We are then rudderless and lost.
- Not being able to even incrementally increase the output level of a salesperson. It fosters a feeling of being stuck in the mud once the basics are learned, and there's no advanced output.

According to a *Forbes* article, up to 55% of salespeople lack basic sales skills. Yet it's sales professionals who bring essential and vital products and services to the general population. Just imagine if that statistic could be said about doctors or firefighters. How scary would that be?

The Perspective of the Hiring Manager— It's for Everyone

As we move through the pages of this book, I often speak to the concerns of a hiring manager or a sales trainer, but I'd like to state something important up front: If you're a team member not yet involved in management, don't consider glossing over these materials to get right to the pages that seem particularly pertinent to you—because, in fact, it *all* pertains to you. Understand both sides of the coin. A team member who succeeds at selling, after all, will most likely be called upon one day to step up to a teaching or coaching position to bring up new talent into a process of sales that are quality and consistent, adding to the bottom line that drives a company both now and securely into the future. Wherever you are on the spectrum of sales teaming—a junior member, a veteran salesperson with a list of consistent sales numbers, or the manager who's advancing as a leader—the entire breadth of this book's discussion on sales perfection indeed pertains to your personality.

What We Will Cover in This Introduction

Throughout this Introduction, we'll cover the following:

- How to look at hiring from the hiring manager's point of view
- Why our personalities run deep with early roots
- Why our nature can be in or out of control
- Why a new level of thinking can change everything
- Why the right path is imperative
- What is revealed in the LEAD Personality Profile
- How to engineer a new outcome

As with all job performances, the journey begins with the hire.

Looking at Hiring from the Hiring Manager's Point of View

Due to the drive of the daily grind, it's beneficial to maximize your making the right hiring decisions in the least amount of time. It would help grow your business in an orderly way, while avoiding some chaos.

You need a plan and a change in the way you think. Same thinking means same results, again. Different thinking means different results—and growth.

By understanding up front a little more about the people you hire, you can better avoid the problem brought on by a non-virtuous hire to begin with.

Hiring Failures

If you're like most people, you probably think you can tell when someone has that certain panache to be a good salesperson—the one who is outgoing and always laughing, slapping backs, and telling stories. I'll bet you think, like most people, "That's the person we need to hire!"

Yet many companies that have based their hiring on similar criteria have found it turned out much differently than they had expected. If finding happy-go-lucky salespeople is your strategy, you won't get very far. Premade talents that work in virtue, dialed into great process-driven techniques, *are not a dime a dozen*. People like that are developed, not found.

Perhaps you've experienced hiring people who seemed promising, but soon after, they were lost in the shuffle. They encountered difficulty selling, and you came in just a little too late. The signs were there, but you missed them; the metrics weren't being properly tracked and discussed. As a result, another person with potential was gone too soon because you didn't have a good enough plan. And once that ship sinks, it's all but impossible to retrieve. When important key indicators are ignored for even a short time, salespeople become disconnected and harder to reach.

Successful selling requires a quality process and a mindset that's committed to following it. Yet according to the technology company Mediafly, 27% of companies do not offer any type of sales onboarding program to new hires. That's a disturbing statistic! When salespeople are not given proper attention or are mishandled, they more easily dismiss the importance of following the process. And it's unfortunate that many companies (and salespeople) don't even know the difference between a truly great training program and one that's poorly designed. When salespeople sense that managers are making up the rules as they go along, those salespeople slowly lose respect for their employers. And typically, a company has no more than three months to rent space in the heads of new hires before they quit. If the company is not engaged in the mindset development of its sales staff early on, it might as well replace its front door with a turnstile. When that happens, do you chalk it up to "them" not getting it?

If you'd noticed what was going on earlier, you'd have stood a better chance at making it work. It is important to see when salespeople are in decline *while* it's happening—and critical to catch it before the enervation is in free fall. When you use a process that tells you the right kind of information, those things are less likely to happen and are much easier to fix.

But first, a primary focus should be placed on the question of whether you are recruiting the right people, the right personalities. You need good information to avoid regretful hiring.

The Right Recruits

In the chapters that follow, we'll focus on understanding more about who these sales candidates are. We'll cover how they think and how to rein in any excess to ready them for better performance. (By "excess," I mean any characteristic of someone's personality that's become a bit out of control.) Then, we'll focus on how to prepare your chosen hires to learn the five nonnegotiable stages of development required to become great at selling. These stages not only are transferable but need to be internalized and committed to as *core-belief thinking*—a mindset that's a powerful force.

Using the LEAD Personality Profile Program

Of course, every individual has a unique personality, and yet there are similarities in people that are nuanced. That's what makes hiring so difficult. This is where the LEAD Personality Profile Program comes in. The LEAD Personality Profile Program contemplates four areas of concentration that, when combined, make up a person's selling personality. LEAD is an acronym for *leadership, extroversion, attitude,* and *disposition*. We delve into the LEAD Personality Profile Program in more detail below, but for now know that it helps you to identify a little more information about a selling candidate, so you'll have a better starting point at the interview and, if they're brought on board, at the hire and the first 30 days and beyond.

To be clear, not all things that make up a personality are inherently good or bad. It's only when certain traits are pulled to an excessive level that people become out of control or unreasonable. And if you are a hiring manager, you might find it hard to decipher the *true* personality of the candidates you are interviewing. Applicants are consciously at their best while interviewing, so a natural read is more difficult. What's worse, you might be the last one to realize your mistake.

Ask yourself if you think you have been getting it right. Are the people you've been hiring turning out the way you thought they would? You can only measure how well you're doing by the results you're getting. If you are currently hiring the right people, and they are working out gloriously, you probably have a good sense of how it's done. But for many, that's just not the case. According to *Forbes*, 97% of weak salespeople lack the minimum required sales DNA for success in their roles. We believe that perhaps 50% of that is avoidable up front—with the right information.

With the LEAD Personality Profile Program, it's possible for a hiring manager to possess insight into candidates' traits—both empowering and limiting—which will affect how well they are *likely* to perform. Candidates' LEAD profiles will reveal their personality or classification, then place them in a color—Red, Orange, Yellow, or Green.

Each category offers information that, up until now, has never been a part of hiring or training calculations. By knowing the color (or colors) that salespeople possess and by embracing the meanings that are behind those colors—as this book explains—you will be on a clearer path to making more precise hiring decisions and developing the *right* staff.

Once hired, it's then critically important that your sales trainees know the exact steps to take in order to keep them focused, growing, and on path. They'll need the kind of engagement the LEAD program provides. By maximizing your standards for hiring—through defining personalities—and training those right candidates to develop into performing salespeople, you will begin to sow the seeds of growth.

So, what to do first? The first step is seeing a candidate's personality. Certain information will lend insight into whether a sales candidate is likely to follow your company's selling system, its process. It's only by following the process religiously that you'll be able to create an approach that has a *constancy to purpose,* which makes selling a more predictable science. It's important, therefore, to consider if a candidate's personality will naturally work with or against this.

Personalities Run Deep with Roots

Personalities vary greatly. Some are friendly, outgoing, and charming, while others are private, negative, and angry. There are even blends of both. Some aren't obvious and forthcoming, while others show themselves more easily.

Personality is said to be more important than looks. A great one can make someone with an average appearance seem very attractive. But unlike your looks, your personality is only partially genetic. When we were young and growing, we were sponges open to influence. Whether those influences in certain circumstances were positive or negative leaves an impression that's burned into our mindset, and from that, a personality is born.

Early Influencers

Our early influencers had a lot of impact on who we are today. I have a theory that a person's favorite color reminds the person of something that was comforting as a child. I like blue, and I think it's because I loved the feeling of looking at a blue sky. My wife loves yellow, which is probably because she connected youthful drawings of the yellow sun as a part of having a perfect beach day. She's a beach girl. One of my daughters loves green. I'm guessing it was from looking at fields of grass and finding serenity there. Have you ever noticed that most people never change their favorite color in life? Early influence is like the concrete in our foundation of being. It is massively powerful. It is our personality's favorite color.

Additionally, we were all influenced by others, such as our parents and relatives, guardians, teachers, friends, and/or employers, who at times might not have *consciously* considered the impact that their approval or disapproval had on our developing minds. Yet we attempt to affirm or disprove the questions they had of our worthiness throughout our lives. It shows up in our actions, purpose, decisions, and direction. Our upbringing is the groundwork of how we reason, act, and decide things as we do. That's exactly where it begins.

Influence could be something as simple as a memorable sentence, said to us at a critical moment in time. Or being treated in a certain way when we were growing up that either made us feel strong or groomed us with thoughts of insecurity. That is all it takes to set off a prolific subconscious quest for the upholding or correcting of our defining record. Our influencers' opinions of us become either our strength of purpose or our struggle. And whether our will is strong and confident, or weak and timid, it sets the initial intensity of its meaning for each of us.

As an example, let's hear Mark Deluzio's story. I think what's particularly pertinent is his eventual response to the opinion of one important influencer, a struggle that grew into his strength of purpose.

Mark's Story

As a business student in the late 1970s at what is now Central Connecticut State University, I had a finance class with a professor I'll call Mr. S. I was the first to go to college in my family, and it was a big deal for me to break out of the lower-middle-class world in which I grew up. My father taught me a great work ethic, and his dream was for me to go to college. I did not want to let him down. I thought the world would open up to me, until one day my dreams were shattered, but only for one moment.

One day in class, Professor S. told us the following: "If you guys think that you will rise to the top of a corporation, you have another thing coming. You are going to Central, and the top jobs only go to those who go to the best of schools, like Harvard and Yale."

My classmates and I were totally deflated. He took the winds right out of our proverbial sails. Some of my friends even contemplated quitting school.

After about a day of depression, I became extremely angry. I vowed to prove this professor wrong. I used his little speech as a motivating factor not only then, but throughout my career. It has been a career in which I became a CFO of a $250 million division of a major corporation in my early thirties, was the first to learn Lean management from the originators of the Toyota Production System in Japan, became the architect of the world-renown Danaher Business System, took a role as a general manager of our division's Asian operations, and became a corporate officer and vice president of Danaher Corporation, reporting directly to the CEO. In my industry, I have risen to the top as being one of the foremost Lean authorities globally. In fact. I'm known as the father of Lean accounting throughout the globe.

In 2001, I started my consulting practice called Lean Horizons Consulting. I am now asked by CEOs of major corporations to be their mentor as they transform their businesses with Lean principles. Ironically, many of these CEOs are MBAs are from those esteemed schools my professor mentioned. I did a webinar for Harvard Business School, and I have spoken at MIT, Kellogg (Northwestern University), RIT, and many other fine learning institutions.

Just think—not only did I destroy his paradigm of a Central student making it to the top, but these Ivy League CEOs are paying *me* big money to be their mentor!

When I became a corporate officer, I took the liberty of calling Professor S. to tell him of my success. He was still teaching at the university on a part-time basis. He never returned my phone calls and was probably embarrassed to face me, since I did leave a revealing message about what I wanted to tell him.

The bottom line is that I could have taken my professor's advice and never thought I'd make it big. However, I took his ill-conceived words and turned them into rocket fuel that propelled my professional career beyond expectations . . . especially for a poor boy from New Britain, Connecticut, small town U.S.A.

It is always a choice for the individual in how to respond to the negative talk from others. While some of the students were discouraged and thought of quitting, Mark quickly reversed his thinking and took the negative words of this early influencer and turned them into his rocket fuel.

Our Nature in Control, and Out

For people to unlock their full potential, like Mark did, they'll need to come to terms with anything that's in the way. The setting of any mindset either creates a desire to achieve or embraces the **excuses*** made for why it's not possible. Initially, it may sound harsh, but it's actually good news. It means you have choices to make.

Our nature, when in control, makes us feel like the world is filled with possibility and there is order. When out of control, it builds in us an alter ego of pseudo-superiority (an attitude that's as fake as a $3 bill) that **justifies** laziness and creates chaos and deficiency. People who deem that trying something new is *not worth their time* simply because they might fail are **justifying** not even bothering to try at all. But what drives that attitude?

Think back to how you were raised. Who were your influencers early in your life? How were you trying to impress them? How well did it go? Think back to moments when an early influencer may have made a comment that stuck with you: an empowering remark that built your confidence, or one that lacked tact and was devoid of the nurturing you needed. Either way, think back to something that struck a chord and stayed with you.

How did it make you feel? Uplifted? Or left wondering if you were any good? Did it provide you with a feeling of buoyancy to believe in yourself, or did it make you painfully question whether you were even worthy of being loved? The impact is huge. The question of your personality is so prevailing, it becomes your nature and your mindset, and it affects everything you say or do. Whether it is kept in check or let to run wild, it holds for you both promise and disappointment.

---

* Just so you know: Throughout the chapters, four words have been consistently bold-faced—**blame, excuses, justifications**, and **rationalizations**, to draw attention to negative behaviors. I consider these four words to be the most destructive words to any person in forming a personal identity. This is explained in detail in Chapter 3.

You cannot erase your past, and your past is quite relevant. Even before you arrived at the age where you might reason through the difficulties of acceptance and rejection, you had the beforehand mission of trying to please your early influencers. Without understanding why some people are impossible to please while others are maybe a bit too easy, you still attempted to accomplish this. These considerations can cause chaos and uncertainty for years, as you try to place where it all fits in your mental configuration.

And here's how it continues to carry such weight for you today: If you were made to feel special and worthy, your efforts will work to affirm and uphold these opinions of yourself. But if they got you wrong, and you felt unfairly treated, it will cause you to either disprove their feelings by taking proactive actions like Mark did—make rocket fuel—or tune out and become disillusioned, disinterested, lazy, detached, closed off, or **excuse**-driven. It sets the tenor for how you see things.

This powerful programming helped shape your personality. All of this took place during a time of intense neural processing and development, so it's there, interwoven like mental DNA. Perhaps that's why there are generational examples of both hopelessness and positivity—fight or flight, accept or reject. The choices we make become who we are.

Another significant element of a personality is worldview, and everyone has a worldview. A worldview is the pattern of thinking that connects logic, and when something or someone agrees with that view or challenges it, it incites emotion automatically. Your worldview is the crux of your logical and emotional reasoning. Worldviews are hard to change, and we measure our intellect by our beliefs. If we were made to feel that we should change our worldview, it would feel as if we were being told that we aren't smart enough. This is why *what* we believe has such power over us.

And this leads our discussion to coping and defense mechanisms. All people naturally need to live at peace with how they see themselves, and we accomplish that early in life by developing coping and defense mechanisms that are designed to get us through difficult passages. By nature, we adopt ways that will reinforce whatever would protect us from too much challenge.

A criticism, for example, can be filtered through a defense mechanism and perceived as an insult. Then, once we feel the insult, we cope with that feeling by defending ourselves through visceral knee-jerk reactions. The criticism/insult keeps us from taking too hard a look at our responsibility for our own outcomes. *However, what would happen if we were to decide to be more open about letting in certain criticism? Suppose we were to view it as a constructive way to become unstuck from where we are now?* When we unblock what holds us back, we become open to new ideas. We gain the benefit of new thinking as fresh neuropathways are built to think more productively. That sure beats sitting in neutral, **justifying** fear and laziness.

A New Level of Thinking

You cannot grow and excel when you fight against recognizing the role you play in whatever is holding you back. You cannot master a new level of thinking that can be highly beneficial if you're making **excuses** or defending nonproductive behaviors. Laziness and fear are the root cause of blocked advancement in anyone. It isn't fun to hear, but we must embrace this reality before we can improve it.

Even though your worldview remains a by-product of early influence, you can still change the less-productive elements of that programming. In order to learn anything new that will challenge you—and challenge is how we learn to better ourselves—you must be willing to face the information that you'll need in order to grow. Do so, even when that information isn't what you want to hear at first. I can guarantee you that by having a willingness to adapt to new information, you'll eventually become stronger and more secure with yourself. And that will lead to mastering virtue and mastering selling.

Mastering selling really isn't a difficult concept, but it requires that you drop your opinions and your ego and be open. You must be willing to be fully committed to empowering change in yourself. If you're not ready, close this book now, and go back to your old way of thinking, the one that got you to where you are now and promises to keep you from growing beyond your current reality. And yes, *getting past your present situation will be painful. That's the hard part. Change can be uncomfortable.* However, in the end, prevailing in something new, like selling, will build your confidence. It has changed countless lives for the better.

The Best New Hires Need the Right Path

For a sales manager, it's easy to get frustrated about how some people never make it at selling when they seemed so promising at first. It wasn't until I began studying the common traits of individuals—while developing the LEAD Personality Profile Program—when I started noticing how different personalities had their own way of processing information. It varied greatly. And among the things I learned was that finding personalities with very well-developed virtues is rare—nearly unheard of. A virtuous approach to life is an exceptional one. And besides, even when you find the best personalities for selling, they still need coaching to maintain high performance standards. Even Michael Jordan had a coach, as did Rocky had Mickey. Then there's that little disturbing fact that top performers often come with great challenges—*excessive* and *deficient* behaviors.

Ultimately, though, failures arise not just for lack of coaching but for many reasons. Chief among them are:

- Companies don't do enough of the right kind of vetting of the personalities they hire. The result: not understanding *who* the candidates really are or how to maximize their natural personality into a state of virtue. Then, missing a golden

opportunity for advancing trainees through a planned process for growth.
- Managers and owners don't understand how to effectively develop potential salespeople in ways that actually work.
- The environment lacks structure for stability and growth. A company needs a great program for sales rep development and a top-notch selling process. The program *always* involves a good selling process, which includes contemporary and effective techniques. You need a program that teaches salespeople how to handle objections skillfully and explains good selling philosophy. You cannot succeed with an outdated or lackluster selling process. Times change, and so do our customers. Change, or get left behind. *Remember:* The only thing that is constant is change.
- The right company culture for long-term success is not developed.
- Communication is poor between salespeople and managers, office staff and employees, company and customers. Improving communication should be a forever quest every day in every way. You are only ever as good as your weakest communication link.
- Both managers and salespeople suffer from being closed to new learning.
- The fast-acting creative is let loose. Salespeople who are very creative take a little information and prematurely run with it, without taking the necessary time to learn it all. This will cut short the full impact and benefits of a potentially good process. These individuals might be highly creative entrepreneurial types, but they are less focused on becoming good technicians first. If they don't have the discipline to learn something in its entirety—because they think they already know enough—they'll struggle to become process-driven salespeople who can do the job and teach it, too.

- Trainees or trainers show excessively obstinate behaviors. When you know everything, there's little left to learn. But it's never actually true.
- People suffer from fear, and for many reasons. Core reasons can include feelings of inadequacies (not being good enough) and fear of loss of love or respect. People rebel or retreat in the face of fear. It's a big driver.
- An under-developed mental acuity and/or a lack in discipline to stay focused can place instinct over process. Your brain needs to be rewired for an expected success, especially if you have a relationship with any avoidance behaviors. By doing the things we know we need to do, instead of finding **excuses** to avoid them, we build the neuropathways required to think more productively, similar to developing a muscle memory.
- Salespeople are not actively participating enough in their own careers. It's a laziness. There is nothing worse than seeing a remarkably talented person mail it in. It's a total waste of superior talent. This is a problem in nearly every sales organization.
- Employees and managers are stuck in a **blame**-game mentality, which wastes valuable time on a focus that is nonproductive, instead of one that targets growth and accomplishment. People lose their way because of a lack of clarity. For example, people who answer *why* to a question of *how* have a need to explain themselves in order to protect themselves against **blame**.
- Companies shoot from the hip and don't know enough about their hires to manage and train them effectively. Winging the growth of your company—and your career—is not a good plan for ensuring you'll arrive where you want.

This list illustrates the importance of learning as much as we can about who people actually are, so that we can properly assess their chances of succeeding at selling. And it underscores that even when a person with a natural skill is found, it's easy to screw it up with a weak selling process and/or with poor leadership running the show.

The goal, then, is to find the right path that directs the best new hires toward mastering selling-greatness. *Master Virtue, Master Selling* and the LEAD Personality Profile Program will give you the information to do exactly that.

Your LEAD Personality Profile

We noted earlier that the LEAD Personality Profile system considers four areas of concentration that make up a person's selling personality and that LEAD stands for *leadership*, *extroversion*, *attitude*, and *disposition*. Here we explain in detail each element of LEAD.

Leadership

Leadership encompasses a person's *natural* abilities to become an authority of direction. Can this person lead a sales presentation naturally by directing the efforts through a preplanned strategy and engagement?

What many people get wrong about selling is that they think it requires you to develop a selling persona. In fact, a selling persona is the very thing that will limit you from becoming great. You must learn to be in state with your selling career by approaching it as *you*. Selling is not you trying to be someone else.

Selling with virtue is tantamount to living a righteous life. In both sales and life, you must lead from an honest position. For example, if a meaningful conversation is to take place, a person with a strong point to make will sometimes run up against another person who has an opposing point of view. In order for a position to win out, the one with the most compelling logic must not shy away from providing superior clarity to gain influence over the other.

Somewhere between the low position of calling the person you are debating an idiot and the better position of influencing the person's faculty of reasoning, a measure must be taken to sway the other person's opinion. If someone is not likely to make that effort, results will suffer. The LEAD Personality Profile Program examines a person's natural tendency to challenge and ultimately influence others, which is very important to selling.

Sometimes, salespeople might hold back. They might have a strong opinion about the value of the offer they make and yet be unwilling to lead by taking on what needs confronting. Holding back can cause internal conflicts for a person holding back, such as anger, cognitive dissonance, built-up resentments, and a host of other negative feelings.

At the other extreme are those who come across in an excessive manner. They don't hold back, and they believe that they are leading by telling us *exactly* how they feel in no uncertain terms, sparing no feelings in the process. Thus, they've isolated themselves from those whom they intended to persuade.

Will a candidate or trainee hold back, confront others, or see leadership as a more virtuous way? Knowing a bit more about how a person thinks about leadership will help a hiring manager or sales trainer to break through and get to the bottom of that pivotal question.

Extroversion

Most people think of *extroversion* as a highly sought-after character trait in someone who sells for a living. While extroversion *in virtue* is a strong plus, extroversion *in excess* yields a cascading deficit in results. As covered in more detail later in this book, out-of-control extroversion is a sign of a different problem.

Excessive extroversion can be the result of someone building defense mechanisms, designed to protect one's feelings of self-worth. It can be a signal of someone needing to be accepted or liked at a dangerously high level, especially in selling. For example, when maintaining relationships with prospects becomes the very rationale for *not* serving them, something is amiss. The need to be liked outweighs the salesperson's goals and responsibility to the company.

The LEAD Personality Profile shows people's natural level of extroversion—where it is too high or too low for them to likely follow a process and if they would default to instinct. Understanding this is one of the keys to unblocking process and excelling in life and, especially, at selling.

Attitude

Selling giant Zig Ziglar is quoted as saying, "Your attitude, not your aptitude, will decide your altitude." *Attitude* is far more important than natural ability. Yet what determines a person's attitude?

This topic has been widely studied by many psychologists and behavioral experts throughout time. The LEAD Personality Profile looks at a person's level of true openness and compares it with the person's potential and perceived abilities at selling; this is called *disposition* (the "D" in LEAD and discussed below). This comparison is tricky because the two factors—openness and abilities—must be compared against each other in order to make that determination.

But one thing is crystal clear: There is a certain level of openness that keeps a person grounded and less blocked from following process. It is a sweet spot. Too high, and people get in their own way with their opinions and individualization of approach. Too low, and they are unfocused, unwilling to learn, and quick to dismiss the value of elevated reasoning, philosophy, ideas and/or concepts that seem foreign or abstract to their own way of thinking. Attitude, as profiled by LEAD, is something that can predict how well someone will tend to accept and adapt to training. This is valuable information.

Disposition

By studying *disposition*, LEAD probes into how natural a personality might be for selling. In and of itself, it is not a terribly important number to track. However, it is quite useful when compared against attitude.

Without an openness to learning, a person will get stuck and be immobilized against growth. In a vibrant company culture, a closed-minded and immovable individual will show erratic behaviors that interfere with a sales team and its objectives. This kind of disposition also has the same effect in life. Closed-mindedness and unwillingness will produce nothing. Avoid being that way at all costs.

Get Your LEAD Personality Profile Now

If you haven't already done so, go to MyLEADprofile.com, and complete the LEAD Personality Profile. Once you have your results, you'll be ready to learn how to unblock process and excel at selling.

And please remember: This is *not* a test. There are no right or wrong answers in a LEAD profile. There is never any shame in the way a person is profiled. It is a specific set of questions that are focused on the things that relate to selling attitudes. It explores who a person *really* is in a way that's useful to that person's development in sales.

And once you have completed the LEAD Personality Profile, whether you're a sales candidate or a sales trainee or whether you're an experienced salesperson who wants to seriously advance your career, you'll find in this book two helpful and insightful sections under each personality: the first clearly explains *what you need to focus on*, and the second details *what you will have to be willing to do*, based on your particular personality, to be successful in process selling.

Learn to Engineer Your Outcome

When someone is said to be *on* a system or *off* a system, understand that technically the person can be both. However, philosophically it is wise to believe that if you are a little off a system, then you are 100% off. This is particularly true with a step-selling process, where each new step builds on the last. This philosophy considers the system, the process, to be all of its parts, not just some.

Selling systems are composed of little segments, detailed steps, that work together to form a perfect union. Whenever that union is performed with precision, predictable results happen on a consistent basis.

The danger comes in when people modify systems with their own individualized ideas. While some ideas are less dangerous than others, the point is, *why would a proven system need to be altered to begin with?*

Those who are new to selling will be tempted to find their own way of conducting business by following what *they* think makes sense. What's more, the "experienced" individuals who go to work for a new company will likely bring with them some old ideas. Some will struggle with a new process when it conflicts with the approach they've already developed. New or experienced, bringing your personality to a state of virtue requires a great deal of willingness to learn and apply what is needed to achieve it.

Don't Fight the Process

If your company has a proven system, and it works well when it is practiced, you won't benefit by fighting it. Here are some common reasons salespeople fight process:

1. Salespeople feel uncomfortable and are afraid to follow things that challenge them.

2. Salespeople have a strong need to individualize their approach, sometimes simply because they are bored or excessively willful.
3. New salespeople are too inexperienced to recognize the amazing empowerment that's to be gained by following a proven process.

If you aren't willing to follow *all* of your company's selling process, think hard about why. If it's because your company's system isn't designed well enough to produce the kind of results it should, feel free to reach out to us at *info@MyLeadProfile.com* for advice. We can discuss options that can help you build a solid selling system that is well crafted and highly effective.

However, if the reason you aren't following your company's process is because you have a strong need to individualize, our advice is to put aside your skepticism and opinions. Put down your ego, and learn to engineer your outcome by unblocking your path to greatness. If you are simply bored, understand that a good salesperson is a technician. An actor cannot simply change lines in a play because of boredom, nor should a process-driven salesperson.

Love at First Sight: Fall in Love, Stay in Love

If boredom translates into allowing yourself the freedom to change your presentation—to keep it interesting to *you*—think of it this way: Try to remember the first time you laid eyes on your presentation. Think of how impactful it was to you that very first time. If you deliver it exactly the same way to your prospects, they're going to feel the same way you did that first time you saw it. If you were blown away, they will be, too. So, why change that feeling? Don't let your boredom chip away at your process. Be disciplined enough to keep a great presentation sounding and looking sharp and enthusiastic. Don't change it. Master it!

Besides boredom, there's a second problem. You're tainted. You're tainted by anticipating objections that you might have already encountered on occasion. It might have stimulated a need to change your presentation to avoid the same objections, something that didn't factor in when you first started.

Plus, since you know what you are going to say, your mind races ahead. It cuts the presentation off at the pass, triggering you to say something better, different, and more clever. Experience is now interfering with process, and you're overthinking, which is probably causing a decline in your results. As you adjust and make changes, your new approach moves farther and farther away from the one that blew you away that first time you saw it. Be aware of this, or you'll change your presentation to a point where it doesn't work at all. Renew your vows to your process each and every time you perform it.

Personalities in Virtue, and Out

As defined by Aristotle, moral virtue is the "disposition to behave in the right manner and as a means between extremes of deficiency and excess, which are vices. . . . We always choose to aim at the good, but people are often ignorant of what is good and so aim at some apparent good instead, which is in fact a vice" (you can find the full quote at www.sparknotes.com/philosophy/aristotle/section8/).

Why do people often miss the mark in deciding what is actually good? By nature, human beings are flawed and lack proper judgment, especially when making certain decisions. Often, promoting an instinctual self-interest over a philosophy of structure might *feel* like a "good" aim; however, it lacks virtue. If people operated with a strict allegiance to a universally understood "good" that kept their judgment in perfect working order, there would be no need for laws. People would just do what is right all the time, and everything would just work out. Perfect thinking would produce order.

Unfortunately, judgment is open to interpretation and falls prey to our self-interests and instinctual perceptions. That's why we need specific processes that will correlate our actions to a desired outcome, which is something that can be understood as a common objective, a good. Anything that threatens to block a process leaves us vulnerable to making decisions that feed our instincts and our need for self-preservation. Thus, to stay on the right track when attempting to achieve something sustainable and repeatable, process is the key, and it helps us to avoid confusion.

Each personality model in our LEAD profile holds virtue, deficiency, and excess. It is virtue that makes a personality the most organized and productive it can be. And to understand virtue, one must consider the extremes: deficiency and excess. A deficiency is a fear to act when one should, and to **justify** acting cowardly when a situation calls for strength. It should be compared with possessing a trait in excess, evident in the unproductive behaviors of a personality that are out of control. An excess sometimes serves our own interests rather than following a process. The key to virtue, then, is judgment. To master virtue is to remain open to all information from others—to strive to understand things around us in a way that is genuine to the way something is, rather than the way we want to see it.

It's no surprise that some personality types are more *naturally suited* to selling than others. The LEAD Personality Profile Program simplifies understanding the different characteristics and personalities by categorizing them into four colors: Red, Orange, Yellow, and Green (each of which is covered later in the book in its own chapter).

If you are a hiring manager or sales trainer, deciding on which sales applicants to hire and how to approach their training starts with the profile, followed by an interview. By subscribing to MyLEADprofile.com, you'll be given access to *carefully crafted interview questions* that explore each of the personality types, along with *a list of global questions* that every good interviewing process should include. Once a new salesperson is hired, you can then use what you've learned in this book to focus on systematically developing them into virtuous sellers.

Red, Orange, Yellow, and Green

Simply profiling someone isn't going to make a person great at selling. It's knowing what to do with that information that makes the difference—for both the hiring manager or sales trainer *and* the candidate or employee. It's about identifying which traits show potential for a career in selling, which ones are signs of caution, and which ones indicate that a company should probably pass on a hire. The profile is the first step. In LEAD, we explore 14 different personality types and four classifications.

LEAD will sometimes pick up on more than one personality/classification in a profile. This is good information, because people aren't just one thing; they are multifaceted. There are one personality and one classification in Red, three personalities and one classification in Orange, five personalities and two classifications in Yellow, and five personalities in Green. Ordinarily, we'll eliminate the red candidates as unsuitable for process selling. Then, we'll work to turn the Orange and Yellow into Green.

The goal is to first turn any profile into virtue. We focus on that while learning the first two stages of Green, *demonstrative* and *advantageous*, described in Chapter 4.

Teaching the Virtues in Order

Ultimately, to gain mental mastery at selling, salespeople need to learn the five Green stages, and in the correct order. Once a virtuous Green stage is understood and mastered, the next one can be taught. By the time people are at the fifth Green stage (called *persistent*), they will have developed a master's level of selling philosophy and mindset. Trainers must direct their trainees with clarity in their pursuit of selling excellence. Cut through the clutter. Using *Master Virtue, Master Selling*'s program, coupled with a killer selling process, should produce incredible results for your efforts. Just keep it understandable and simple.

Following the Process in Virtue

Learning and mastering a process—in virtue—is *much* more important than selling. *Master Virtue, Master Selling* strongly expresses the essential need for a process-driven selling system. When salespeople fall out of favor with results, it's typically because of a lack in their willingness to follow some aspect of the sales process. Some treat process as more of a suggestion rather than the sole focus, which is a huge mistake. Companies that lack a good process aren't helping their cause, either. You are free to excel to new heights only when you have the right process in place and learn to trust it above following your own instincts.

It's imperative to remember: To sell something off-process informs your mindset that instincts can be an option. And it will happen again and again, except without the better results. If strict adherence to a process is not reinstituted quickly, the countdown clock to the end of your selling career has begun.

In the big picture, selling on-process will always turn more sales than selling off-process. In reality, *following process is more important than the selling itself.* It is the lifeblood of a healthy selling career, which is far more important than losing any one *sale* on occasion by following process over instinct.

Instinctual selling will wire your understanding the wrong way. Your brain needs to develop productive neuropathways in order to sell on-process. Don't throw your ability to sell into chaos by making that one-off sale the wrong way. Your mind needs to accept that selling on-process is the *only* way to sell, if you are to enjoy the benefits of a long-lasting and stable career. Short of that, a person can only flirt with success by hoping for luck. So, if you do that—good luck!

The Power of Learning to Trust Process

Picture yourself swimming when, all of a sudden, you're caught up in a riptide. The first thing that kicks in is your instinct, which is telling you that you're in trouble, so you try to fight the current. As you fight the current more and more, you get tired and find that you're not advancing back toward shore. Instinct served to alert you to the danger—and many dangers are, of course, overblown today and are only lingering remnants of our early ancestors' fears. However, instincts are nonetheless present.

What you really need in a moment like this is a good process. If you knew a process to release yourself from the pull of the riptide, you could literally save your life.

For one, you can preserve your much-needed energy and stop fighting the current. Let yourself float to the surface. Next, you could swim sideways to detach yourself from the pull of the current. Neither of these things is instinctual. They are a learned process. They feel quite unnatural in the moment, but they are the right process to save your life. In almost any circumstance, process—a systematic approach—will serve you better than instincts.

TRUSTING THE PROCESS: A PERSONAL STORY

There was a time when I couldn't bring myself to drive over a bridge. It was a totally irrational fear. I knew in my logical brain that nothing was going to happen to me, and yet I panicked every time I approached a bridge. I would sweat; my heart would race; I felt like I might pass out. While that panic was senseless, the fear was real to me. And that's all that mattered.

One day I asked myself, "What is a bridge?" It's just a road connecting two pieces of land. It was developed by highly trained engineers who followed a sound process. They certainly didn't build it by winging it. Once I decided to let go of my unreasonable anxiety and simply trusted a process—mentally acknowledging that those engineers followed a process—I was then able to overcome my panic disorder.

By placing my faith in the process of driving over a well-engineered bridge, today I can drive over any bridge without even a trace of fear. I simply thought it through and fixed it. I didn't need to understand the mechanics of engineering a bridge. I didn't need to question the philosophy of the engineering principles. I just needed to use trust. That's how impactful it is when we *decide* to completely trust a process. It's life changing.

How to Begin

The LEAD Personality Profile Program and this book work together to reach one specific goal—to identify an individual's personality traits and put the person on a unique and effective path toward working in virtue, from a particular personality's starting point all the way to the apex of mastering salesmanship. Thus, *Master Virtue, Master Selling* is a tool of great importance to both the manager and the team member, even to a new hire who's embarking on learning sales skills for the first time. This book will guide you through every personality category we've established at MyLEADprofile.com and illuminate how to address and correct excesses while tapping into and expanding natural virtues.

And the book's structure is intentionally simple, like all things that are carefully crafted.

In a nutshell, here's the plan: 99.4% of the time, our LEAD profiling process will pick up on certain personality traits that a salesperson or candidate is suspected of possessing, and categorize the person as Red, Orange, Yellow, or Green. Next, the individual will work a primary personality into *a state of virtue*—which we discuss for each personality—while learning to master the first two stages of Green. For example, a salesperson who profiles as Yellow (respectful) will work on the virtue of courtesy while mastering Green Stage 1 (demonstrative) and Green Stage 2 (advantageous). When all three are accomplished, the person will move on, in order, to Green Stages 3, 4, and 5 (serious, influencer, and persistent, respectively).

To aid in this process for every personality type, I also wrote special features. These are based on pertinent findings from my 30-year career in sales and my work with studying personalities—findings that I openly share and urge each salesperson and hiring manger to embrace and utilize, if they intend on succeeding in mastering virtuous selling and building a team of virtuous salespeople. I've alluded to a few of these features earlier, and here's the complete list:

- What you need to focus on
- About this personality type
- What you must be willing to do
- The Six Global Interview Questions (available at MyLEADprofile.com)
- Specific interview questions (available at MyLEADprofile.com)
- A manager's 30-day assessment after hire (available at MyLEADprofile.com)

I've also included a single and powerful special feature that I entitled "The 92 Undeniable Core-Belief Statements for Selling-Mature Salespeople." I'll give you more details on that list, and how to apply it, later in the book.

But an important reminder: As I've underscored many pages ago, don't skim through these chapters in search of what seems to pertain only to you, your personality, your role within your company, or your hire candidate's specific profile. I know it's tempting, but you will miss out on so much! As I wrote *Master Virtue, Master Selling*, I carefully curated topics that I believe every virtuous salesperson must tap into and reflect on. (These topics go farther than the special features I listed above.) As you progress through the book, I'll take you deeper and deeper into discussions about developing the mature and persistent mindset of selling—a maturity and persistence that will serve you in a virtuous life, both professionally and personally.

Let's get started!

CHAPTER 1

Red Personalities

Red personalities account for 13% of all the people we've studied using the LEAD Personality Profile Program. While many who profile as Red are certainly wonderful and bright individuals, they aren't recommended for hire in a selling position, especially not a one-call approach. There are two concentrations in Red: One is a personality called *preparer*. The other is called *not for OCS* (*one-call selling*). If your company performs one-call sales, and someone profiles as not for OCS (without any other traits that show in LEAD), my advice is to save the time, trouble, and aggravation of hiring the person. The odds are stacked against it working.

Red: A Nonstarter

"The statistics show that 1.2 out of every 10 people who apply for a sales position will likely not succeed. Imagine that you could prevent these people from being hired in the first place simply by profiling them on LEAD." Now, think of how it would feel to make that decision with confidence. By understanding a personality profile and weighing it against what it means to master selling by following specific steps, you can confidently rule out the candidate. The reason—in the world of LEAD, Red is a nonstarter.

People who are less natural at selling will require learning and applying *adaptive behaviors*. This is common. In the construct of LEAD, adaptive behaviors are learned behaviors that, with practice, will be accepted by a person's logical and emotional reasoning. Some people can adjust better than others to applying what is counterintuitive to their own natural behavior. People can adapt if there's enough meaning in it for them. The question is, how much does something mean to someone?

In the LEAD personality model, Red candidates would be hard-pressed to make changes that run so counterintuitive to their natural way of thinking. *If being right holds more meaning for someone than a need to advance—by applying adaptive behaviors—that person will not develop.*

For employers, hiring salespeople who profile Red is unlikely to work. It's not only risky for your company but bad for the Red personalities themselves. Why waste their time learning something that they are unlikely to make good? The truth is, by *not* hiring them, you're doing them a favor. Let those individuals go on to find something at which they can better excel.

If you're considering trying to train people with unnatural abilities into something that they are not, think about this: People can change if *they* want to, but most won't, and most don't. So, don't lay odds against yourself. Spend your time where it's most likely to pay off.

As you advance through the chapters that follow, you'll learn that Orange and Yellow personalities also require adaptive behaviors, and even Green players will have to adapt to unnatural thinking where needed. Red personalities, however, are the least likely to internalize the need for change and to actually do it *your* way. They are resistant because they're very independent and like to decide things for themselves rather than use your sales process. When the patient controls the diagnosis, the cure is based on their own biases and, thus, has its limitations.

If you're an employer, you should ask yourself: "If the objective is to build a winning sales team, do I have the luxury of spending large amounts of time on such questionable propositions?" Best leave Red personalities to make their mark in the world where their *natural* talents and ambitions can shine. Selling on a process is almost never the right fit for someone who is profiled as Red.

RED

Classification: *Not for One-Call Selling*

86.8% of Red; 10.9% of all profiles

VIRTUE

For salespeople who are lacking in the desire to work using a one-call sell, it is likely that they are proud of not being pushy, and they see it as a virtue. However, when your company has a conversational selling process that avoids pressure, there should be no concern.

DEFICIENCY (THE OPPOSITE OF THIS CLASSIFICATION)

Not applicable.

EXCESS (THIS CLASSIFICATION WHEN OUT OF CONTROL)

Believes that all one-call selling is a pressure sale. Therefore, sees all one-call salespeople as pressure sellers, such as used-car salespeople, which, of course, is a sweeping generalization.

About *Not for OCS*

There are great people to be found in *every* personality profile, including Red, but some just aren't going to fit into the world of process selling or one-call selling. To the untrained eye, people look similar. But the differentiating factors are found beyond what the untrained eye can see, and those factors heavily contribute to who will make it and who won't.

Even companies that use a personality profiling program such as LEAD will not always bowl a strike. Not every time. Yet how would things be different for you if you bowled a strike every three frames instead of every five? What if you could bowl a spare every two frames instead of every three? In time, your overall scores would improve, and you'd eventually be considered a bowling champ. It's the same using the LEAD system for finding, hiring, and developing the right salespeople for your company. By cutting out whatever is wasting your time and focusing on the right stuff, your odds of achieving success increase. In the big picture, small but steady increases are big steps forward.

In following the lessons of *Master Virtue, Master Selling*, and by using the LEAD Personality Profile Program for selling, we first weed out the personality types who stand very little chance at making it in process selling. We also don't want to hire those who do not have a desire to influence the thinking of others. By avoiding those hires, you'll save a lot of time and money.

How to Play Good Odds, Instead of Chasing Exceptions

Of course, when it comes to dealing with people, there are always exceptions, but why not invest your time and energy into playing good odds instead of chasing those exceptions? Some people think that successful selling requires being pushy, and too many companies give this idea validation, especially for one-call closers, who are thought to be the paragons of pushiness. That's not salesmanship. That's manipulation. While many companies perform their selling duties in this way, it is not at all what *Master Virtue, Master Selling* promotes. *Selling is the ability to influence, plain and simple. And mastering selling is to do so conversationally, person-to-person, and without pressure.* In fact, pushy salespeople give one-call selling a bad name. Mastering selling at the LEAD level would mean *not hiring* a typical used-car salesperson of any kind.

When I use the term *one-call selling*, I'm describing a sale that is started and completed with a written contract signed on a first visit. Mastering it takes a willingness to comply with order and a process and certain personality traits. In our program, one-call selling doesn't necessarily have to mean writing the contract on the same day. It can be thought of as *selling that requires the ability to impactfully influence another person in one visit.*

Selling is about being an agent of influence and interpreting value for a prospect. It is not about being pushy or, at the other extreme, merely providing information and acting as an agent of acceptance, essentially taking orders. Selling involves a transference of feeling and emotion that methodically creates influence, through a process of thoughtful steps.

At this point, I hope that you're starting to realize that learning to sell at a master's level might not be what you thought it was. Therefore, the people who you might have thought would make great salespeople—the pushy ones—are now suspect.

The advice I'll offer is this: If someone profiles as not-for-OCS and with no traits in the other color categories, take a pass on hiring that person for a job at direct selling. Bear in mind, however, that people who profile as not for OCS could very well be beneficial in other roles. They might possess strong professional traits that make them very steady and meticulous employees who are competent and capable in a wide variety of other responsibilities, including management. Some will outshine salespeople in those particular areas many times over. Like they say, if you judge a fish by its ability to climb a tree, it will live its whole life believing that it's stupid. If you've got the wrong species for the job, then this book will help you get it right more often.

No Interview Questions

At www.myleadprofile.com you'll find the Six Global Interview Questions that I believe should be posed to every hire candidate. I've also provided probing interview questions that are specific to each personality. These questions are free to anyone with a myleadprofile account. However, since I recommend passing on hiring the Red personality in a sales position, there are no interview questions necessary for the not-for-OCS personality type. If someone profiles with other traits along with not for OCS, use the other traits' interviewing questions.

RED

Personality: *Preparer*

12.6% of Red; 1.7% of all profiles

VIRTUE
Practical

TRAITS USUALLY ASSOCIATED WITH THIS PERSONALITY
Planning
Inquisitiveness
Autonomy
Caution
Skepticism

VIRTUES HELPFUL TO SELLING
Good organization
Curiosity for learning

DEFICIENCY (THE OPPOSITE OF THIS PERSONALITY)
Extemporaneousness
Spontaneity
Impulsivity

EXCESS (THIS PERSONALITY WHEN OUT OF CONTROL)

Challenges to Selling
Overthinking
Worry
Stubbornness
Strong instinct
Opinionated by gut feelings

Overcaution
Below-average empathy
Skepticism
Insensitivity
Lowered self-awareness
Inflexibility
Unwillingness to follow someone else's process
Difficulty subordinating opinions in order to capitalize with protocol

TRAITS SIMILAR TO PREPARER'S

In this case, there is only one—instinctive.

MOST RELATABLE GREEN TRAIT

Based on the individual

The *Preparer* Candidate

Carla's Story

My grandfather was a great guy. A salt-of-the-earth type of person. He wasn't a big hugger or the highly emoting type, but you always knew where you stood with him. He was even-tempered—didn't yell much or feel the need to raise his voice—but he was always clearly the one in charge of his house.

Being the rugged military type, he mostly hung out in a boys' club. Boys do certain things, and girls do other things.

My granddad was a smart guy who could fix anything mechanical. He ran his own autobody shop for years and retired early.

I think similarly to him. His voice is the voice in my head, telling me whether I'm doing the right thing or not. I also have a knack for fixing things that are mechanical. I'm a lot like him in that way. My friends call me their go-to girl when anything needs fixing.

I always knew I was as good as the boys, and I can do anything they can do, probably even better. Of course, if my granddad ever noticed it, it would have felt really good to me.

About the *Preparer*

There is nothing holding a preparer back from being a good or even great salesperson. A preparer is a meticulous aficionado with skills that shine when requiring in-depth focus and study. And by that definition, a preparer sounds like a good bet, and I'm sure that many companies have preparers who are successful salespeople in their rank and file. They sound ideal, actually. Ideal, that is, unless you want to grow a process-driven sales organization.

Preparers are instinctual and independent. They have a strong mindset about doing things their own way. If you're a sales trainer, they may hear you out, but they'll conduct their business however they choose. Lone wolves have what is considered a nontransferable style in the way they work.

Preparers are practical to a fault; they are not idealists. Things have to make sense to them, or they won't get on board. If they do, it'll only be in part. Your ideas and your strategies, they are but mere concepts to preparers. Since they are stubborn personalities, convincing them of something conceptual can be difficult.

All healthy and growing sales organizations need structure. For a regular, predictable number of sales to be made, sales training must be process-driven with detailed steps that are performed methodically in an order. Those steps are called a *process* or a *system*. Adherence to a great selling process leads to a winning sales team.

Preparers take your ideas *under advisement*, but not as their gospel. They might succeed at making sales, but at what cost? *It takes only one off-process success story, just one individual in your company, to rattle the institution of process to the ground.* If preparers are allowed to sell off-system, and they succeed, it will come at the great expense of losing belief in your process for all the other salespeople who have been tasked to follow it. Why should someone listen to you when a coworker is showing that successful sales can be done without your so-called process?

Having a specific process also provides an important benchmark for measurement. It will give you the advantage of gauging the successes and the failures of your team by way of discernable metrics and proven techniques. If you know where someone is off, you can then direct that person to get back on track. Preparers, however, by and large are unwilling to follow a process—at least the ones that they themselves didn't create—and this makes measuring their success in a factual way that much more difficult.

With that said, what makes someone a preparer? The answers are wide and varied, but one thing is for sure: Preparers need to prove to themselves that they can achieve. And they take that challenge seriously.

Acceptance and Rejection: Two Sides of the Same Coin

People naturally seek acceptance, whether or not they do it consciously. It's not that every person relies on the opinions of others—that is an unhealthy way to live—but people still feel unsettled when they are considered unworthy. That is why one fear we all face is the idea of not being good enough.

Much has been written on the topic of *fear of rejection*. Some hide it well, and it bothers some less than others. Some are more confident, and sometimes that confidence is real. Other times, however, it's a faux confidence that is referred to as an *overcompensation* for whatever people feel they lack.

For those who are bothered the most, extroversion can be a coping mechanism. It's developed over time, as an involuntary response to help deal with deeply rooted feelings of inadequacy. These feelings, felt early on, are some of the things that can lead to the preparer personality.

Certainly, all rejection will cause some degree of hurt and disappointment, whether it is being snubbed for a job or a loan, failing a driver's exam, having little success at dating, or receiving the disapproval of a parent or an authority figure. Personal rejection is rarely ever a positive experience. Yet preparers can sometimes take rejection differently than others. Depending on their individual will, it could actually spur them on to achieve.

Accomplishments

Preparers are the ones you would want around in case of an emergency. They are ... well ... "prepared" and probably better than you are. Many virtuosos are among the many great preparers. Consider the work that has to go into becoming a genius, such as a great pianist, guitarist, athlete, or comedian—the study and the research, even a myopic laser-like focus, in tune with the perfection of small details. Think of the amount of preparation that goes into mastering something special at an amazing level. To a preparer, accomplishment feels meaningful, and rightfully so.

Preparers like to follow their own instincts. When making decisions, they are comfortable going it alone. They can be noncollaborative and often feel they can accomplish something better alone than to have to explain their plan to others, who wouldn't do it as well as they would anyhow. It's common for preparers to have an attraction for things that satisfy their own interests and can be enjoyed by themselves, alone.

Why Preparers Struggle When Working with You

As noted, preparers are very independent people. They are known to be stubborn and have strong feelings about being right. They are, therefore, not always open to a challenge posed by another point of view. This is especially true if the preparer has built an identity around being right and is proud of it. But when a person is not open enough to incoming ideas from others, it creates in that person a skepticism that is hard to break, and presents a struggle in communicating. A person must be open in order to grow. Without an openness to some collaboration, you cannot avoid self-limitations.

Being less open can lead to an isolation with others, an uncomfortableness that forms a thick air among varying points of view. Preparers can at times become adversarial in their own environment. An attitude that can feel less welcoming, less empathetic, and less caring to others. This is not to say that preparers are less caring; they're not. For some, it is about awareness. Like other people, preparers can be unaware that they are not showing enough empathy or do not realize the importance of it in every case.

The potential paradox is: If a preparer *needs* to be right, then those the preparer believes are wrong must *stay* wrong. Otherwise, it's the preparer who will be wrong. This is a dichotomy that prevents progress from being made—a stubborn and classic stalemate.

A lack in empathy at key moments in life will limit a person's capacity to forge trusting relationships. Empathy requires nonjudgmental awareness. It is the ability to develop a noncritical response to the feelings of others, despite whatever opinions, thoughts, ideas, and advice you may want to give. It involves acceptance without conditions, which requires you to place your own feelings second to those of another person, regardless of how hard it might be.

Salespeople need to connect with their prospects and customers. They need to inspire, to show the way. Keeping in mind that prospects and customers are just people and might not take kindly to being *proved wrong by someone who has a strong need to be right. If preparers are demonstrative enough and can connect at that level by picking up on social cues, they might overcome that shortcoming.*

A NEED TO BE RIGHT BLOCKS THE BASICS

For a constancy-to-purpose approach to prevail—which is the key to successfully mastering selling—following deliberate steps in an exact order is necessary. Without doing that, salespeople would easily get worn down by having to reinvent themselves in every new selling situation. Can preparers adapt to a selling system that they might not agree with 100%? If they fail to perform a process they haven't accepted as gospel, it will be easy for them to place the **blame** on the prospect or on a lead itself when they fail. If they don't like to be wrong, then the question is: Can preparers take an open inward look and make internal corrections without it threatening their sense of security that's brought on by needing to be right? It would undoubtedly be challenging.

My being a musician means I've spent some time in recording studios. I have one at home. At times, software issues and other various recording problems come about, setting off a mad dash to find out what's wrong. From experience, I can tell you that when something mechanical isn't working, it's normal to check the installation of software, open the backs of equipment, check fuses, and bring things to repair shops—all in an honest effort to fix whatever is wrong. Yet, it's funny to say, the best and most consistently productive people always tell you to *check the basics first*. Oftentimes, they'll suggest that you check whether or not you're even plugged in, to begin with. Probably 50% of the time that I've experienced studio gear issues, something simply wasn't plugged in. It's the last place I expected to find an answer, but the first place I should have checked.

Always check the basics.

And this prompts the question, are preparers, who do not want your advice, open to going back to someone else's basics when things are not working? People in a slump wouldn't be best served when they've limited themselves to a self-diagnosis. This doesn't just apply to preparers, it also applies to anyone else thinking of selling.

If you are unwilling to go back to basics to improve, you might be stuck for a very long time. Preparers are smart people, but they are sometimes the least willing to open their minds and commit to a distinct process (one that they themselves didn't create) as a baseline for judging whether they are on or off their game. If they want to do things their own way, they're not likely to value your process or your advice as the right way to achieve consistent and predictable results. This doesn't make them wrong, just wrong for joining a team that's directed by you in your own specific way.

If you were to introduce your own process thinking as a means for recovery, it might produce a fight-or-flight reaction from the preparers, depending on their level of sensitivity. The trouble is, when people are underperforming, isn't it reasonable to assume that they are missing something that they themselves have yet to pinpoint? Being open means that collaboration could more easily bring about solutions. But are they open to it?

Preparers usually express their honest opinion. Sales trainers can be challenged by preparers as they inject their opinion—some can't help it—and question whatever they disagree with. Being vocal in that way is the very behavior that puts a selling system on trial, with the preparer as the judge and jury to decide the system's merits and worthiness. Preparers are apt to pick apart a selling process and perform, or be faithful to, only the parts they agree with. However, as I underscore throughout this book, *if a person is a little off a process, then the person is actually 100% off that process, and it won't work in the big picture.*

No company can afford to constantly fight a conflict from within. While good sales organizations should welcome a challenge to prove the value of their wisdom, no company wants to be judged for worthiness or legitimacy by the very people it hires to do a job.

Many times, preparers first identify with the opposing consideration of someone's idea. It is their nature to play the devil's advocate. While this can be useful in real life, in a fast-paced business world, it can feel like a negative weight, especially if it interferes with making progress.

OVERLY CAUTIOUS AND NOT IN A HURRY

When making decisions, preparers are predisposed to being overly cautious. They're not known for jumping at things impulsively. They go at their own pace, despite how others around them might feel. This makes them prone to bouts of procrastination. They aren't usually the showboating type, so they aren't looking for your approval. They think hard, consider options, weigh considerations and analyze the costs and benefits, contemplate the information more, then make decisions at their own pace. They are gut-driven and over-practical to a fault, even at the risk of being considered nonempathetic.

Being excessively practical is a challenge to openness and entrepreneurial thinking. Therein lies a dysfunction of rejecting the abstract, the unusual, the farfetched vision, the ideas that challenge a more conventional approach. While learning to sell is not necessarily entrepreneurial, the teachings that comport well with learning to sell are similar. Selling in itself is the function of a technician; and learning the information that's needed to become a technician is specialized, the specifics of which can be rejected by a preparer, who's not open to it and sees it as unnecessary. It's hard to get off the ground when learned behaviors are challenged at the start.

The fastest way to a destination is a straight line; yet preparers might complicate that map. Doubt reduces the speed of progress. Instead of accepting knowledge, they challenge it by injecting personal opinions.

In addition, the cautious preparers will privately reflect about something, using the information they discover. They might not even be sure how to use that data or how it applies to solving a problem. They take time to seek out a *quantity of information*, whether or not it's relevant to the questions before them.

THE FRICTION BETWEEN THE ENTREPRENEUR AND THE PREPARER

Preparers think out loud, which at times makes them seem deliberately confrontational. Yet they are usually only fact-finding in an effort to gather information by questioning what they are curious about through a verbal stream of consciousness. They ask questions that a more process-driven personality would think of as a distraction from an end-game strategy. This is so, in theory, because preparers aren't playing *your* game of "selling-chess." They compile information—whatever comes into their mind—and sort it out later. This is opposed to a process salesperson, who would be more apt to think in that chess-like manner, asking only the questions that are pertinent to an end-game strategy.

Entrepreneurs think of this as a lack of vision because they think with vision first, but often leave the details of an idea for others to figure out later. Not the preparers; they have to consider everything carefully, whether it's relevant or not to the entrepreneurs.

Since preparers are not impulsive but are instinctual—they don't make quick decisions; they make gut decisions—they can privately ponder solving a problem over a period of time, just to be as right as they feel they need to be. This is sensible and practical. It is, however, not how entrepreneurs think. They move faster. Sometimes they leap, then look. Preparers take their time and cannot be rushed. They take apart data and analyze it. That's why they are challenged when asked to blindly follow a system, such as a selling process. They are skeptics of other's blind beliefs. They'll pick apart a process and question the relevance of the portions they disagree with, despite the fact they might not have any hands-on selling experience. Unfortunately, for preparers, that approach is a nonstarter to making progress.

Preparers are skeptical. They question and dismiss a great deal of entrepreneurial thinking, which often deserves that kind of scrutiny. They can be closed to "concepts" that seem abstract to them. Yet to the entrepreneur, it is an irritant. For sales trainers, preparers aren't easy disciples, since they ask a lot of questions and challenge information they are given. For *excessive preparers*, that approach will lead to analysis paralysis and make progress virtually impossible.

Remember, entrepreneurs start businesses. To organize their vision, they hire managers, who in turn hire technicians to carry out that work. The job of a salesperson is not an entrepreneurial station. It is that of a technician, a person skilled in the technique of a craft. That craft is mastered by way of a process and the delivery of a specific preplanned presentation. If a sales organization is to grow, a selling process must be transferrable to others in order for it to be scaled. It is not something that should ever be winged by instinct.

No Interview Questions

While interview questions are available online at www.myleadprofile.com, since I recommend passing on hiring the Red personality in a sales position, there are no interview questions necessary for the preparer personality type.

If You Were Profiled as a *Preparer*

If you were profiled as a preparer, you must be willing to do the following:

1. Admit that you have trouble following other people's directives when they conflict with your own view. Then, change that.
2. Be ready and willing to accept that you will have to embrace new ideas and directives that are counterintuitive to your own. Work on becoming more collaborative.
3. Limit your skepticism about following a process that you did not develop yourself. Learn to embrace information, a system of thought, with blind acceptance.
4. Focus on problem-solving, and avoid problem-dwelling. Think in terms of solutions. Don't get caught up on problems. Make a solution part of the process when there is a problem or disagreement. Make the solution inextricable from the problem. Be open-minded to make this work.

If you cannot bring yourself to do all these things, I recommend you not work at a company with a process-driven approach that you did not create.

CHAPTER 2

Orange Personalities

Orange symbolizes a place in between yellow and red. It means either don't take a chance *or* proceed with caution and with some caveats, such as employing tight time frames to check progress, looking for exceptional cooperation, willingness, openness, responsiveness, engagement, urgency, work ethic, and punctuality.

Many Orange personalities have shown that when they're willing to make necessary *adaptive changes,* they can break through and become very successful at selling. *It's powerful to have a willingness that's strong enough to succeed, despite one's own natural skepticism.* In our studies, there have been numerous Orange success stories. They make up 12% of sales applicants, so they are an important group to work with.

Before deciding whether they are a good fit, however, Orange personalities must be given a definitive time frame to adapt to necessary changes. This could mean days, weeks, or even months. With skilled management, it could happen. Just don't drag it out by romanticizing the notion of someone becoming successful at selling when there is no real evidence to support it. Make no mistake: The odds of success are higher with Yellow and Green candidates. However, a knowledgeable trainer—one who imparts great wisdom to someone who is willing to listen and apply—can be all it takes for an Orange to succeed.

ORANGE

Personality: *Sensitive*

73.4% of Orange; 9.0% of all profiles

VIRTUE
Focused

TRAITS USUALLY ASSOCIATED WITH THIS PERSONALITY
Passion
Empathy
Seriousness
Care

VIRTUES HELPFUL TO SELLING
Focused on achievement and results
Responsiveness

DEFICIENCY (THE OPPOSITE OF THIS PERSONALITY)
Emotionally unresponsive

EXCESS (THIS PERSONALITY WHEN OUT OF CONTROL)
Challenges to Selling
Complaining
Judgmental/Hypercriticism
Moodiness
Reacts to critique; shows sensitivity
Emotional thinking
Problem-dweller
Cutting

Insensitive
Below-average self-awareness
Passive-aggressive behaviors
Focused on comfort before success

TRAITS SIMILAR TO SENSITIVE'S
Respectful
Instinctive

MOST RELATABLE GREEN TRAIT
It depends on the *individual*.

WHAT YOU NEED TO FOCUS ON

Sensitive people tend to be serious. Seriousness is a very professional trait, and serious people tend to be more focused and dedicated in their work. Just remember to breathe and smile and have some fun, too. If you can balance your seriousness with a pleasantness and patience for others, your personality will be at its best.

The *Sensitive* Candidate

Mary Ellen's Story

Mary Ellen's Side of Her Onboarding Story

A few months ago, working in inside selling was a whole new thing to me. I'll admit, it was a little scary at first. I felt picked on when I did something wrong. My manager was very direct when she trained me, and at first, I didn't know if this was going to work for me. With my doubts, I was probably a little hypersensitive to her critique.

A week in, I made a conscious decision to trust the training I was getting. It definitely took me out of my box, and I'm glad I stuck with it. If I had fought it, I would have quit or gotten fired. Then what? The truth is, I've become a stronger person by trying to learn something new in a very short period of time. It all felt unnatural to me, but I thought about it and went "all in." I trusted my supervisor and followed her process.

The training, and the company, and, most importantly, our process have been proved to me that it all works. I now train others to learn how to succeed using that same process in our inside sales department.

An Analysis of Mary Ellen from Her Direct Supervisor

Mary Ellen presented herself fine in our in-person interview (for an inside sales position/phone work). She seemed like a serious candidate. She asked good questions and looked like she'd make a good team player. In her first few days, I had Mary Ellen shadow other people to see how our process worked. I always do that, so a new person gets a taste of what is expected on the job. We in inside sales can't afford to have brand-new people call prospects until they have enough training to navigate those calls successfully. We just don't want to burn through our database of leads.

On the third day at work, Mary Ellen began making calls. She made a few mistakes, so I quickly corrected her. I detected a slight sensitivity while giving her directives. It seemed to grow a bit more into a defensiveness by the end of the first week. In hindsight, knowing she profiled as sensitive, I probably should have kid-gloved a bit more of the initial critiques.

By the time her first month was complete, Mary Ellen no longer seemed defensive or sensitive. She really stepped up. I no longer feel any sensitivity coming from her to any subsequent critiques. Maybe we just got used to working together, and she became more accustomed to my style. I know I can be direct, but I take what we do seriously. Today, Mary Ellen is growing in her new position as the head of her department.

About the *Sensitive*

Mary Ellen's story has a happy ending. She made a conscious decision to accept the initial discomfort of learning something new, and she trusted her training. As she said, it felt uncomfortable in the beginning, but once she got past the direct nature of her supervisor, who had the experience and was teaching her in a transferable way, she absorbed the training. And boy, did she thrive. Today, she sounds talented when training others. Imagine if she were closed-minded and questioned everything to the point of exhaustion. She would not have achieved that happy ending.

Using an Operations Manual—It's How We Do Things Around Here

Mary Ellen's story illustrates why it is so important to run every department of any company with a well-crafted operations manual, something that can be referenced easily and used by each department. Every directive is clear, every task is understood, every piece of the puzzle fits, and no judgments need to be made about the supervisor's training. Simply put: *It's the process, it's how we do things around here, and it works.*

A good operations manual helps make a business scalable. It protects a company from liability by instituting clear directives. It adds market value to a company in the event of a sale. It also saves a lot of time.

Had Mary Ellen's employer not had such a clear operating process, Mary Ellen would have had to recall her own interpretation of the training she received whenever she trained someone new. Instead, she just consulted with the manual, followed the process, and found every answer she needed. When something wasn't in the manual, she'd bring it to her supervisor. That action creates the impetus for new additions to the manual as needed. That's how these things get built and stay current. By following a clear process, every answer she gives is the right one.

Running a company with an operations manual will give employees a feeling of security. Their knowing that the company has a method that is consistent makes the business run like an engineered design. And people are more apt to trust an engineered design than some supervisor's personal opinion.

The Value of Virtue: Clearer Thinking and Better Judgment

Mary Ellen had the strength to come to terms with the decision she had to make—either to play ball by learning and taking her company's process seriously or to leave. Too many people, especially those who profile as sensitive, would have chosen otherwise, but where would that have led?

She decided not to let her pride get in the way. She kept the virtue of her sensitive personality in check—empathetic, caring, responsive. And never let its excesses become debilitating—reactive to critique, complaining, judgmental, moody, hypercritical, focused on comfort before success, emotionally based thinking.

This demonstrates how, by building your personality into virtue, you are provided with clearer thinking and better judgment. It benefited Mary Ellen and her company for her to stay. She turned out to be a great contributor and an essential employee. She is growing into a very good manager because she remembers her own difficulty at the beginning and is willing to show empathy for the people she hires while training them on a proven process.

If You Were Profiled as a *Sensitive*

If you were profiled as a *sensitive*, you must be willing to do the following:

1. Focus on two things simultaneously: Monitor your own performance, and develop professional and positive relationships with those you work with.
2. Be hungry to learn new things. Completely embrace your training material, and agree to follow it without exceptions. Avoid individualized thinking, especially in the beginning.
3. Recognize that you might take things personally. Awareness is the first step in solving a problem. Be aware of your own sensitivities, and don't let them block you from growing.
4. Go *all in* and place yourself in the hands of a process that you might sometimes disagree with or only agree with in part. Agree to follow it without making any changes.

If you cannot bring yourself to do all these things, I recommend that you not work at a company with a process-driven approach that you did not create.

Questions for Someone with a *Sensitive* Personality

There are three sets of questions you should ask that have been designed for the specific profiles in this book. Ask the first two sets before you hire an applicant (global and specific interview questions). And ask yourself the third set (30-day review questions) 30 days after hiring. You can access the questions and the 30-day reviews at www.myleadprofile.com.

As an example of the questions you will find at the website, here are the three sets of questions: The Six Global Interview Questions, The Interview Questions Specific to a *Sensitive Personality*, and *A Manager's 30-Day Assessment of the Sensitive Personality*.

The Six Global Interview Questions

Begin any interview with six global questions that provide general information and cover expectations of reliability.

1. Before we get into the questions I have for you today, I just want to go over some of the basic requirements of hours we would be looking for in a work schedule. Are there any days of the week, or times of the day, when you are unavailable to work?

    Go over the basic requirements of time commitments you'd expect of a new hire, and make sure your candidate doesn't have restrictions of days or times that would compromise what you would need to fill in this position. If the candidate cannot work the required hours, the interview is all but over right here.

2. **Are you currently working?**

   Review your candidate's work history. This presents an opportunity to see if the candidate's in-person recollection matches the written résumé. If there are glaring inconsistencies, probe them. Most people buff up their résumé a bit. While we wish they wouldn't, it's a common occurrence. If the buffing is excessive, it's a problem.

3. **What brings you here today? Why did you apply to our ad?**

   This is a simple and good question designed to gain a basic understanding of your candidate. Be sure to professionally spin your responses off the answers you get, and never ask anything that is inappropriate or illegal to ask.

4. **You mentioned that . . .** *or* **It says here that . . .** (*looking at the application*) **you worked at the XYZ Company. Tell me about a problem you had there.**

   The purpose of this question is to see if the candidates answer as a problem-solver or a problem-dweller. If candidates give you a solution they implemented to fix the problem, they are most likely problem-solvers. If they dwell on the problem as being something tough, but they never come to the solution they applied to overcome the problem, they are most likely problem-dwellers. In a good culture, we want problem-solvers.

   Remember not to ask this question differently, by saying, "Tell me about a problem you had and how you solved it." Candidates will follow the tip that you want to know how they solved it. Let them answer it exactly as Question 4 is written. If the candidates state they don't understand the question, just re-ask it in exactly the same way without any extra elaboration. This approach tends to work.

Probe their handling of problems and conflicts at least two or three times. That way, you'll see if there's a thought pattern surfacing, of *working on the fix* or *dwelling on the problem*.

This global question is especially important with a sensitive personality. Sensitive people usually avoid confrontation. Yet we all have to deal with it in our work. If these candidates are problem-dwellers (offering no solutions without your prodding them to do so), it is, at the very least, a solid clue as to how they'll likely deal with conflict. Mishandling conflict is a reason a sensitive person might leave a perfectly good job. Developing skills in conflict management can help advance a sensitive person's career.

5. **What's a misconception that some people may have about you?**

   Get the candidates to open up and willingly share information about themselves. The misconception they bring up may be the very thing you'll need to probe. It relates to the mindset they'll likely bring to your organization.

6. **Do you have a defining moment in your life? Something that made you who you are today?**

   While it sounds like a towering question, its purpose is to begin to understand what motivates or frustrates the candidates. For example, if someone overcame a life-threatening ailment in childhood, the person may feel like a fighter who cannot stand feeling helpless, which is a potential sign of strength. If a parents' divorce was the defining moment in the candidate's life, because it tore the family apart and created a battle of pleasing two parents, this person might have a heightened state of fear that continues to guide their direction in life.

Based on this person's LEAD Personality Profile, this information will serve as a useful guide to where you might take a line of questioning.

Although it is not true for *potential* profiles (for whom there's limited information), each of the other personality profiles has a virtue, a deficiency, and an excess. If this person fits a personality type that is workable in a selling role, questions like these will help you probe for excessive and deficient behavioral traits (those not working in virtue), thus avoiding a mess after you've hired someone you shouldn't have.

The Interview Questions Specific to a *Sensitive* Personality

Probe these questions that are specific to a *sensitive* personality trait until you are satisfied that you understand the applicant better:

1. **What are some potential work-related issues in your past that may have caused a sensitivity for you?**

   Come right out and ask this question as if you ask it of everyone. Don't give a clue that it pertains to only the sensitive personality profile. You'll want to make applicants comfortable with opening up and talking with you. Keep in mind that many interviews fail when the applicants pick up on the reasoning behind certain questions. They begin interpreting what *you* want to hear in an answer, and then you'll learn very little about them. You want to make interviewing an actual discovery of who they *really* are—this person you might hire—not an invention of who you *want* them to be.

2. **Have you ever walked away from an opportunity because you felt you were treated unfairly in some way, in comparison with others? If so, please elaborate.**

   What we focus on will manifest itself, and a focus on fairness can be an inhibitor to personal empowerment. Sensitivities can come about by focusing on an unfairness when the issues that trouble us feel unmanageable. For people to get over a focus on unfairness and clear a path for more productive thinking, they'll need to put away any defensiveness and negativity and find answers through humility and a probative mind. Listen carefully to how candidates answer this question. Are they stuck, or did they rise above the perceived unfairness through a more productive focus?

3. **Tell me about a time when you felt picked on.**

   This is a spin-off of Question 2. If you sense that your applicant has a history of trouble taking a critique and reflecting toward self-accountability, you might be onto a serious problem that can prevent growth.

4. **Where do you see yourself professionally in the next year or two?**

   This is asked to see if the candidates have any thoughts of advancement—and to learn what is most important to them, what they want to get out of an opportunity like yours. If you probe this and cut through the obligatory answers they might give you (such as, "To give a company my very best . . ."), you might get to know the candidates a little better. This can be helpful in recognizing how to best work with them, or if it's even possible.

   In the end, the sensitive personality seeks comfort and peace, which is fine, so long as it is not at the expense of growth and the proper use of corrective thinking when dealing with a prospect.

   Note: Beware of hiring salespeople who have jumped around from job to job, whose main goal, they tell you, is to find a home from which they can retire. They'll tell you they're looking for that last place where they can dedicate the rest of their working lives. But it's almost always *a projection of their fear that you'll see them as a job-jumper, which they likely are.* Given their history, they'll probably treat your company the same as the others.

A Manager's 30-Day Assessment of the *Sensitive* Personality

Ask yourself the following questions 30 days after making the hire to determine the progress of the *sensitive personality you are working with:*

1. How does this person take to constructive critique? Is the person open to it, or do you sense that the person shuts down when being confronted about something that needs adjustment?

    For the trainer: Check your own delivery of critique to be sure it is never cutting or offensive to your trainee. That's a very difficult thing to do for a person who has trouble with employee retention. If your own EQ score (emotional intelligence) has been tested and is too low, you might not be aware of how you come across. Fix that, or you'll never grow a team. Please make sure you are well versed in what someone might legitimately consider to be attacking. Don't attack. Consider the trainees' feelings and recognize their need to feel that they belong and fit well with your company's culture. That's any good manager's job.

2. Are *you* being patient while training this person? It can take weeks or even a couple of months for someone to come around. Be patient, so long as there are signs of progress. Work hard with people who are a cultural fit to your company. Hiring someone new is expensive.

3. Do you feel that this person legitimately wants to do well? Does this person appear to be *committed* to doing well?

4. List the signs you've noticed that indicate this person's willingness to learn and follow your company's system.

5. List the signs you've noticed that indicate an unwillingness on the part of this person to learn and follow your company's system. Is there anything blocking this person from becom-

ing process-oriented? If so, how is this being worked out?
6. Do you feel you are developing a trusting relationship with this person?
7. Do you laugh along with this person in the course of a normal workday? (You should.)
8. Is this person progressing in results—in measurable metrics—on the job?
9. Would you buy something from this person? Is the person convincing and trustworthy? Is the person likable?
10. Do you sense that this person would support your leadership with others, or is there reason to doubt that?
11. Has this person's sensitive personality been dialed into a state of virtue?
12. What is the next step you have in mind for this person's development?

    Please note: Avoid answering this question lightly. It should be well considered and filled with details. A blanket answer such as "For them to produce more leads" is *not* a good manager's answer. If you do not know the steps to develop someone in your department, you're lacking vision. As the ancient proverb states, "Where there is no vision, the people perish." Put together a model for growth in your department. One that may include helping someone to graduate from your department, onward to your employee's next monetary gain. Losing good people to upward positioning in your company is a sign of your superior developed management skills. It's a big feather in your cap. Losing people who quit the company, if reoccurring regularly, is not.

13. Does this person offer ideas to improve the mechanics of the salesperson's role in your department?

    If yes, are you willing to be open to new ideas? That doesn't mean you should embrace all new ideas. You want conformity to process, especially at first. But if you are the only one coming up with ideas to improve your system for delivery, you will be limited by your own vision. Great ideas come from unlikely sources. Are you, as a manager, open enough and secure enough in yourself to embrace them? If your department isn't considering ways to improve, are you under the belief that you have a perfect department? You should always work at improving your system of delivery, or in time you will be left behind by an ever-changing consumer marketplace. Keep fresh and encourage new ideas. Becoming antiquated is the result of managing without a vision.

14. In your opinion, if you were trained by this person, would the person do a good process-oriented job of training you?

ORANGE

Classification: *Inconsistencies*

11.6% of Orange; 1.4% of all profiles

VIRTUE

It's not a virtue, but it's not dishonest when people answer profile questions the way they see themselves, as compared with how others see them. The problem is that the people who are doing this run the risk of being less self-aware about how they appear to others. It's innocent but requires training and awareness to improve.

TRAITS USUALLY ASSOCIATED WITH THIS CLASSIFICATION

Not applicable

VIRTUES HELPFUL TO SELLING

Not applicable

DEFICIENCY (THE OPPOSITE OF THIS CLASSIFICATION)

Not applicable

EXCEPT (THIS CLASSIFICATION WHEN OUT OF CONTROL)

Challenges to Selling

Deliberately attempting to cheat the profile to look more like a qualified salesperson than is the case

Lying for sport; untruthful

Willfully obstinate when convenient

The Candidate with *Inconsistencies*

Ken's Story

Ken's Version of Himself

I've always been successful. No matter what I did, I always found a way to maximize any opportunity. My boss shared a story with me the other day about how he made $500,000 one year. I told him about the first time I did that, too. Our experiences are actually pretty similar.

I do whatever it takes to keep being successful. I have an outstanding work ethic. I have a little fun along the way, too.

Someone Who Knows Ken Gives Her Version of Him

Ken is thought by many who know him to be a pathological liar. He comes across the way he wants others to see him. He's a likable enough guy. I mean, he laughs and stuff, but you can never trust anything he tells you. I suppose he might have privately held feelings of low self-esteem, but he certainly tries to overcompensate for it by putting out an aura of being more than he really is. He tried selling, and within a month, he talked himself out of the opportunity, making **excuses** that weren't real. My guess is, he feared failure and let his laziness win out. All talk. No action. His numbers looked like those of a pro on his profile because he answered the questions to make himself look stronger.

Mario's Story

Mario's Version of Himself

I had a few people in my life who really helped me to become a better me. I know I can do whatever it takes to succeed. I just need some training and some encouragement to keep going. But when I have that, no one will put more into being great at selling than I will.

Someone Who Knows Mario Gives His Version of Him

Mario is an exceptionally nice person. He is someone who wants to please others. He's a gentle soul whose demeanor is kind and considerate. I really believe that he believes he is a strong salesperson-in-the-making. If I'm being 100% straight with you, I think he's too nice to learn how to hold his ground in a closing situation, but he's convinced himself he can. His numbers looked good on the profile because he sees himself much differently from how he comes across—perhaps not too self-aware. I think he'll push himself, but I'm just not sure he's got what it takes. I think he wants to improve his life, and yet I sense a part of him is restlessly wandering in self-doubt and lacking confidence.

About *Inconsistencies*

The ominous-sounding word *inconsistencies* doesn't appear as a Red trait, because it's more complicated than at first glance.

Inconsistencies is a classification, not an actual personality, meaning it doesn't note that people are inconsistent in everything they do. *Inconsistencies* hints at some kind of cheating of the profile, although that's not necessarily true either.

There are two types of people who show inconsistencies when profiled:

1. Those who deliberately try to beat the profile to compensate for a strength they know they don't have. A misguided attempt at papering over the truth about oneself for the purpose of preserving self-esteem and pretending a vigor that really doesn't exist. This is dishonest.
2. Those who see themselves differently from how other see them. A false sense of self, not meant to cheat. It's honestly and simply what they believe. They are not self-aware.

It's difficult to guess a person's motivation for showing inconsistencies until we get to know the person a little. In the cases of Ken and Mario, the two are very different. Only one of them has a chance of making it at selling, and that chance would require a sincere commitment to change, which can be very difficult for some.

First, Ken, who is deliberately deceitful, is bad for company culture. If you allow *known liars* into your organization, your company will be quickly and thoroughly infected. You and your company have to stand for something, and it can't be the condoning of dishonest people or their practices, no matter the volume in revenue they might bring to you. For every dollar they bring in, they cost you triple that in trouble, damaged growth potential, sullied reputation, and chaos and dysfunction.

As for Mario, while he doesn't raise the concern of jeopardizing a company through dishonest behaviors, he presents another challenge. He is unaware of how he comes across to others, which is a symptom of a bigger problem. He is lacking self-awareness and, therefore, direction. He hasn't taken a critical enough look at his own challenges to devise a good enough plan to overcome his restless uncertainty. He has a view of himself that he believes to be true; yet everyone around him sees someone who's completely different.

Mario is kind and thoughtful, probably too kind. He's actually so nice that he'd likely have major challenges applying corrective thinking with a disagreeable prospect in a sales presentation. He runs the risk of being trampled, the result of being too understanding and respectful to be honest with someone when it is needed. By feeling fear, he might conduct himself as valuing prospect relationships *more* than turning prospects into customers. And if you don't make customers, you will be out of business.

For Mario to become successful at selling, he would need to adjust his personality for growth and change through the use of some very important *adaptive behaviors*. His direction would have to shift toward something that holds a lot of meaning for him.

First, he would need to find a greater purpose in his work, something that gives him a sense of mission and completeness, a purpose so strong it's bigger than his reluctance to educate recalcitrant prospects when they need correcting. He needs to be taught and to internalize seeing selling as helping and serving, not just as selling. It would have to be bigger than just wanting to do something good; it would have to become his *mission to help.* To make it more meaningful for Mario, he would also need to connect in his mind a sense of fulfillment for his efforts in selling:

Selling = helping = virtue = a good feeling back to Mario

Shortened, it simply means selling = doing good. If he could get that lodged firmly in his head, he could use it as his newfound mission to becoming great.

There is a profound tenet of philosophy that states, "Fulfillment is growth directed to purpose." Certainly, Mario has some growing to do if he is to become successful. He needs a purpose that can change his life. The odds are never promising with anyone who needs to change at an unnatural and heightened level. Applying adaptive behaviors is difficult, because they are always counterintuitive to the thinking of those needing to apply them. *Very few people are determined enough to change their paradigm.* However, while challenging, it *is* possible.

Since Mario needs a purpose that is stronger than his fear, let's dive into the philosophical tenet pertaining to what gives a person a real purpose: how the spirit of fulfillment is found in the spirit of growth.

Understanding True Fulfillment

What is fulfillment?

Many can't put it into words, or it sounds a bit utopian and unrealistic when they try. Some think that if they had a certain material possession or if they were to win the lottery and became rich, then they would be happy forever. The more farfetched the answers are, the less likely that people have spent much time thinking about what true fulfillment is or what it means to them. Fulfillment is essential because it means finding actual happiness in life; yet, unfortunately, so many cannot define it.

Fulfillment may not be what you think it is. It's not always about reaching the apex of a big goal. You may be happy or even euphoric to reach that goal for which you've worked hard, but unless there's something to follow it, fulfillment would be unsustainable.

Most people work at jobs that take a lot of their time. *We become focused on our work, which sometimes has little connection to our real selves.* It's easy to go adrift in the big world that's filled with deadlines and bills to pay, and in the chaos, we lose a part of ourselves. We get farther away from our own sense of purpose and lose touch with who we really are, or don't give much thought to who we could be—*an important consideration to anyone having to apply the use of adaptive behaviors.*

Ask yourself, *Are you living the life you used to dream about when you were younger, when problems were small and financial debt wasn't a consideration?* If you are working in a field where there is little to no fulfillment or enlightenment in it for you, aren't you just trading hours for dollars? Is that really all you want? Is that enough to drive you to challenge yourself to become great at something? The problem is that we only have so much of that time to give anyhow, which is easy to forget.

Your outcomes will reflect the choices you make. Be aware that your views affect your self-talk, what you say to yourself that enters your subconscious mind. This self-talk helps to form your hardened beliefs, both empowering and limiting. You can talk yourself into something that requires determination and discipline just as easily as you can talk yourself out of it.

What Blocks Achieving Fulfillment

If everything in the universe is either growing or dying, what happens to a person who is no longer growing? Inside, the person is dying.

Depression, a lack of excitement, loss of a sense of self, no true purpose: All are signs of someone who isn't growing and is likely dying inside. Complacency, by its nature, is an uncritical look at oneself. Therefore, because it involves no growth, to be complacent is to suffer a slow death of will. Your potential doesn't matter if you don't care about it or act on it. Yet you can't grow into something bigger or better until you understand who you are and what you need.

If all people have the *capacity* to develop and grow, why do so many people seem to go through life standing in place? If we lack motivation or don't understand who we really are, we might exist, but are we really alive in the truest sense of the word?

Without sufficient motivation, eventually we even lie to ourselves to find the external reasons to **blame** for why things aren't better in life. Yet we are the only ones who can solve those problems. Some people are chronic complainers, which limits their potential of finding answers. They suffer a deficit of positive passion, the kind of passion that feels self-empowering, so they're not truly inspired and excited. All of this affects how they see themselves and the world they live in. Former business owner Robert Quillen remarked, "I have noticed that the people who cry, gossip, and complain the most are the ones who possess the least amount of personal hustle and internal fortitude." We can easily mask what we want to deny, but it won't improve unless we understand the way it really is.

Cliché or Not: It's the Journey, Not the Destination

By accepting the tenet of philosophy that "growth equals fulfillment," we see how being in the moment and feeling a sense of moving forward is the part of our journey that speaks to our happiness. We've all heard the saying, "It's the journey, not the destination." While it might sound like something you'd find on a greeting card, that statement holds great meaning for us all.

If you look for fulfillment as something that comes with a huge happy ending, you might be too influenced by Hollywood. When the story is over and the credits roll, leaving a great movie is uplifting, but you're lucky if that feeling lasts till the next morning. This isn't to say that you can't find amazing happiness in real life, but you need to understand what it is you're looking for and what it could actually mean for you.

Euphoria Is Not Fulfillment

If you don't spend the time to craft a vision for finding the real purpose of your journey, you're not likely to find long-term fulfillment in your life. You might begin to seek short bursts of what you think is fulfillment, a euphoria, which is little rushes of dopamine, an organic chemical produced by the human body. But fulfillment doesn't happen in short bursts. Fulfillment is about growth over time.

Seeking euphoria over fulfillment is a dangerous path to take. For example, drug addicts look for euphoria. They crave the high high, but without the next high ready to go as they begin to drop, they sink to a low low. Even a natural euphoria is a short climb to a very tall place, which is followed by a quick, precipitous drop down. It's only a temporary shot of dopamine, and an occasional natural high is not a worthy pursuit as a mainstay purpose in life.

Another example of euphoria is the billionaire who buys an island, thinking he needs this enormous purchase to be truly happy. At first, there is undoubtedly a sense of euphoria, but unless it is followed by some way to sustain it, it eventually becomes boring, and even depression sets in. How many of us think that if we had our own paradise island, we could find a way to be happy? Well, it wouldn't last. Eventually, it would just be a mailing address and not much else. In time, you would need more.

Euphoria may be an amazing feeling, but a roller-coaster ride only lasts a short while. You get a quick burst of dopamine, but then what? Euphoria has no journey. And since we are going to spend the lion's share of our lifetime on the journey, doesn't it make sense to find fulfillment along the way? That's why it's important to connect your selling career to a purpose, by developing the right system-driven protocols and procedures that work and ultimately heighten your growth and level of positive feeling.

Let's examine this a little further. Suppose, for example, you were to put together a fund-raising team for a charitable event. What would it involve?

At first, you might feel excited at the idea of taking on such a noble responsibility. You'd start by making a number of calls to assemble a team. There would be conversations and meetings, and people would come to the table with their ideas. There might be some who would be a bit forward with their opinions, and there would have to be some give-and-take, but you would be working a plan and would be *in the moment*.

While there would surely be challenges, you'd have a sort of jingle in your pocket—little flutters of dopamine firing off while the creative juices are flowing; working on a mission, giving you a sense of purpose; giving you a feeling of being part of something that's working toward a goal. A stream of ideas will flourish; a movement will be born. You'll laugh, you'll strategize, you'll even become frustrated at times, but you'll be surrounded by meaning. Each step, big or small, that moves you closer to your goal involves growth.

Then comes the day of the event—the walkathon that will raise the needed funds. The number of calls proliferate as last-minute arrangements are addressed. The excitement builds as you begin feeling the anticipation about the big event, and the dopamine is firing more rapidly throughout the day.

You'll rehearse your speech for when you represent your team while presenting the check for the team members' efforts. Your team members assemble the tents they'll sleep in that night. Then you notice a few young children playing on the running track where people are starting to walk laps, which reminds you that you're doing something important (more dopamine). Excitement continues to build as you await the moment when your team's name is called, and the presentation of your efforts is complete. Everyone on your team is proud, and the atmosphere is electric, even euphoric. You deserve that feeling. You've earned it.

The next morning, everyone packs up, drives away, and goes home tired. But it's a good kind of tired, a feeling of euphoria. That morning, you'll take a number of congratulatory calls from team members about how wonderfully everything went and how proud everyone is of all that was accomplished. You're still riding that high. The following day, you take and make a call or two.

A week later, you see someone from your team at the grocery store. The person glimpses you and yet literally passes you by, without even a hello. What happened? The euphoria has dissipated.

The euphoric drop occurs because there is no immediate plan to continue the movement forward. The feeling of growth is lost. The dopamine isn't there anymore. That destination is concluded. The jingle in your pocket is gone. Your purpose is over. Euphoria has ceased, and the sense of fulfillment is no longer present.

As if euphoria were all we needed, we can so easily overlook the importance of our journey when we're only fixated on getting to our destination. However, even during the most challenging times in planning the event, you had focused on the purpose—the reason to be in the moment working toward a goal, on a journey, and it mattered to you.

Growth Directed Toward a Purpose Equals Fulfillment

When you feel an awareness that you are in the moment and taking some action, big or small, toward accomplishing something, or working in any way toward an eventual accomplishment, it will create a sense of purpose. Any action you take toward satisfying a sense of purpose is fulfillment. That action forward is your growth. Growth directed toward purpose equals fulfillment. Therefore, to continue feeling fulfilled, you need to keep doing something that involves growth. It's that simple.

This is a good place to begin if you need the inspiration to accept that you must adapt yourself to challenges and to find meaning. It can be done. It won't be done by most who need it, because they will only talk, and most will never commit to following through on their potential. However, that's not a choice made by society or systemic limitations. It's an individual's decision.

Repurpose Honest Inconsistencies into Productive Change

Since growth leads to fulfillment and a sense of purpose, if you are someone who showed inconsistencies *but are honest*, you can thrive if you are willing to do the following:

- Internalize the idea that growth is the one true goal by firmly connecting growth to purpose.
- Recognize that helping people with your products and services is a purposeful cause.

- Adapt to growth-oriented behaviors when needed, in order to be better equipped for success.
- Disallow yourself to be talked out of opportunities when they become challenging.
- Disallow yourself to be talked out of opportunities by naysayers. There are a lot of negative people. Don't spend your time with the negative ones. They'll only drag you down, and that's *your* choice.
- See sales training as a never-ending pursuit, which means keeping growth at the forefront of what's important. Make growth a constant focus, despite setbacks and bad days.

A tip for hiring managers in spotting the honest versus the dishonest inconsistencies in the reading of a profile: In general, the ones who are being honest might profile with other personality traits, but none higher up the Green stage than *demonstrative* (Green Stage 1). The less honest person is more likely to show traits that may include *advantageous* (Green Stage 2), *serious* (Green Stage 3), *influencer* (Green Stage 4), or *persistent* (Green Stage 5). After weeding out those with dishonest inconsistencies, focus only on those with a low sense of self-awareness.

If You Were Profiled with *Inconsistencies*

If you were profiled with *inconsistencies*, you must be willing to do the following:

1. Be committed, and stay committed, to learning how to sell by way of a process. Commitment is defined as staying with something even after the feelings that initially excited you have gone. You must be *that* committed.
2. Be willing to think outside your box and embrace counterintuitive thinking. Be willing to apply this thinking as directed, without hesitation. Do not confuse your need to grow as a

sign of unworthiness. No one can declare you unworthy if you are willing to participate strongly in your own renaissance.
3. Develop a probative mind. Ask questions that help you understand what you do not know. Become intellectually curious.
4. Go *all in* and place yourself in the hands of a process that you might sometimes disagree with or only agree with in part. Agree to follow it without making changes.

If you cannot bring yourself to do all these things, I recommend that you not work at a company with a process-driven approach that you did not create.

Questions for Someone Who Profiled with *Inconsistencies*

There are three sets of questions you should ask that have been designed for the specific profiles found in this book. Ask the first two sets before you hire an applicant (global and specific interview questions). And ask yourself the third set (30-day review questions) 30 days after hiring. You can access the questions and the 30-day reviews at www.myleadprofile.com.

ORANGE

Personality: *Soloist*

7.0% of Orange; 0.9% of all profiles

VIRTUE
Focused

TRAITS USUALLY ASSOCIATED WITH THIS PERSONALITY
Self-sufficient
Autonomy
Private

VIRTUES HELPFUL TO SELLING
Orderly
Independent; less in need of emotional support

DEFICIENCY (THE OPPOSITE OF THIS PERSONALITY)
Needy

EXCESS (THIS PERSONALITY WHEN OUT OF CONTROL)
Challenges to Selling
Introvert; shy
Resentful
Reserved
Quiet
Noncollaborative
Isolated

TRAITS SIMILAR TO SOLOIST'S

Respectful
Instinctive

MOST RELATABLE GREEN TRAIT

The most relatable Green trait is *advantageous*.

WHAT YOU NEED TO FOCUS ON

Focus your attention on other people. Since you prefer to keep your innermost feelings private, you can turn your attention to your prospects and make it about *them*. This will have to be a conscious effort, but it's a natural way for you to focus your personality to virtue. Ask questions that show interest in prospects. Show how you have their best interests at heart in all you represent. Listening is important in selling; just lead, too.

The *Soloist* Candidate

Peter's Story

I do like doing things my way. I get a lot more accomplished without the distraction of interacting with too many people. I have my own systems for doing what needs to get done. I am very efficient and take my responsibilities seriously. I don't need a lot of supervision. I report directly to the owner of my company. I work hard to make sure I don't have to deliver bad news about not accomplishing some expectation given to me.

I was married later in life, and so early on in life, I learned to spend a lot of time enjoying my own company. I've attended concerts on my own and have gone away on vacations for a few days on my own in the past, too. When I hear that someone could never do that, I guess I get it, but I know that I can. I have a couple of close friends, a smaller but meaningful circle.

I am independent and enjoy a high degree of autonomy.

About the *Soloist*

When thinking about what traits make up the greatest salespeople, "outgoing" is usually considered one of them. Yet there are some very exceptional salespeople who are more private and operate more by themselves.

To sell for a living, the ones who perform with less outward excitement must have something else, a substitute, which can be a well-developed maturity, an intelligence. Often times, they have an impressive vocabulary. They usually appear real and believable to the average prospect, and they show that they care and display a strong need to serve, instead of just selling.

Think of a doctor who gives off a certain look of trust and maturity. Certain soloists can do the same. Admittedly, it is uncommon to find salespeople with such control that they can trade an expressive attitude for the trusted look of quiet sage wisdom. But it can work that way.

In selling, finding someone with a more demonstrative approach is more common. Being demonstrative works well, as most identify salesmanship with excitement. Soloists, however, are usually private and are, therefore, not obvious candidates for selling. Yet if properly cultivated, the doctor temperament can be powerful, too.

Let's avoid confusing a workable doctor's temperament for one that's lacking in personality, one without traits that are personable. The doctor personality can relate to customers, but as more like a respected authority who has a mature, trusted look that can make an impressive impact in the minds of decision-making prospects. Once that trust is established, these doctor-type personalities hold a power. Unfortunately, though, it's more common to find a soloist personality who's less engaging, more like an administrator. And for that reason, soloists are placed in the category of Orange. They should be given only a finite amount of time to prove that they are more like the trusted doctor than a quiet administrator who will more or less, in sales, become an agent of acceptance.

Soloists are mostly introverted. They tend not to favor small talk and see it as shallow socializing, and they're uncomfortable when forced by circumstance to participate in it. Some soloists become exhausted by social interaction. That doesn't mean that they walk around with their heads hanging down and avoid all human contact. Rather, it means they enjoy working without the distractions of having to mingle with others. This is where they struggle. Some people feel anxiety about small talk, fearing they'll run out of things to say. Some fear exposing too much of themselves and their vulnerability, and they might even worry about the awkwardness of how to eventually end an impromptu conversation. Unfortunately, salespeople rely on that kind of interaction to build trust, and that puts the soloist at a great disadvantage in selling. Some soloists develop sarcasm as a coping mechanism to defend against too much exchange of pleasantries.

Soloists can have a higher sensitivity to dopamine, which means that they might need less of its pleasant effects than a confirmed extrovert would need to feel all right. And dopamine can overstimulate a soloist.

Soloists have strong comfort zones that are hard to break, and they tend not to enjoy the challenge of growth. However, if a soloist has a persistent desire for fulfillment, an introverted soloist can lean into becoming more of that trusted doctor type.

Be sure to use the Interview Questions Specific to a *Soloist* Personality, as well as the Six Global Interview Questions. Used together, they will help you to draw out which of the two you are interviewing—the quiet administrator or the respected doctor.

If You Were Profiled as a *Soloist*

If you were profiled as a *soloist*, you must be willing to do the following:

1. Come to terms with the need to be more extroverted. This doesn't mean you need to be the life of the party, but the party needs to know you're alive.
2. Consider how being a bit more collaborative would affect your life for the better. Think of the ways it would enhance it.
3. Learn to become curious about other people. Becoming interested in others is easy. Let it come from your care for people. Allow it to bloom until it is noticeable to others who know you. Be aware that isolation is a warning sign to others that says, "Don't approach!" That is a terrible disadvantage to give yourself in a role that requires communication and a desire to help others.

4. Go *all in* and place yourself in the hands of a process that you might sometimes disagree with or agree with in part. Agree to follow it without making changes.

If you cannot bring yourself to do all these things, I recommend that you not work at a company with a process-driven approach that you did not create.

Questions for Someone with a *Soloist* Personality

There are three sets of questions you should ask that have been designed for the specific profiles found in this book. Ask the first two sets before you hire an applicant (global and specific interview questions). And ask yourself the third set (30-day review questions) 30 days after hiring. You can access the questions and the 30-day reviews at www.myleadprofile.com.

Although it is not true for potential profiles (for whom there's limited information), each of the other personality profiles has a virtue, a deficiency, and an excess. If this person fits a personality type that is workable in a selling role, questions like these will help you probe for excessive and deficient behavioral traits (those not working in virtue), thus avoiding a mess after you've hired someone you shouldn't have.

ORANGE

Personality: *Professional*

8.0% of Orange; 1.0% of all profiles

VIRTUE
Versatility

TRAITS USUALLY ASSOCIATED WITH THIS PERSONALITY
Caution
Proper and structured in approach
Requires orderly work environment
Trust of conventionally accepted approaches
Team player; congruence
Humility
Steadiness

VIRTUES HELPFUL TO SELLING
Less about personal passions
More about steadiness and reliability
Appreciative of good process

DEFICIENCY (THE OPPOSITE OF THIS PERSONALITY)
Amateurish behaviors
Careless in work
Dabbler, without active expertise

EXCESS (THIS PERSONALITY WHEN OUT OF CONTROL)

Challenges to Selling

Inflexibly practical
Less open to unorthodox thinking; more of a conventional thinker
May casually dismiss unconventional ideas and practices
Conformist who can be highly skeptical of visionary ideas
Stiff in relating, rigid, inflexible
Focused on information and data over emotion
Emotionally disconnected in some respects
Might struggle with expression of passion

TRAITS SIMILAR TO PROFESSIONAL'S

There are two:
Respectful
Serious

MOST RELATABLE GREEN TRAIT

The most relatable Green trait is *serious*.

WHAT YOU NEED TO FOCUS ON

Build trust. Connect all the dots. Work the entire presentation to be focused on the needs of your prospect. Take in all the information from a needs-assessment, conversations, product demonstrations, and discussions about the next step that helps a prospect in becoming your customer. Lead prospects into the right buying decisions by gaining their trust and respect for you. Learn how process directs an outcome, and be true to it.

The *Professional* Candidate

Perry's Story

My parents raised me to do the right thing. They are both honest people who are examples of how to follow the rules. After high school, they put me through college, where I received a degree in business. As it turned out, my degree isn't what got me the job I've been at for the past 20 years. It was a job in marketing that was supposed to get me through until I found a better job in business. But I was good at this one, and it was where I wound up.

College was a good experience. I'm a little shy and introverted by nature, so I think going to college rounded me out as a person. It introduced me to some things that were out of my box, and that was good.

I've been serving clients for many years now. I'm diligent at what I do. I've been promoted to a high-ranking position at my company. I am proud to say that I think I've missed a total of two days since I started, 20 years ago.

I'm someone that my bosses and coworkers can count on. I provide for my family, and I do a pretty good job keeping everything going as it should. We're not rich, but we aren't in need for anything.

About the *Professional*

Professionals can become salespeople, but they are far less likely to desire to do so. Most professionals see the world as a place where, if you follow the rules and work hard, the system allows you to eventually retire and live a humble life thereon. Since selling is something that can feel infectious in its pursuit, professionals aren't looking for that kind of stimulation. They want things to be steady and stable. Although they wouldn't necessarily vocalize it as such, many would use modest and conventional considerations when assessing the value of a person's lifetime.

PROVIDERS, NOT RISK TAKERS

Professionals are not risk takers. They want certainty over variety in many of the things they do. Yet they might enjoy variety on matters that are less important than their careers, and they'll exercise that variety where taking a chance would have no negative consequences and might even add a dimension of fun. As long as there's no real risk involved, they're fine.

Professionals take their roles as provider seriously. They aren't known for jumping job to job or seeking major career shifts that could threaten the stability of their family. They faithfully complete their work roles to the best of their ability and are generally approved of by their higher-ups. They will do as they're told, as long as the directives bring a stable life to their universe. Many professionals would be considered salt-of-the-earth types. Honest and straightforward, they trust in the worldly system. Not inclined to rock the boat.

Can a professional do well at selling? Yes, but it's not usually a natural fit. For professionals to become great at selling, they would have to see the art of selling as a worthwhile quest that pays their bills and provides a future. Since they don't usually thrive on or seek out the stimulation of risk, it would have to be more about a conventional approach. A professional who is willing to learn and apply the tenets and structure of a good selling process can do very well.

Since they are more averse to risk and less likely to take chances, professionals can more easily stick with a job (like selling) *as a career*, which would only happen if they follow process and disallow anything that threatens it. If they see a selling process as a conventional means to achieve, it will make sense to them. They are not attracted to lofty-sounding promises of big money and incredible success. They are far too practical to be mesmerized by big-talking ideals. It's not what they care to hear. What they want is to believe that an opportunity to work will provide realistic promises that are steady, stable, and true.

Getting a professional to fit into a selling role at your company can be the greatest challenge, since the perception of the selling industry (so to speak) is made up of so many high-energy, dice-rolling salespeople. That doesn't apply to selling operations that are more sophisticated, but the fast-moving, risk-taking world is the complete opposite of what a professional personality desires. If you find one who's willing to do what it takes, it will require the development of demonstrative skills. Similar to the soloist, the professional can seem more private and reserved than naturally outgoing. That's why professionals can learn to develop their demonstrative skills as more like a trusted and respected doctor, who can look up over bifocals and tell you what you need to know, rather than as an overexcited extrovert.

Our approach is to turn natural personality traits into a virtue, while learning the first two Green stages, which are *demonstrative* (Green Stage 1) and *advantageous* (Green Stage 2). Then, move on to *serious* (Green Stage 3), *influencer* (Green Stage 4), and *persistent* (Green Stage 5). The professional perhaps *can* do it. The question will be, *Will the person want to?*

A GOOD FIT?

If you're a hiring manager, think ahead and ask yourself, *What happens when you hire someone who has reservations coming into your organization? Will sensing those reservations in an interview make you more likely to paint your answers to the person's questions a little more brightly than normal?* You might see something in a potential candidate, but if you're going to have to sell the candidate on the job itself and continue selling the person on the career, is it a good fit? Having to reconvince a skeptic about your opportunity will not produce a winning salesperson. The right professionals will need to present themselves as serious and willing to learn, apply, and work your systems. Never oversell professionals—or anyone else you interview—or you'll work for them.

Since many professionals are seemingly unnatural for a role at selling, also ask yourself, *Do these professional candidates represent themselves in a way that I would buy something from them? Are they asking questions that show they take care to help and serve? Or are they more focused on their own prize for the effort?* Later in this book, you'll note the importance of serving versus selling. Does it look like your candidate can legitimately convey that message of serving? If not, consider the odds of potential success. Weigh it carefully against the time, effort, and energy that you'll put forth in training and management.

I'm not suggesting that you shouldn't hire someone like this, but I am suggesting you should think about it at more of a macro-level. Look at the big picture. Decide if this hire is right for your energy. Be true to yourself in these situations, and you'll avoid a great deal of wasted time. Remember, when you have the right people at your company, you'll move mountains, and the victories will feel more energizing. With the wrong hires, however, you'll be dragged down and spend a lot of time on things that might only frustrate you. Just think about it carefully when you're deciding whom to hire. The people you surround yourself with are your choice.

If You Were Profiled as a *Professional*

If you were profiled as a *professional*, you must be willing to do the following:

1. Adopt a conscious realization that communications require both logic and emotion. Limiting yourself to 90% logic will hurt your chances of succeeding at selling. Consciously consider how you relate to and communicate with others, and add more feeling to what you convey.
2. Read books from the greats of selling. Zig Ziglar is the founding father of modern selling. He is but one author you

can learn from. Become an active participant in your career by seeking out knowledge that can help you to develop your outgoing (selling) personality more.
3. Accept that when a prospect rejects your offer, it's because that prospect needs more information to make a new and better decision. Be prepared. Don't just fold your tent at the first sign of resistance.
4. Go *all in* and place yourself in the hands of a process that you might sometimes disagree with or agree with in part. Agree to follow it without making changes.

If you cannot bring yourself to do all these things, I recommend that you not work at a company with a process-driven approach that you did not create.

Questions for Someone with a *Professional* Personality

There are three sets of questions you should ask that have been designed for the specific profiles found in this book. Ask the first two sets before you hire an applicant (global and specific interview questions). And ask yourself the third set (30-day review questions) 30 days after hiring. You can access the questions and the 30-day reviews at www.myleadprofile.com.

Although it is not true for potential profiles (for whom there's limited information), each of the other personality profiles has a virtue, a deficiency, and an excess. If this person fits a personality type that is workable in a selling role, questions like these will help you probe for excessive and deficient behavioral traits (those not working in virtue), thus avoiding a mess after you've hired someone you shouldn't have.

CHAPTER 3

Yellow Personalities

Allow me to direct your attention to a simple fact: If a personality were completely natural to selling, the person would have likely profiled on the Green scale. Yet Orange and Yellow have many success stories—when the proper willingness meets with great training.

Yellow symbolizes caution. People can drive through a yellow traffic light and make it, but sometimes they get a ticket or collide with another car. Yellow personalities are varied. A full 61.26% of the people who apply to most companies have shown to possess some Yellow traits.

Never write off 61.26% of your potential staff. To build a sales team, you will need to learn how to develop Yellow and sometimes Orange candidates into Green. It would be much harder to build a large team if you rely on hiring only Green personalities. If you cannot learn to turn Yellow personalities into winning salespeople, you are essentially writing off the majority of applicants, and that would not be advisable.

The key is working with Green, Yellow, and Orange personalities. Together, they constitute 87.1% of the people who apply for sales positions. You can write off the 12.6% who are Red—and you'll actually save a boatload of time by doing so—but you cannot afford to write off the rest. That doesn't mean all the people who apply can be turned into winning salespeople. First, you have to know who they are. The LEAD Personality Profile Program for selling will give you information that's important to know, and when you master learning all the personalities in LEAD and in this book—and understand the virtues, excessive behaviors, and deficiencies—you'll spot some of these traits in an interview setting, maybe even subtle ones that our profile program hadn't detected. If you ask the right questions during an interview, offer great training, and use skilled managers who understand LEAD, your developmental onboarding process will be firing on all cylinders. There's no more need to chase your tail. With the right information and focus, you can build that sales team quickly and efficiently.

YELLOW

Personality: *Willful*

33.7% of Yellow; 20.8% of all profiles

VIRTUE

True believer

TRAITS USUALLY ASSOCIATED WITH THIS PERSONALITY

Strong beliefs
Strength of conviction in self
Potential leadership skills
Highly focused
Perseverance
Entrepreneurial-minded

VIRTUES HELPFUL TO SELLING

When strictly following process, thinks most like persistent (Green Stage 5)
Critical thinker

DEFICIENCY (THE OPPOSITE OF THIS PERSONALITY)

Meek

EXCESS (THIS PERSONALITY WHEN OUT OF CONTROL)

Challenges to Selling

Too open to influence that is not thoroughly considered
Impressionable
Stubbornness
Strong opinions

Inconsistent discipline
Instinctually uncommitted to process
Sees process as only a guide
Trusts intuition over process
Rationalizes knowing "enough," thereby shortcutting properly learning of a selling process, selling philosophy, and selling psychology
Inattentive to protocols
Long-term commitments challenged by constant change
The managing of emotions
The need for excessive autonomy
Can be distracted and become bored
A strong need to be right
Closed-mindedness/closed attitude toward critique when in conflict with own thoughts and ideas
Careless behaviors
Independent streak; follows own path
Hubris
Argumentative

TRAITS SIMILAR TO WILLFUL'S

Instinctive

Activist

Persistent

MOST RELATABLE GREEN TRAIT

As previously noted, the most relatable Green trait is *persistent*.

WHAT YOU NEED TO FOCUS ON

Learn to faithfully follow a process as it is written, without individualizing it to fit your comfort level, opinions, or creative ideas. Turn willful into willing. Be open to new ideas, and embrace new learning through honest application. Learn not to change something you have yet to perfect. Listen without defensiveness. Avoid creativity when learning a new process. Do not challenge the process, but spend enough time mastering it to a point of excellence. Then make suggestions. Challenge yourself to be disciplined enough to follow system process, without any exceptions.

The *Willful* Candidate

Robert's Story

I've always marched to the beat of my own drum. I am very independent, and don't like to rely on others. I've always had a restlessness in me that makes it hard for me to keep still and sit back. Time is passing, and I want to do things. Too many rules are unnecessary. If I don't agree with something, I don't have to shout about it; I just don't follow along.

About the *Willful*

By definition (as found in *Lexico*), the word *willful* means "having or showing stubborn and determined intention to do as one wants, regardless of the consequences or effects." It carries a notable level of intensity, which can be applied to a number of different character traits in the LEAD Personality Profile Program for selling.

But the way it is used in LEAD speaks to its intensity—to think and to act as a force that sometimes, when out of control, disregards following a process due to thinking that one knows better. When excessive, *willful* means acting without allegiance to a set process, ignoring established protocols, or, as we put it, either not knowing (understanding) or not following on a consistent basis the mature principles that are directed to a purpose.

A NATURAL TENDENCY TO CHALLENGE THE CONVENTIONAL NORMS AND THE PROCESS

Why would someone not follow established principles that have been proved to work? It could be that a willful person has not yet been taught the importance of certain selling principles. Some willful people get there later because they have to learn it on their own. Or they have been taught the principles but have not yet internalized following them with precision; they'll treat them as suggestions, not as hard rules of protocol. Or they'll refuse to follow system protocols whenever the urge to ignore the protocols suits them; they are determined to be willfully resistant to someone else's process as *they* see fit.

Mandy Hale, best-selling author of *The Single Woman*, said, "When nothing is certain, everything is possible." Entrepreneurs see the world as an endless sea of ideas, a world of ever-changing possibilities. A place where you are free to make changes on the fly. An open road, a bounty of dreams waiting to be realized. When entrepreneurs do what they do best, they create. To them, fixed principles are but malleable structures awaiting another look, a more complete analysis, open to interpretation, reinterpretation, and exploration. All of this is true for entrepreneurs, but what would happen if we applied the same thinking to soldiers in battle?

Soldiers fighting for their lives need structure. They need to understand what to do when confronted by a force that is unsympathetic to their existence. In battle, it's life or death, and the stakes of winning or losing the battle are high. Would any great general ask soldiers to take a hill just any old way? Would a general simply ask troops to do their best and not worry about procedures and protocols? If generals did this, they'd increase the chance that the soldiers would wind up as casualties.

The architects of warfare are tasked with designing strategies. In many ways, they are the entrepreneurs of a war: the planners, the strategists, the best prepared, and the most trained to limit the loss of life while accomplishing the objectives they desire. There needs to be structure to create an end-game strategy to win. No one with a functioning mind would run such a thing by simply winging it, and soldiers must be certain that the plan is the best it could be, or it could cost them their life.

When we apply such thinking to selling, the general is the entrepreneur, and the soldiers, are the technicians. The soldiers must be ready at the quick to follow orders that were designed to create an intended outcome. In selling, the intended outcome is to serve prospects by selling to them something they need and want. If the approach is less systematic, it will prove to be less reliable. If it were war, the cost would be bloodshed. In selling, the cost is failure to sell, failure to serve.

When we follow a well-developed process and master it well, we become experts who perform with predictable, consistent results. The problem is that in selling, the entrepreneurs and the salespeople each have their own ideas. If the soldiers aren't going to follow the general's plan, they're going to have it tough, and in come the **excuses**. As in Aesop's fables, when the fox couldn't reach the grapes, he simply **rationalized** that they were not ripe.

Being willful means a person has a natural tendency to challenge the conventional norms, and being around people who break the rules makes it that much more tempting for others to do so, too. That's why you can't have a bunch of salespeople in your organization who act with excessive tendencies, *even if they are selling*. If they appear to be successful to a willful personality, they'll influence the willful person away from following your process. It'll bring out the rebel in them all, and you'll have unmanageable chaos.

When people are selling on instinct, they might or might not be able to become effective at selling. However, if they do, they will never be able to teach that instinct to others. That is how renegade, gunslinger-style performers operate. Lacking adherence to an established process—no matter the individual effectiveness of one person—is but a recipe for stalled growth at any business. Instinct simply isn't scalable.

On the other hand, scalability is at the core of a selling process. What exactly is a selling process? It's a series of steps of a sale, taken in order and performed in a distinct way, with certain checks and balances along the way to test how it is working. Any quasi-system that relies on a gut feeling to build to a selling climax (a close), and with no real checks and balances to test its effectiveness, will degenerate to a game made up of rules governed only by a salesperson's individual mind. Not only is it impossible to duplicate in others; it's hardly repeatable by the gunslingers themselves.

Fear, Laziness, or Egotism Can Be What Holds People Back

Fear, laziness, or egotism: These are the main reasons salespeople would opt to not follow a proven system for selling. For example, in certain cases, if salespeople have challenges retaining what was taught to them, they might choose to hide their difficulty for fear of looking foolish to others.

Some salespeople are unfortunately lazy, too. Some come into professional selling because they feel they have the gift of gab but are too lazy to work at a job that seems boring or difficult, like sitting at a desk all day. Selling, for some, just seems a lot easier and more of a natural fit. Of course, that is a myth. Selling, at a true professional level, is a career that should come with a master's degree in psychology.

Immaturity Can Be a Problem

Another reason why some salespeople refuse to follow process is their immaturity. They have fun selling to prospects by telling tales that might have no basis in reality, all in an effort to heighten a prospect's admiration for them. Telling a prospect that you were a Navy SEAL, when it isn't true, might make a prospect feel a sense of respect for you, but it's despicably wrong to do. Only the most immature salespeople would do such things. Having to portray yourself as something you are not is a sign of being uncomfortable with who you really are. For those who follow process and sell comfortably in their own skin, dishonesty would never be a burden that they would have to carry. Being confident in yourself means that you don't need to pretend to be someone else. Maturity isn't a condition. It's a choice requiring courage.

Comparing the Yellow Willful and the Green Persistent (Stage 5)

Leadership is the ability to direct a sales presentation. Willful personalities show strong leadership traits, too strong in some cases, where those traits can turn into pushiness. In the case of non-process-driven willful salespeople, leadership could show up as strong opinions, not necessarily productive ones. In fact, in this willful example, the salespeople could present an obstinate resistance directed at authority, such as their manager or their company. If they're picking a fight with their manager, instead of redirecting their effort to correcting a prospect who needs more accurate information, they are misappropriating their strong leadership skills away from productivity. Obstinate resistant attitudes threaten the benefits of process selling.

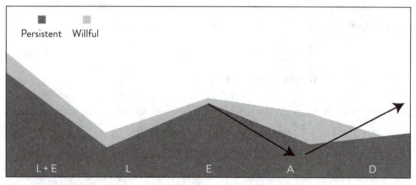

FIGURE 3.1 Comparing Yellow, willful, and Green, persistent.
Key: L+E—leadership + extroversion combined, L—leadership, E—extroversion, A—attitude, D—disposition.

Figure 3.1 shows the relationship between willful and persistent. In comparing the two personalities, it becomes apparent that the extroversion levels between the willful and the persistent (Green Stage 5) are not far apart. The persistent's extroversion was a little more on the serious side, while the willful personality leaned into being more demonstrative (Green Stage 1). That's okay.

In this graph, the biggest difference between them, however, is found in the willingness to perform as a trained procedure would require, a willingness that's present in mature persistent personalities but not in willful ones.

Willful personalities have an A that is higher than the D. In other words, their attitude (opinions) towers over their disposition (natural ability). This shows a closedness to accepting and applying what is learned, which is a serious block to faithfully following a process without making **excuses**. Without that A level falling below the D level (preferably by around 8 points), the willful person is not ready to work toward becoming the more persistent one. The arrow on the persistent model (A to D) shows that a willingness to accept training and apply it as taught is going in the right direction. The arrow points to the direction the line should go. Notice that on the persistent graph, the D is higher than the A. The disposition (natural ability, which continues to grow with training) of a persistent is above the person's attitude (opinions). That's the goal.

In general, a willful person's intensity is focused on opinions, and opinions are subjective. Persistent people dedicate themselves to process, not their own opinions. Process is transferable, opinions are instinctual. Developing a strong loyalty to system thinking is the key to changing everything for the better.

How a Willful Person Can Become Persistent

A willful person can become more influential and persistent only after accepting and internalizing the serious trait of selling maturity, which is Green Stage 3. Willful personalities are potentially junior persistent people because they have some of the same driving forces at play. They each have a strength of passion and a lot of drive. The willful person is like a stallion that's yet to be broken. The persistent personality is at the very top of the Green scale (at Green Stage 5) and follows process as their *only* guide, a perfectly seasoned player.

One distinction between the willful and the persistent is their emphasis on their tasks of selling. *Willful personalities are more focused on selling, whereas persistent personalities place the emphasis on maximizing helping a prospect by way of process.* Persistent personalities know that when you focus on doing the right things—the things that value and respect others—success follows. *Selling is helping. It's a matter of developing a genuine servant's heart and directing it toward a purpose through the person's actions.*

It is not surprising that willful people sometimes have roots in being difficult in their youth. Do you know of any old friends from your childhood neighborhood who were basically troublemakers but later in life became police officers? That's a classic example of willful turned persistent. At some point, those willful people realized that they needed structure (process in life). They figured out there was something greater than their own instinct, something bigger than themselves. They harnessed the force of their own nature, turning it into something far more mature and productive. The ancient Chinese philosopher Lao Tzu offered this: "When I let go of what I am, I become what I might be."

Selling is no different. The best thing that can happen to willful personalities is to get on a path to become persistent personalities. The worst thing that can happen is for willful personalities to buy into a rationale for feeding their own egos. If you think you already know everything and see yourself at the top of your selling, you have nowhere to go but down. More selling careers are killed off by big egos than for any other reason. Ego is not your amigo. Persistent people are often willful personalities who have matured.

Choose Your Elevation, and Select the Influencers in Your Life

You will be most affected by those you choose to associate with and who influence you the most. If your closest friends are not adding to your elevation, you may want to rethink those relationships. To work toward becoming more persistent, make a list of the five people with whom you spend the most time. Those individuals will have plenty of influence over your feelings and direction and your attitude in general. Being around them will build you up, bring you down, or keep you the same. They'll add to your enlightenment, or they'll make you feel strange for trying to elevate theirs.

Write down the names of the five people. Evaluate your relationships, and consider in which direction they take you. Are you able to grow from their influence, or are those relationships uninspiring to your future? Maybe even bringing you down? I'm sorry to say, but we do outgrow certain relationships over time. If you find that you are the main influencer in your peer group, it might be good for the others to be around you, but you need elevation, too.

The goal is to be the strongest salesperson you can become, and in the world of LEAD, that also means becoming the strongest *person* you can become. Being persistent requires that you keep moving forward. Are these friends helping you move forward, or is their influence part of what's holding you back?

Life opens a whole corridor of new possibilities when you elevate the company you keep. Seek out people who can elevate your perspective and inspire your persistence. Make a list of five people with whom you've come in contact who inspire you to be better, and work to grow these relationships. This is a very proactive decision that people can make to change their perspective for the better. Start your own mastermind group. Meet once a week or once a month. Get and give ideas to elevated thinkers. Things will change quickly, and your mindset will become stronger when you commit to this. It's your choice to be proactive and make that happen.

Get Out of Your Own Way

If you are willful, ask yourself, *Am I trying to learn from the instructor, or am I trying to* be *the instructor?* If you are trying to be the instructor before you have the information you need, you are simply challenging authority. If you are trying to learn from an instructor, then you're on a quest for knowledge, which is selling maturity. The former path is just an effort to show that you are smart, while the other offers real advantage and gain. Think about it.

In today's information age, people like to put themselves in charge of finding whatever information that they think they'll need in order to advance. But if you're the one who needs the coaching, you don't know what you don't know, so what do you search for in order to progress?

Allow a good manager or coach to help you work your way up the Green scale. While managers can only assess a salesperson using what they deem important to cover, managers who subscribe to the LEAD training approach have a much clearer direction from which to lead. You can trust a well-versed LEAD manager to understand your personality and take you up the Green stages, where you can become great, *provided you are open and willing.*

Don't challenge your coach because you think you are in the trenches while your trainer is sitting behind a desk. I'm sure Coach Geno Auriemma wouldn't be able to keep up as a player in a UConn women's basketball game, but you'd be hard-pressed to find a coach who can do a better job advancing the players of a team. Listen to those who are there to lead you. Change as they direct you to change. Become a willing student. Apply what they teach you. *It's easy to be obstinate; it requires nothing but skepticism and negativity. It takes true courage to be willing to put aside your own ideas and find enlightenment through working a proven process that you did not create yourself.*

If willful people don't at some point evolve to persistent (Green Stage 5), they will become what sales aficionado, Zig Ziglar referred to as a "wandering generality." Complacency will settle in, and they will think they know everything but know not nearly enough. They'll eventually get bored and become disengaged, and they'll drop out.

Being willful means a person has passion and is unafraid to confront what others might shy away from. Those are great qualities to develop, but that's not the place where your efforts should end. The willful person's goal should be to get moving onto the Green stages of selling and to master all five. Until that happens, a willful person is not yet of the mindset to master selling.

Decrease Hubris and Increase Confidence

Hubris is excessive or exaggerated pride or self-confidence. Confidence is a firm trust, the state of being certain about the truth of something. There's a fine line between the two. What's the difference between hubris and confidence? Your success.

School is never out for the pro. Learning isn't over after a finite amount of time. It's a forever kind of thing. Believe it or not, even when people have mastered our entire Green platform, if they don't continue to revisit that training, they will eventually fall out of favor with their own success. People must stay open-minded, willing to revisit what they've learned, and embrace more learning. Refusal to do so is to your own disadvantage.

Hubris is a block to continued progress. When students feel that they've outgrown their teacher and start to tune out and stop listening, hubris is not far away from taking over and destroying the gains they've made. Unfortunately, poor training from instinctual management doesn't help either.

Though many don't, some willful personalities have great potential for becoming wildly successful. That advantage comes in the form of a self-assuredness. In fact, willful people can make great entrepreneurs. All entrepreneurs are a little crazy. You'd have to be to think that you can start a business from some idea or vision and actually make it happen. Entrepreneurs start businesses with odds stacked against them. They must be willful just to get past all the naysayers who point out how irrational it is to take the risk. Otherwise, they'd cave to the negativity and fold. Being willful is a part of their initial strength. Elon Musk is undoubtedly one example. Many people want to be like him, and yet very few are. For your path, you will need to self-reflect and ask yourself if it's working for you, or if you need a more transferable and scalable approach to selling.

Willfulness must adjoin with openness, which is usually the main struggle. Being willful, you think you know better. But once you've mastered the five stages of Green, it's remaining open to ideas, accepting input from others without defensiveness, and being willing to adapt that would prevent you from losing your way, becoming obstinate, and beginning to think that you know better than the training that got you there. A clear sign of closedness is, for example, having to get in the last word in a disagreement. Getting in the last word might even involve storming off to end a conversation or hanging up on a call. When we don't want to understand someone else and are unwilling to engage, we are closed off. This is a serious problem. It will interfere with people's ability to grow and will ultimately block them from finding any true sense of fulfillment in the big picture. People who react like that aren't truly happy. They may *manage* their instabilities, but they aren't *conquering* them.

Then there are people who will try to pick and choose what they like about a process—another sign of closedness. They'll follow one step but not another. To that, I say this: If your goal is to buy milk at the corner store, would you succeed if you drove only part way there? I mean, you can't say you didn't take *some* action to get the milk, but did you come home with milk?

If you want to become successful at selling, or anything else, it requires a strict adherence to a process. Anything—and I repeat, *anything*—*that causes you to close out to a proven process is a block to your own success. It will slow it down or kill it completely.*

Process requires an all-in approach. What willful people must understand is that they need to follow each and every step in a process and do it in the intended order. Shortcuts are individualized thinking, and they shred process altogether. Willful individuals must respect their company's process and those who teach it, and must work to persistently master it. I know that I've missed sales by adding one extra line to a close. One line! That's how important it is to become succinct with a selling process. And without a process, I wouldn't have even known to reflect on that *one solitary* line. Process provides reliable benchmarks for measurement.

To increase your confidence, keep your hubris in check. Don't throw cold water on your enthusiastic personality and entrepreneurial spirit; just work it in virtue by following and respecting all of what you should be doing. If you don't like string beans, eat them anyway if they're on the plate of process.

Be Open to Believing

One thing that gives a tremendous advantage to willful people is that they tend to have good imaginations, and like entrepreneurs they are visionaries. They imagine what something might be like, then try to create it. They can get behind these visions and, thus, become true believers in a process—that is, when they are convinced.

Consider religion, for example. I will not elaborate on my own personal beliefs here in this book, but consider the different mindsets of people who are atheists and those who believe in a higher power. Consider the difference between people who need constant proof of something in order for them to believe in it and those who go on faith.

While I'm certain that there are many willful people who are atheists, faith requires imagination to believe in something or someone you have not physically seen yourself. This comes more naturally to the willful personality. Someone who's strictly focused on science might point to organized religion as mythology and folklore. But whether there is a higher power or not, those who deeply believe in a philosophy of religion can gain a sense of power, feeling that they are in a relationship that is directed and guided. Yet it requires a leap of faith to get on board.

When a mind is open and believes in something strongly, it lets in the benefits of core-belief thinking, an enormous strength that comes only from belief. When people are strong believers in something, there is little that can stop them. Therefore, wouldn't those with strong core beliefs in selling fare even better when they believe strongly in following a proven process 100%? And even more so if they are also open to more knowledge and growth? Very definitely. It would lend great advantage in all things they focus on accomplishing.

Again, I'm not advocating belief in religion or otherwise, but consider how someone who is rooted in a science-only attitude—with a show-me-the-proof skepticism—would compare with someone capable of true belief. Power is cultivated by strong core beliefs.

Consider, too, the magnitude of Alcoholics Anonymous. It is a 12-step program that requires a buy-in of faith. Faith does not require proof. It requires belief. If people go around questioning everything that they *could* accept but choose to be filled with doubt, they'll find themselves at a disadvantage and will more easily tumble into obstacles. Doubt generates hesitation. Belief creates forward movement. It's as simple as that. Like most ideas in this book, these are choices for you to make.

It Takes a Great Willingness and Openness to Grow

Willful people who remain willful can easily become skeptics over time. They run the risk of becoming self-righteous and self-absorbed know-it-alls. Their accomplishments remain unrealized and trail off into the dustbin of potential. However, if they continue along the path of growth and remain open to ideas—even the ones that challenge what they thought they already knew—they will benefit from expanding their thoughts. It takes a great willingness and openness to grow from being willful into becoming persistent (Green Stage 5), but they're two of the most aligned personalities to compare.

Maturity is the bridge from willfulness to persistence. Mature determination is derived from being exposed to new ideas and embracing possibilities. Developing good judgment comes from knowing which things actually make sense. With a keen understanding of selling philosophy, a good grasp on selling psychology, and a cooperative spirit to follow all the steps we are taught, we grow. One cannot make the leap from willful to persistent without having a strong maturity and discipline. Reaching and maintaining persistent (Green Stage 5) requires unusual dedication.

If believing that a 12-step program can keep someone who's suffering from alcoholism from drinking, then there's no denying that belief has power. It's life-altering. Believing in a sales philosophy—such as LEAD—holds that same power. It offers clear direction and certainty for those who follow it. It will help you to accomplish great things. And to get there, you must choose to buy into the program and believe in it.

If You Were Profiled as *Willful*

If you were profiled as *willful*, you must be willing to do the following:

1. Be "hone-able." Be open to accepting that you do not already know enough, regardless of how much you know. There is always more to learn.
2. Tame your temperament to go the distance. Understand that you need great discipline to make it big. If you are willful, you probably already have great determination, but it may not be properly focused on the things you say you want. Discipline is a forever thing. If you are not disciplined to work by way of a process, you will bounce around from success to failure based on your mood. Discipline yourself for the long haul.
3. Avoid the temptation of making changes to process. Even slight changes can produce unintended consequences. Being willful means you feel confident in your judgment. However,

you do not know what it is you don't know, and as you build your experience, you must remain cooperative with the direction you are getting from your manager, especially if your manager is LEAD-trained. Selling is a process. Creativity should be left to the entrepreneurs.

4. Go *all in* and place yourself in the hands of a process that you might sometimes disagree with or agree with in part. Agree to follow it without making changes.

If you cannot bring yourself to do all these things, I recommend that you not work at a company with a process-driven approach that you did not create.

Questions for Someone with a *Willful* Personality

There are three sets of questions you should ask that have been designed for the specific profiles in this book. Ask the first two sets before you hire an applicant (global and specific interview questions). And ask yourself the third set (30-day review questions) 30 days after hiring. You can access the questions and the 30-day reviews at www.myleadprofile.com.

YELLOW

Personality: *Respectful*

33.4% of Yellow; 20.6% of all profiles

VIRTUE
Courteous

TRAITS USUALLY ASSOCIATED WITH THIS PERSONALITY
Values relationships
Likable
Kind-hearted
Caring

VIRTUES HELPFUL TO SELLING
Cares for others
Personalized warmth
Good listener

DEFICIENCY (THE OPPOSITE OF THIS PERSONALITY)
Bullying behaviors
Disrespect
Inconsideration

EXCESS (THIS PERSONALITY WHEN OUT OF CONTROL)
Challenges to Selling
Passive
Shyness
Introvert
Values relationships over results (a false choice; it should be both)

Compromised negotiating
Timidity
Fearful to impart corrective thinking when a prospect is misinformed
Virtue-signaling behaviors; does not want to be seen as a "typical salesperson"
Shyness
Excuse-making
Justifications for failures (It's not me; it's something else)

TRAITS SIMILAR TO RESPECTFUL'S

Professional
Instinctive

MOST RELATABLE GREEN TRAIT

The most relatable Green trait is *advantageous*.

WHAT YOU NEED TO FOCUS ON

Learn and internalize the value of applying corrective thinking to a prospect. Understand and internalize the difference between helping people and being confrontational with them. See courtesy as a human kindness and helpful to selling; just don't let it interfere with your ability to help people by telling them the truth. Focus on serving over selling. Remember, selling is how you serve.

The *Respectful* Candidate

Shawn's Story

I am always respectful of other people. I listen to what people have to say. I don't believe in pushing people into buying something they don't want or need. I am definitely not pushy. If someone is interested in something, I'm always happy to help. I just wouldn't want to make people uncomfortable by pushing my product or service at them. If my product or service has the right value for my prospects, I'm sure they'll see it and want to buy it. And when they say no, it means no.

I can remember when I was young, my family bought a used car from a dealer. We never had a new car, but a good used car always felt new to us. Anyhow, the dealer promised my dad a lot of things, and he believed him. That dealer never delivered on half of what he promised. The car was a clunker, a real lemon. My dad was so mad at that salesman. He would swear about him whenever it was brought up. He made sure we all knew that he thought salespeople were all crooks.

I'm sure they're not all crooks, and my dad's opinion was his emotions getting the best of him. Unfortunately, it's hard to trust a salesperson. If I were to sell, I would never be anything like that used-car salesman. I would listen to what my customers tell me they want, and I would make them happy!

About the *Respectful*

Good and naturally inclined salespeople have that something special. It's hard to define, but it's easy to detect when you're in the presence of someone who's got "that thing," that certain charisma. It may not even look like a tremendously noticeable personality trait before it is fully developed, but inside that person, there is a quality that's brewing, a craving for a definition, a meaning, a desire for significance, and a way to show its importance.

Successful career salespeople aren't selling because they couldn't find anything better to do. They are *passionate* about selling. Communicating effectively and influencing others *is* their life. They cannot picture themselves doing anything else.

Sometimes it takes getting that first job in sales to realize your passion for it. But once exposed, if you're the right type, there's no turning back. If you think of selling as a pushy, negative job, however, then you've got it all wrong.

Let's discuss what it means to be respectful in selling, in the first place.

Everyone knows that being respectful is in itself a virtue. We are taught at a young age, for example, to respect our elders; and as we grow into adulthood, most of us are fairly well rounded in the way we treat other people. To respect others is to show you care. Therein lies the virtue of being respectful, and it's good.

In selling, however, respectful personalities might confuse challenging a prospect's incorrect and preconceived ideas as a form of disrespect. Remember, the saying wasn't "Respect others *unless they're wrong.*" We are taught that it is virtuous and respectful to allow others to have their own opinions even when they're wrong. Yet that's not being respectful in selling.

For example, let's say that you have a high-quality product, such as a replacement window that's far more insulated than anything else a prospect could purchase. It looks incredible, comes with a high pedigree, and has a 100% lifetime material and labor warranty that completely covers those who invest in it. The warranty is even transferable to a new owner when the house is sold. Let's also add that there are 10 more attributes that far outweigh even the next best window available. Now, picture a salesperson—whose idea of respectfulness equates to not challenging inaccurate preconceived notions—meeting with a prospect who thinks all windows are reasonably close in value and is highly suspicious of salespeople.

The prospect tells the respectful salesperson, "All windows are basically the same to me. I'm sure yours are great, but just give me a price. Anything would be better than what I have now. I don't want to hear all this stuff you're covering about your window." What does the respectful salesperson do?

If lazy or easily discouraged, which is common when not fully committed to following a specific selling process, respectful personalities will use the prospect's unwillingness to listen as the **rationale** to avoid covering everything that they should. They'll skip parts of their presentation and take shortcuts to move their presentation along. Thus, turning a potentially great and convincing case into an individualized facsimile of the process. And without the designed delivery as it was intentionally written, the outcome flops. A respectful salesperson who has slipped into laziness would **rationalize**, "They didn't want to hear my presentation." And **justify** it by reasoning, "It would be disrespectful and rude for me to ignore their request to stop covering information."

By covering less than the entire presentation, the salesperson is 100% off the company's process. This is a critical point to internalize. If you are off your selling process in *any* respect, you are 100% off that process. Stop to think about that.

It is crucial to accept this idea as your core-belief thinking. For a true pro, this kind of thinking is nonnegotiable. A process for selling should never be compromised by a **justification** to preserve your ego or acquiesce to fear. The question should never be about what to cut out. It should be redirected to asking yourself, "How do I get back into my presentation, despite my prospect's unwillingness to listen?"

How to Drive the Selling Highway

Think of the sales process as a highway. You learn to drive that highway as you learn to master delivering all your presentation exactly as it was written. After some experience, the drive is easy and smooth. Then comes an objection. An early objection may be insignificant, which only requires you to nod that you noticed it as you continue driving down the highway.

But then you're given a *real* objection. Think of it as a need to take an off-ramp, and once at the bottom of that ramp, the only thought you should have in your head is about finding an on-ramp back onto the highway. You answer objections with skill that comes from preparation—your training and experience—then smoothly merge back into the selling process. You cannot allow yourself to take a detour or an alternate route because of an objection that took you off the highway. If you take another route, your process-driven presentation will fail, and you will not be helping anyone today.

If respectful personalities are afraid to merge back onto that highway, they might handle this objection by making an **excuse** to themselves of not wanting to be disrespectful to a prospect. Are these salespeople **justified** in their decisions? Only if their objective is to try to sell something by choosing to follow their intuition over their company's process.

If you don't want to be seen as a typical sales rep, no prospect will *catch you selling,* so to speak, if what you're doing is *serving*. So, you have nothing to fear about getting back on the highway to your process-driven approach. But it takes commitment and learning how to apply the skill of corrective thinking. It also requires that you have it in you to be a leader.

ARE YOUR PROSPECTS BEING HELPED BY NOT GOING WITH YOU?

What happens when prospects don't go with your high-quality window and settle for something less? Will their outcome be better? Will their warranty last longer? Will they get the same level of service they would have gotten from you?

Will the best product always win the sale? No, but the company that sent the best interpreter of value will. And the best interpreter of value is a process-driven salesperson, hands down.

The establishment of value is essential to a sale. Without it, your efforts will degenerate into a price-only bidding war. No prospect is helped by ignoring value. Losing a sale to a lower price is something to notice. It's a signal that you need to show your prospects more value in your company and product.

When working in virtue, you serve people by selling to them. Imagine if your company had the best product and the best service and offered the best value. Who wins? The prospects who invest in your product. Therefore, if you are a respectful salesperson and suffer from an excessive fear or laziness, are you actually respecting your prospects if you don't persist with your offer to help them? Of course not. Respectfulness becomes the block to following your company's system for selling, and it's nothing more than an **excuse** to **justify** fear or laziness on the part of a weak-willed salesperson. In this way, *respectful personalities who do not gain a strength of purpose—by consistently following process—can only sell but never serve.* Prospects are the ones who get the short end of the stick. There is no way to work in a state of virtue if you think being liked is more important than really helping someone. Stand up for what is right, and always let doing what is right be your guide.

When going up against other companies, I've found that many of the salespeople we would compete against are performing a lazy "pitch." I can't call what they do a presentation. They are in and out of a prospect's home in little time. Sometimes they sell, but then the prospect who just made the purchase continues shopping, knowing there is a three-day period during which the sale can be canceled. That selling effort isn't solid and often unravels. Then, in walks a company, such as ours, that performs on-process and makes the sale.

THREE IMPORTANT QUESTIONS

In the replacement window field, our specialty, a complete sale from beginning to end takes as much time as needed and covers the details. A one-call process-driven presentation must answer three important questions:

1. Why should the prospect go with your company to the exclusion of all others?
2. Why should the prospect go with your product to the exclusion of all others?
3. Why should the prospect become your customer today, on the initial visit?

First, the company. A salesperson must make a complete and outstanding case for why a prospect should go with the salesperson's company, to the exclusion of all others. This should include trial closes, a technique of using mini-commitments throughout the presentation, to which the prospect agrees. These will ensure that your company is the *only* company the prospect would consider.

A trial close used after making a big point might sound like this: "Now that you know there are companies that only warrantee their product for 10 or 20 years, and only give you a one-year guarantee on labor, and now you know you can have a warranty that covers materials and labor for a lifetime, is there any way you would ever settle for only a 10- or 20-year warranty?" The prospect says no, and the trial close is accepted.

It's important to use a delivery style that includes tie-downs, such as, "It's noteworthy that our company has an impressive A+ rating with the Better Business Bureau, wouldn't you agree?" Including "wouldn't you agree" at the end of the statement makes prospects comfortable with accepting the points you are making. This technique sets little markers of agreement from your prospects, of which they could be reminded later, should they forget. Other similar tie-downs include "Isn't it?" "Shouldn't it?" "Wouldn't it?" "Aren't they?" "Can't you?" and "Won't they?" Even asking—"Does that make sense to you?" after making a point can create the same kind of acknowledgment from a prospect. Note: If there are two prospects, ask them both separately, or you may unwittingly alienate one of the two.

Without making a substantial presentation that seals the fate of the competition and secures your company as the only real choice, sales might be made, but they'll be compromised by price, weak terms, pointless promises, and unnecessarily high cancellation rates. If you resort to using a lazy pitch, you'll make it easy for another company to come in, unravel your lazy contract, and cancel your lazy sale. Thus, bringing that prospect over to becoming another company's customer.

The good news for many of you reading this book: In today's world, you'll run up against a lot of poorly trained, unskilled, and lazy salespeople who work more like estimators and don't deserve to make the sale. If you're prepared and well versed in your company's specific way of conducting business—assuming it's good—you'll clean up on your competition.

Next, the product. There are a lot of products competing in today's marketplace. It's advantageous if your product has features that can be considered exclusive. If someone cannot get a feature from anyone else but you, and if you make that feature attractive enough to your prospect, it'll make the decision to invest in your offer that much easier. In the window business, we've found that a good number of prospects held the incorrect opinion that all windows were pretty much the same. Whatever your industry, there's probably a similar misconception. In the absence of a value interpreter, such as yourself, that incorrect assumption will be accepted by your prospect if it's left unaddressed. You must carefully differentiate your product from all others, and your company should have a sales presentation that addresses the need for *exclusivity* and *differentiation.*

If your product is not properly differentiated against others, your presentation will degenerate into a price war. If you're selling cheap materials and cheap labor for a low profit, I would argue that you are not genuinely serving your customers well. If you honestly respect them, you would want them to make decisions that would truly benefit their lives, not just make a quick buck by taking advantage of an uninformed consumer. Only fear or laziness would drive a selling effort that's based on fighting a price war with your competition.

Last, why today. Your prospects must feel a sense of urgency if they are to invest in your product or service at your initial meeting. Without urgency, prospects will have plenty of reasons to wait and keep shopping. If you want to master one-call selling, you must include an urgent element that provides compelling reasons why it should happen today.

In the case of respectful personalities who don't understand that true respect means actually helping their customers, these salespeople will have difficulty explaining the reasons why investing today is so important. That reluctance to provide prospects with a better value for a same-day purchase will feed into human nature, which is to procrastinate. It is, after all, unnatural to decide to move ahead with something right away. Buying decisions can feel somewhat painful to people. We all want the benefit of a product without having to pay the price. And there is never a good time to write a big check or make a sizable commitment. So, *the value of your company and product must outweigh a hesitancy to proceed. Value is the only antidote to a price objection.* Deciding to move forward today involves investing money, so your case on *value* must be airtight.

If a prospect thinks that the price is too high, a masterful presenter will drill down on what the prospect's idea of what the price should be and will ask where the figure came from. Then it can be challenged without pressure by simply giving your prospect a new perspective.

In other words, if the price your prospect thought your product *should* cost is lower than the value the prospect derived from your presentation, first fix your presentation to show more value. Next, take whatever your prospect thought the price should be, and add in the features that differentiate your product. Assign a dollar amount to each feature. Exclusive features are especially useful in reframing the value of any offer. Add these features to what the prospect thought it should cost. Then, it becomes a question of features versus value, which means price versus value. By taking a prospect's expected price and adding in your extra features, you can increase the *perceived value* of your offer and bridge the gap. Once a prospect feels that the value of your offer is greater than the price, it will make sense logically.

And this takes us to the other important factor in closing a sale—emotions. For prospects to decide to move forward today, they must embrace doing so logically *and* emotionally. Therefore, selling requires that you connect both the logical and the emotional reasons for investing in your product. Reinforcing this belief is Mark Curry, CEO of Your Remodeling Guys, LLC: "People will make decisions to buy a certain thing based on emotions; however, they need to justify that decision logically. The most effective means of selling will appeal to both the right and the left hemispheres of the prospect's brain."

Not buying today must be seen as more painful to your prospect than moving forward with an order now. There is a lot written about two important driving forces: the fear of loss and the hope of gain. For most consumers, a fear of loss is a stronger motivator than a hope of gain. It has been said that people will fight harder to keep $20 from falling from their wallet than they will to put $20 in it. Fear of loss is emotional and therefore highly impactful. When such loss feels unnecessary, it becomes even more important to the consumers to solve their problem right away.

PRACTICE, AND PRACTICE AGAIN AND AGAIN

To become a long-term success, all salespeople must study and practice mastering their company's selling system. This is something that requires revisiting often. Too many don't reread their training once they hit the road. That's like seeing one weather report and feeling prepared for life. You're going to get wet.

Perfect practice makes perfect, and, therefore, the approach to performing these steps must be made automatic through repetition. Once you spend the time to cut those neuropathways in your brain to work your company's process automatically, it will be hard to fail. After performing the proven steps of selling enough times, it becomes a committed muscle memory. A higher level of success is available to anyone who has the discipline. Success begets success, and more will follow. Achievement feeds on success.

It Is Mentally Exhausting to Constantly Reinvent Your Approach

Can you imagine just winging all the psychology that's needed to sell or having to make it up as you go along? When respectful salespeople get knocked off the highway of process, too often they take the back road to their destination and wing it. Salespeople who don't follow process have to reinvent their approach each time they are in a new selling situation. Just because you get an objection in one particular presentation doesn't mean you should alter your approach the next time you perform it. Noodling with a presentation isn't being true to it.

It is mentally exhausting to spend so much brainpower coming up with new approaches to sell just because you haven't committed yourself to selling on one good one. If this is your style, you are spending precious time reinventing the wheel and far too little time building and serving a client base. When it gets right down to it, consumers want honesty, which is a real virtue.

God help salespeople who have individualized opinions about everything. When complicating so much of the selling process, the lack of consistent net results will speak for itself.

If You Were Profiled as *Respectful*

If you were profiled as *respectful,* you must be willing to do the following:

1. Conduct yourself by way of action. Accept that showing respect does not mean you should retreat in the face of objections. True respect is to believe in what you are offering. When guided by real belief, persisting in the face of

objections is the best kind of respect you can offer to anyone. Don't merely understand this: *Act* in a manner that says you do.
2. Don't fear a prospect who acts like a bully. People make decisions based on information. Lead a sales presentation as the one person carrying the needed information. Convey that information to your prospect without giving up before you should (which is based on your company's process).
3. Avoid using the **excuse** of not wanting to be rude as a reason for giving up before you should. Believe in yourself as an agent of influence. Be someone who is legitimately trying to help others. Let your passion and genuineness be a catalyst for influence. Focus on helping your prospects, even when they don't realize, as you do, that they need the help.
4. Go *all in* and place yourself in the hands of a process that you might sometimes disagree with or agree with in part. Agree to follow it without making changes.

If you cannot bring yourself to do all these things, I recommend that you not work at a company with a process-driven approach that you did not create.

Questions for Someone with a *Respectful* Personality

There are three sets of questions you should ask that have been designed for the specific profiles in this book. Ask the first two sets before you hire an applicant (global and specific interview questions). And ask yourself the third set (30-day review questions) 30 days after hiring. You can access the questions and the 30-day reviews at www.myleadprofile.com.

YELLOW

Personality: *Instinctive*

18.8% of Yellow; 11.6% of all profiles

VIRTUE
Natural

TRAITS USUALLY ASSOCIATED WITH THIS PERSONALITY
Casual
Visceral
Subliminal
Self-sufficient
Impulsiveness
Spontaneity

VIRTUES HELPFUL TO SELLING

Instinctiveness is not a good or bad thing; what matters is how it is developed to meet a specific purpose. Reprogramming components of a person's instinctiveness towards process-driven behaviors can make a belief in process exceptionally strong.

DEFICIENCY (THE OPPOSITE OF THIS PERSONALITY)
Overcalculating
Rationalistic
Induced
Careful
Overanalyzing

EXCESS (THIS PERSONALITY WHEN OUT OF CONTROL)

Challenges to Selling

Highly opinionated

Unconscious justifier

Challenged by following another person's deliberate process

Irrationally negative

Impulsively reacts from feelings

Worry

Comfortable with complacency

Insecure

Reacts to a challenge, instead of responding to one

Resistant to change

Fearful or lazy

Rationalizes not bothering to try

TRAITS SIMILAR TO INSTINCTIVE'S

Sensitive

Willful

MOST RELATABLE GREEN TRAIT

The most relatable Green trait is *demonstrative*.

WHAT YOU NEED TO FOCUS ON

First, show an honest willingness to consciously direct your efforts to a cultivated process—instead of making spontaneous, individualized decisions that interfere with following a process. Be certain that you are willing to put in the work to follow your process. If not, a career in selling stands little chance of getting off the ground. Learn to trust process more than your own instincts. Make an agreement to follow process over instinct for one full year without question. If that commitment is kept, you can then develop into a naturally accepting, process-driven salesperson who will likely become successful. Since what you feel is what you go with, you need to make what you feel align with process selling without exception. By doing so, you can become very strong.

The *Instinctive* Candidate

Sammy's Story

There is a lot of political division in the country, and that's because there is only one party that does the right thing. It is my party. They are for the good people. Those who believe as I do are good people. They made our country better. I have no respect for the people in the opposing party. They are brainwashed. I know what I feel, and I've held these feelings for a long time.

I love music, but not all music. I know good music, and I know what bad music is too. I sing in a band from time to time. The problem is always in finding the right people to form a band. Too many crazy ideas. I can't be around that for too long.

I don't have much, but I find a way to get by. Unfortunately, sometimes I have to lean on my friends to help me out, but I have very good friends who are there for me when I need them.

About the *Instinctive*

Sammy listens to his feelings. He is less proactive and more reactive in his approach to life. He does not have great ambition. He was brought up in a way that allowed him to develop lazy habits. His routine lets life go on around him without him having to take responsibility in ways that grow strength of character. Being allowed to disengage socially, Sammy could do whatever he pleased, however he pleased. He didn't need to work, since his parents never made it a point to teach him the value of hard work or the virtues of contribution. They never expected him to work. They weren't well-off, but they lived on less and never gave it much thought.

THE EXPECTATIONS OF EARLY INFLUENCERS

Expectations play a key role when determining what is possible. Revisiting the expectations of your early influencers, if there were few expectations to none, the inspirational seed lay dormant. If there were high expectations placed upon you early in life, you were probably challenged to break from your instinctual comfort zone and expand. The manner in which that expansion took place would have affected your desire to be accomplished or your fear of failing. How you got there can be explained. The question is, *What do you do with it?*

When *under-cultivated to a real sense of purpose*, instinct is a default setting. For the instinctive person, it can mean living by way of **excuse**, brushing off the idea of potential growth as silly and unnecessary. Skepticism fills the void of curiosity, and people are less likely to take chances—**rationalizing** basic risk as unimportant and unworthy, an unwanted intrusion to living a life by way of default.

IS RISK DANGEROUS?

Instinct is important. It alerts our nervous system to be fearful in the face of danger. That is why, without good internal programming, we have a harder time separating a challenge from a *true* danger.

Danger in the physical sense is obvious. If you live like Keith Moon, the former drummer of The Who, who edged his way from a seventh-floor hotel balcony onto a three-inch ledge just to tap on someone's window, dangerous risk is obvious and physical. But what about applying for a job in an unknown field? Is that risk a danger, or is it merely a challenge? What about contemplating going for a promotion to become a manager? Even greater, what about the risk involved in becoming self-employed, where your risk to reward is heightened, and your responsibilities to others are intensified? Danger and challenge are clearly not always the same thing.

WE CAN LIVE OUR LIVES BY DESIGN OR BY DEFAULT

Consider Sammy's story. Since his parents were largely absent, he had no disciplined direction to guide him. He instinctually overcompensated for a lack in confidence, which gave him an ugly arrogance to defend against perceived attack. There was nothing productive in his life that steered him toward an accomplishment. Ironically, it is the feeling of accomplishment that would have helped him to gain confidence. Instinct needs to be formed and informed if we are to design the outcomes we want. When we understand what is at stake, it seems plenty obvious that either we design our lives, or our lives will become unguided by default. The good news: It is a conscious choice to make.

In selling, a process gives salespeople specific things to do to move strategically toward a sale. It requires following deliberate steps that are precise and philosophically, psychologically, and logically considered—not unlike a structure of good parenting that will aid the development of a child. Process provides a clear set of expectations that produce an intended outcome.

The pivotal questions for instinctive personalities are simple: Are they truly willing to follow a process that they did not create? Will they follow it faithfully? Or will they break ranks with structure and apply their own way of thinking in the moment?

A QUESTION OF WILLINGNESS

Everyone's personality has a virtue, a balanced, productive place to be. Instinctive people are accustomed to following gut impulse, so developing their excessive behaviors into their particular virtue will require a shift in paradigm, one that accepts that a learned process is something that's more important to follow than gut feelings. Each person, however, is different, and that is a challenge. Instinctive people can use the four levels of development—which are covered in Green Stage 3, serious (see page 191)—as a structure to grow. It is a question of willingness.

If You Were Profiled as *Instinctive*

If you were profiled as *instinctive*, you must be willing to do the following:

1. Place your *complete* trust in a process that you did not create, even when you question an approach. If you do not understand something, ask for clarification—but be willing to follow process, nonetheless.
2. Commit to your success. You cannot have just one toe in the water. You have to commit to achievement at a level you might have never experienced before. Dedicate yourself to it like it's a matter of life or death.
3. Agree to being uncomfortable with ideas that do not necessarily fit into your current comfort zone, so that you can expand it considerably. To get new and different results, you will need to think in new and different ways.
4. Go *all in* and place yourself in the hands of a process that you might sometimes disagree with or agree with in part. Agree to follow it without making changes.

If you cannot bring yourself to do all these things, I recommend that you not work at a company with a process-driven approach that you did not create.

Questions for Someone with an *Instinctive* Personality

There are three sets of questions you should ask that have been designed for the specific profiles in this book. Ask the first two sets before you hire an applicant (global and specific interview questions). And ask yourself the third set (30-day review questions) 30 days after hiring. You can access the questions and the 30-day reviews at www.myleadprofile.com.

YELLOW

Classification: *Potential*

9.3% of Yellow; 5.8% of all profiles

VIRTUE

The candidate has not been ruled out for hire. The graph in Figure 3.2 displays a level of potential in any or all of the following: leadership, extroversion, attitude, and disposition—LEAD.

DEFICIENCY (THE OPPOSITE OF THIS CLASSIFICATION)
Unknown

EXCESS (THIS CLASSIFICATION WHEN OUT OF CONTROL)
Unknown

WHAT YOU NEED TO FOCUS ON

Learn what selling leadership is really all about. Think about what influence means in your connection with others. Be ultra-cooperative in your training and your selling duties. Be supremely willing to follow instructions and show eagerness about doing everything necessary within your power to learn and apply your company's selling process. Stand out as someone who is committed to following process.

About the *Potential*

A potential candidate might not fit into any of the personality profiles. Therefore, we'll discuss potential not as a personality but as a classification. A potential profile is categorized as Yellow because while it doesn't show a specific personality, it does make apparent a compatibility to a standard one-call selling model and the potential for selling success.

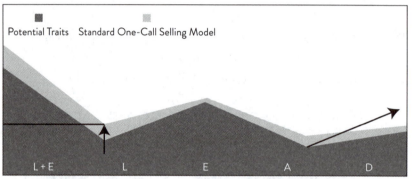

FIGURE 3.2 The *potential* classification graph comparing the *potential* traits with the standard one-call selling model.
Key: LE—leadership + extroversion combined, L—leadership, E—extroversion, A—attitude, D—disposition.

Figure 3.2 shows the profile of someone who was categorized as a potential. None of the numbers are spiked too high or shown to be too low. For those candidates who are classified as potential, it's important to pinpoint their attitude, willingness, and openness. There isn't much else to go on, as the profile of the potential shows neither an obvious promise nor any evident disqualifications.

In the figure, the potential candidate doesn't show a strong intensity in the categories of leadership (L) and extroversion (E), nor does the curve from attitude (A) to disposition (D) show quite the level of openness we would want to see for someone learning how to sell. What it does show is *potential*, a nine-letter word that could mean a lot—or nothing at all.

LEADERSHIP

If the candidate passes the scrutiny of a professional interview and then takes well to sales training, the leadership number should grow. This can take some time. The graph shows leadership (L) at 26. While not bad, it could stand an increase of up to 39, which would signify a stronger style. In time, without an increase in leadership, this potential salesperson runs the greater risk of standing down to a prospect who's misinformed or who's using skewed logic.

Low leadership numbers will show up in low net sales rates and an unacceptable NSLI (net sales per leads issued). This is addressed over time when a salesperson develops and internalizes the needed key core beliefs.

As we discussed in the section on the respectful personality, a potential's main mission is to answer three key questions:

1. Why should a prospect choose your company to the exclusion of all others?
2. Why should a prospect choose your product to the exclusion of all others?
3. Why should a prospect become your customer today, on the initial visit?

Good leadership is like a magnet in that all people are inclined to follow strong and trustworthy leadership. It's not that we go to bed each night praying we'll find a strong leader, but when we meet one, it's noticeable, and it creates an attraction. Once salespeople truly believe in their own answers to these three questions and have internalized them as gospel, they'll communicate with a prospect with *stronger* feelings that show a credibility and a zealousness that live at the salesperson's core. It's real.

EXTROVERSION

In Figure 3.2, the extroversion number (E) for the potential is 56. It is well within the margins we seek. The range of 53–60 shows a level of seriousness that's workable but never crosses over into excessiveness. Anything above 60 would indicate a stronger need to be liked. By staying under 61, this person shows more seriousness and less gregariousness. At 53, there is a sign of greater seriousness. Closer to 60, however, the person will be more enthusiastically demonstrative.

ATTITUDE AND DISPOSITION

Attitude levels (A) are more established when over 20, even 30. Measuring the importance of attitude is a factor of disposition (D). Where A sits in relationship to D is important.

The attitude on the potential's graph isn't really weak, but the natural disposition of this potential candidate would be much better if it were increased by another 5 points, but not higher than another 16 points. Ideally, we would want to see A somewhere around 30, but 23 would be fine, provided it's within 8–19 points lower than D. This shows a really good level of openness in the mindset of the candidate.

However, when A is more than 19 points lower than D, candidates are more guarded, we lose their openness, they tend to be less responsive to working "concepts" (which is what your selling process is), and they are less likely to share what they feel about what they casually ignore. Many will keep their personal opinions private, which makes those salespeople harder to train and assess. Communication is important to training and learning.

So, what happens if A is higher than D? Candidates with a potential profile would never show that characteristic. But briefly and for the sake of this discussion: When A is higher than D, the candidates are showing signs of not being open-minded enough to learn and work with a selling process that they did not design. They're more likely to openly show skepticism, possibly putting your whole process and its worthiness on trial. This is not a winning formula for hiring a new salesperson. But again, this wouldn't apply to the potential profile.

Three Important Considerations Before Hiring a *Potential*

For the candidate who's classified as a potential, there is limited information, so an in-person interview and the interview questions are especially important. Since potentials are a bit of a mystery, we want to ask questions that will help them to open up. Be sure to review and use the Six Global Interview Questions and Interview Questions Specific to Someone Profiled as a *Potential*. Ultimately when hiring, we want to keep three important considerations in mind:

- **Is this person a cultural fit?** Does the person possess the four Hs? Is the person honest, humble, hone-able, and hungry?
- **What is this person's aptitude for working in sales at your company?** LEAD can usually help with that. In the case of the potential salesperson, it's about probing to find out who the person is, what the person knows, and if this person is a fit for your company. Is the person open, willing, responsive, engaged, and urgent? These five considerations are important for all hires but particularly so with those who profile in one of the three categories: potential, novice, and inconsistencies.
- **Is this person reliable?** Be sure to use the Six Global Interview Questions to cover expectations of reliability and general information.

If You Were Profiled as a *Potential*

If you were profiled as a *potential*, you must be willing to do the following:

1. Demonstrate that you are serious about a career in selling. Accept and embrace the protocols, philosophies, psychology, and principles of selling that are taught to you. There can be no question about your willingness to embrace those things.

It must be shown up front and kept in practice throughout your development. It is mandatory.
2. Demonstrate a high-level of openness to the training you are given. Someone with potential is a bigger mystery with respect to dialing into a specific virtue. Thus, a company is taking a chance with you, and there is less tolerance for disapproval of process.
3. Go the extra mile to prove that hiring you was the right decision for the company. Work to show you are committed to your own success. Be willing to do things that less successful people would not. Be active in the development of your career. Be responsive and engaged.
4. Go *all in* and place yourself in the hands of a process that you might sometimes disagree with or agree with in part. Agree to follow it without making changes.

If you cannot bring yourself to do all these things, I recommend that you not work at a company with a process-driven approach that you did not create.

Questions for Someone Who Profiled as a *Potential*

There are three sets of questions you should ask that have been designed for the specific profiles in this book. Ask the first two sets before you hire an applicant (global and specific interview questions). And ask yourself the third set (30-day review questions) 30 days after hiring. You can access the questions and the 30-day reviews at www.myleadprofile.com.

YELLOW

Personality: *Activist*

2.8% of Yellow; 1.8% of all profiles

VIRTUE
Passion

TRAITS USUALLY ASSOCIATED WITH THIS PERSONALITY
Motivated by feelings
Driven by cause

VIRTUES HELPFUL TO SELLING
Care for prospects and the issues that
can be helped by the salesperson

DEFICIENCY (THE OPPOSITE OF THIS PERSONALITY)
Complacency
Getting caught up in distracting personal drama

EXCESS (THIS PERSONALITY WHEN OUT OF CONTROL)
Challenges to Selling
Self-righteousness, feelings of moral superiority
Irrational negativity
"Yacktivism": all talk and no action
Virtue signaling (pseudo-caring)
Too sympathetic about problems with prospects
Not empathetic enough about solutions with prospects

TRAITS SIMILAR TO ACTIVIST'S
Willful

MOST RELATABLE GREEN TRAIT
The most relatable Green trait is *influencer*.

WHAT YOU NEED TO FOCUS ON
Get in touch with what truly motivates you at a conscious level. Learn whether you can become a protagonist in the cause of helping others to improve their lives with what you sell. Stay far away from situations that lend to drama, such as gossiping and making unproductive judgments of others. Do not virtue-signal your willingness to help, but instead make efforts to put in place the solutions that will improve the lives of your prospects. Get behind your company's cause of helping its customers by using empathy and providing solutions, not by offering sympathy and leaving problems unresolved.

The *Activist* Candidate

Marta's Story

I am very big on environmental issues. I believe in green technology. I'm sure that smart people understand, as much as I do, the value of conserving our natural resources and reducing carbon emissions in the environment. I read a lot online and do a lot of research on the health of the planet. I like being educated on important global issues.

As far as selling goes, I don't like pushing people. I have respect for other people's opinions. I believe that people need time to decide what's important to them. If they are shown the value of a good product or service, they'll get back to me when they're ready to go with my product. Why wouldn't they?

I've held a number of jobs over the years. I've been involved in a lot of different things. I'm curious, and I think that it's good to know as much as possible. I have a clear conscience about how I conduct myself.

About the *Activist*

Activists are motivated by cause, and they are attracted to contributing to something that matters. They might see a wrong and want to right it. Or they might be a late-life success story who wants to impart their wisdom to others in a magnanimous way. If they are emotionally connected and can make a difference, activists are motivated. At least, the true ones are.

THE DIFFERENCE BETWEEN AN ACTIVIST AND A YACKTIVIST

To understand what motivates the activist personality, you must first decipher whether you are interviewing a *true* activist or a pseudo-activist. Pseudo-activists are those who virtue-signal just to demonstrate that they are good people. True activists act. Pseudo-activists do a lot of talking and aren't active in the pursuit of their beliefs. I call them *yacktivists*. They are the activists who are excessive, this personality type when out of control. The modern yacktivist, for example, might take a selfie to show off taking part in a march or a cause, but only to fit in or for the accolades.

People who are willing to *act* are true to their cause in a more honest way. People who talk about what everyone else should do and call out others who appear less virtuous than they are aren't true activists; they are complainers.

Talk is cheap!

The Rev. Dr. Martin Luther King Jr. once said, "One of the great tragedies of life is that men seldom bridge the gulf between practice and profession, between doing and saying." For activists with enough passion to follow through on ideas, more power to them. They deserve to be congratulated for creating positive change in the world.

For yacktivists, however, it is unlikely they'll get past their own ideas and opinions long enough to learn new skills, such as selling at a professional level. If they're hired because they want to *try* selling, chances are they won't engage with unfamiliar ideas outside their comfort zone long enough to get anywhere.

ACTIVISM AND SELLING PASSION

Passion is powerful. For activists who want a career in selling, what better way is there than to connect your actions—your profession—to something of purpose, to represent a product or service that makes life better for someone else? Provided their company cares for its customers and carries exceptional products and services, true activists should be able to get behind the idea of bettering the lives of those they serve, a worthy cause. An activist can make a very healthy living in sales by succeeding in the mindset of a win-win arrangement.

For yacktivists, who spend time judging the purity of others, there is little hope for success in the world of professional selling. A virtue-signaling yacktivist is little more than a judgmental complainer, someone with nothing better to do than to label others as less virtuous than the yacktivist. Does that sound like someone you'd want representing your company and serving your client base?

True, there are some customers who can never be satisfied, despite our best efforts. It's unfortunate, but difficult people are a fact of life. Now, imagine a virtue-signaling, excessive, and out-of-control activist—the yacktivist—working in your sales department, angrily bringing you every nuanced complaint from a difficult customer and judging your company as unsatisfactory for not being everything to everyone all the time.

While every good company wants to do right by its customers, there are limits. A good business will usually go above and beyond to help a customer, but some people simply cannot be satisfied. It is rare, but it does occasionally happen. Rather than attempt to quell unreasonable expectations, an excessive activist will likely find fault with your company. And if the person's activism crosses over to politics, the person may see it in a classic mindset of *the little guy versus the big bad company*. It's a problem if your company is doing right by its clients, and yet the excessive activist sees only a disagreement through the eyes of an unreasonable customer.

Additionally, some salespeople are the ones who overpromise and set a customer's unreasonable expectations. They'll then **justify** their own failure at solving a problem by **blaming** the company's protocols and requirements, since some activists can be more likely to fight the process to begin with.

One good way that sincere activists can transform activism into successful selling is by *putting their passion behind the cause of helping prospects—while respecting the virtue of the company they represent.*

Activists should focus not on *selling* to people, but instead on *helping* them, *serving* them. This applies to all personalities and categories of salespeople, but it's a tenet that's elevated for true activists, since they thrive when they have a purpose.

How difficult would it be to work with an activist and not understand what is at the person's motivational core? This is where the LEAD Personality Profile Program for selling provides a better understanding. The activist personality is easy if you can connect purpose to the person's core-belief system.

A HIRING TEST

While interviewing activists, the goal is to determine who they truly are and whether they appear to have any of the attributes of the five Green stages (demonstrative, advantageous, serious, influencer, and persistent) on some natural level. After learning all about the five green stages, use the Six Global Interview Questions and the Interview Questions Specific to an *Activist* Personality. During the interview, always remain true to your mission of hiring those who will best fit your company. If you lose sight of this, then reading this book and working the LEAD program won't save you time or increase your bottom line.

Ideas for Connecting Your Cause to Selling

Start by asking yourself the questions below. They'll serve as a catalyst for exploring what you feel about what you sell, and why. Write down your answers, and examine their meaning. If you can completely buy into your company's mission to serve, then you can channel your activist mindset toward the betterment of others and find fulfillment in the work you do.

- Is your company selling a product or service that is everything you represent it to be?
- How many points of true value can you name about your product/service that outweigh the cost of investing in it?
- What are all the ways your product/service helps a customer?

- What are the consequences your prospects face by not owning your company's product or service?
- What are the exclusive features of the product/service you sell, the things that your prospects cannot get elsewhere?
- How does your company's product/service differentiate itself from other similar products and services being offered in your area?
- How are consumers less benefited by going with your competition instead of you?
- Can you put your mindset on a "mission" to get your product/service to as many prospects as you can so they are benefited by going with you instead of your competition?
- Can you stand up to prospects who do not see the value in your product/service, and can you professionally work to correct their misconceptions?
- Do you empathize with prospects who do not value your product/service as much as they should?
- Are you completely sold on the idea of your product/service, enough to own it yourself?
- Do you currently own the product/service you sell? If yes, why? If no, why not?
- Describe how you feel after you make a sale. Are you mostly happy for your new customer or mostly excited by a sense of achievement and the anticipated commissions?
- Are you satisfied with your company's ability to follow through and serve its customers?
- How could your company better serve its customers?
- What is the number-one thing you offer your prospects/customers?
- Where does your company fall short in meeting customer expectations? Can anything be done to improve it?
- Is there anything about what you sell that makes you feel uncomfortable?

- What about your product/service/company makes you most proud to sell for your company?
- Does your opinion of the product/service/company tend to change from time to time? If yes, why?

If You Were Profiled as an *Activist*

If you were profiled as an *activist*, you must be willing to do the following:

1. Connect your passion for cause to the mission of your company. Sell what you offer in order to help people.
2. Connect yourself to your company. See the two as one. Never disassociate yourself from the company's protocols and the promises made to your customers. If you believe something is being neglected by your company—something that negatively affects your customers—speak to the powers-that-be about it. Express your concerns. Never complain to anyone who is at or below your level at the company. And when a determination is made by the higher-ups, respect it in your actions and your words, and get behind it and back it like it was your idea, even if you disagree with the ruling. If you disagree strongly enough, resign your position before committing a betrayal of the company that signs your paycheck. Work toward perfection, but don't expect things to be perfect. Every good thing is forever a work in progress.
3. Do things to help others. In the world of virtuous selling, selling *is* helping. Don't get involved with any drama. Never think you are acting virtuously if your purpose is only to gain recognition. Mature people understand they do not need to grandstand for compliments. Good deeds rarely go unnoticed by others.

4. Go *all in* and place yourself in the hands of a process that you might sometimes disagree with or agree with in part. Agree to follow it without making changes.

If you cannot bring yourself to do all these things, I recommend that you not work at a company with a process-driven approach that you did not create.

Although it is not true for potential profiles (for whom there's limited information), each of the other personality profiles has a virtue, a deficiency, and an excess. If this person fits a personality type that is workable in a selling role, questions like these will help you probe for excessive and deficient behavioral traits (those not working in virtue), thus avoiding a mess after you've hired someone you shouldn't have.

Questions for Someone with an *Activist* Personality

There are three sets of questions you should ask that have been designed for the specific profiles in this book. Ask the first two sets before you hire an applicant (global and specific interview questions). And ask yourself the third set (30-day review questions) 30 days after hiring. You can access the questions and the 30-day reviews at www.myleadprofile.com.

YELLOW

Classification: *Novice*

1.0% of Yellow; 0.06% of all profiles

VIRTUE

The candidate has not been ruled out for hire. The graph in Figure 3.3 displays some level of potential that might point to leadership, extroversion, attitude, or disposition.

DEFICIENCY (THE OPPOSITE OF THIS CLASSIFICATION)

Unknown

EXCESS (THIS CLASSIFICATION WHEN OUT OF CONTROL)

Challenges to Selling

Unknown

WHAT YOU NEED TO FOCUS ON

Work on growing your skills of influence. Be cooperative, engaged, eager, and willing to do what is necessary to become successful. Make it your mission to follow process without exception. Learn to become an expert at helping people in the role you play.

The *Novice* Candidate

Leah's Story

I am a curious person. I was a reporter for a local newspaper for two years, but I just couldn't really make a living in a dying industry. As an interviewer, I've always been the one asking questions to others, but when I started to think about what I wanted to do with my life, I had to start asking a lot of important questions concerning myself.

I've considered getting into selling at a couple of crossroads between jobs. I've heard it's a lucrative profession. I'm just not sure what I would have a passion to sell. I suppose I could sell almost anything if the money was right.

I'm used to holding people accountable when I reported on stories where people ripped others off, so I know I could hold prospects accountable for making a good decision on buying a good product. I could also hold the company I sell for accountable for taking care of its customers.

There's a lot I don't know, but I'm interested in learning if I could make it as a salesperson.

About the *Novice*

Figure 3.3 shows how Leah scored in LEAD traits. The graph shows that Leah has a decent level of leadership (L) at 30, and her high extroversion (E) number of 64 shows that she's easy to like.

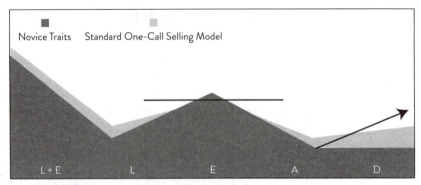

FIGURE 3.3 The novice classification graph comparing novice traits with the standard one-call selling model.

Key: LE—leadership + extroversion combined, L—leadership, E—extroversion, A—attitude, D—disposition.

LEADERSHIP

If the leadership number (L) is 20 to 39, it is a sign that this person might have some natural leadership skills. But if it exceeds 39, it signals a very high level of dominance, and that can be problematic, as the focus of a salesperson can shift away from influence into manipulation. If it is lower, 10–20, leadership can be developed in a person, so long as there are a strong cooperation and willingness to grow.

EXTROVERSION

The ideal level of extroversion (E) is between 53 and 60. If too low, a person's ability to captivate the selling audience with enthusiasm might be lacking, although the person might possess another form of captivation, a sense of respectability like a caring yet authoritative doctor. If the extroversion is too high, over 60, the person's need to be liked is elevated, which can interfere with the ability to influence a prospect.

One important note of caution in this novice graph is the straight line where attitude (A) and disposition (D) meet. This particular line is usually a good indicator of whether a person is open to new information, or whether a person's individualized opinions are too strong and present a challenge to growing openly and willingly. The arrow shows what would be considered a more willing and open-minded sales candidate. But when A and D are equal, and the line runs straight across, as it shows in this graph, we don't have the luxury of that information.

What does it tell us instead? Since A isn't towering over D, it says that this person isn't likely to be excessively closed-minded. However, since A and D are both 23, it doesn't say that the person is open-minded either. And there is a difference between "I'm not closed" and "I'm open."

A person who passively resists—with the attitude of saying, "I'm not closed"—isn't going to jump hurdles to win a race. A race will be won by the person who is *actively open and willing* to do what is necessary in pursuit of excellence. That requires commitment. Be aware of that distinction, and probe it in an interview with a novice. Levels of cooperation and intensity do matter.

DISPOSITION

One thing that seems obvious is that if D were to go up by about 8 points, the graph would look much better in terms of this person's openness.

Why are this person's disposition and attitude numbers the same? It could be because the person is a true novice and knows little about selling. This is fertile ground for a good sales manager to grow someone into a process-driven salesperson, thus raising the level of the person's disposition.

When someone is a true novice but is excited and willing to sell, provided there is not a passive resistance, the person's mind is like clay that's ready for a good sales trainer to sculpt. Certainly, if that's the case, a worthy sales manager would enjoy training a true and open novice. And LEAD provides the clarity to achieve that mission. The difficulty lies in the way people deal with challenges. It is human nature to **blame** circumstances when things don't go as we'd like. Behaviors must be kept in virtue and away from becoming excessive. To avoid passive-resistance or passive-aggressive behaviors, management is also cautioned not to create a work environment where there is a suppression of one's expression.

The Connection Between Personal Accountability and Confidence

If growth is to occur, it's vital that one very important tenet of philosophy is taught, not only to a novice but to *everyone else* going into a sales career. This crucial tenet of philosophy states, "Personal accountability equals self-confidence." Let's explore this in depth:

First, understand yourself. Many people live their lives on autopilot. They do what's safe and comfortable, and they don't give it a whole lot of thought. They get up in the morning, go to work, come home, and go to bed—repeating the same thing each day until they're simply older people. Have you ever talked with someone older who asks, "Where has the time gone?"? It's as if the person were watching life from a seat in an audience, surprised at the time that had passed without a sufficient feeling of accomplishment. Some **blame** fate. Others, circumstances. So many of us spend our youth dreaming about the things we'll do, only to later regret not doing them. But why? To get closer to discovering how to go about increasing your level of accomplishment, start by asking yourself two basic questions: "How well do I know myself?" And "How well do I understand myself?"

To create change for the better, you must first recognize the depth to which your life experiences have programmed your thinking. You'll need to understand the conscious choices that are yours to make that, up until now, have been left to an untrained subconscious, following an intuition that's focused on comfort and not necessarily aligned with what you really want out of life. One thing is certain: The way you think at the subconscious level is the centerpiece to finding answers, which is why you must know *how* to think before you even spend time on what to think about. Your beliefs live in your subconscious mind, and all conscious decisions to make changes have to pass through the subconscious first. This is where they are often stopped from progressing as doubts seep in.

By developing new instincts that serve us better, we then work toward ending our relationship with hopelessness. However, before you decide the details of your plan forward, you'll need to understand what's working for you and against you, and it might not be what you think.

As you begin to study what influences your thinking, you might be surprised to find that some of the coping mechanisms you've built up in the earliest years of your life might still be in play, ones that no longer serve any real purpose for you today. Until they are identified and addressed, they'll block the road to your growth.

The things you'll tell yourself to feel better about a poor outcome could be the very things that stop you from getting a better one. Over time, we form patterns of behavior that are repeated regularly, until they become patterns of unconscious activity, unconscious habits. In other words, we do many things without even thinking about them, and yet these things steer our path.

You should also become aware of the dangers, the pitfalls, of **blame** and **excuses**. Let's bring you back to the years when you were very young. You probably don't remember this, but at some point, somebody, probably an adult figure, became upset with you about something.

Maybe you did something you shouldn't have, perhaps unintentionally. It can be something as innocent as spilling a drink on a carpet. Something happened, and that adult approached you, wagging a finger in your face, rhetorically asking in anger or frustration, "*Why did you do this?*" It was an aggravated attempt at holding you accountable for the very first time. And it scared you.

It could have been a teacher or an employer who frightened you, but somewhere along the line and early on you encountered that finger wagging in your face. Anyone who confuses personal accountability with a personal attack will become defensive. Complicating it further is the tone of the angry adult figure, which can be too much for a young mind to process.

Today, as an adult, when we deflect the responsibility to our outcomes, it creates an on-ramp into a world of **blame** and **excuses**. Like a shield of protection, that deflection becomes a coping mechanism. At first, we see the action of someone pointing out our own accountability as undue criticism, sharply aimed and designed to make us feel bad, a sort of power control that someone has over us. And when our knee-jerk intuition drives our actions, we **blame** anyone and anything around us for things that went wrong. The **excuses** we give aren't really what we make them out to be. We go right back to our early programming, where we felt scared hearing that we were responsible for something that went wrong. We're all wired to look for ways around the things that make us feel uncomfortable. It's just being human.

So, here you are, living in a world of **blame** and **excuses** that you probably didn't even know exists. You've built up a shield to deflect criticism to protect your feelings and emotions. It starts to build an ego and a closed mentality. You become hardened against hearing a critique that would hold you accountable. Your (A) line (attitude) towers over your (D) line (disposition) on the LEAD Personality Profile graph. You then go about your life dealing with difficult situations in this manner. In all these years, you felt **justified** in telling yourself that you were the victim of undue criticism, and it made you feel better. Right? Wrong.

The truth is, while it feels good to say that it's not you, your problems aren't getting solved. If you're not the reason something went wrong, then you also don't have the power to fix anything. You can go through life valuing your sense of security above the fact that you're not getting things done, but it renders you helpless. Ironically, by protecting yourself and your feelings, you think you're increasing your security, but you're actually building a stronger *insecurity*.

Ask yourself, *Has deflecting responsibility ever actually solved anything for you?* Deep down, past the façade of our egos, we all know the truth. When you allow yourself to become comfortable with deflecting responsibility, you create a cognitive dissonance, holding two contrary beliefs in your mind: the lies you tell yourself and the accountability you avoid. You develop a restlessness and a stress that can create depression. Conflicting beliefs are never at peace with each other. Even worse, if you attempt to reconcile this restlessness by denying your responsibility even further, you begin to believe your own **excuses**.

That's when you learn to explain away your lack of success with bravado and righteous indignation. But it'll cost you a productive future.

As we get older, simple **blame** and **excuses** become fancier words like **justifications** and **rationalizations**.

THE FOUR WORDS THAT ARE THE MOST DESTRUCTIVE TO YOUR GROWTH

Blame, **excuses**, **justifications**, and **rationalizations** are the most destructive words around which to form a personal identity. Anytime you hear yourself using any of those words in a sentence or applied to a point of accountability, you can assume that something is not right. These words are triggers and need to be noticed and then avoided at *all cost*. Using any of them will let you know that you're on the wrong track in your thinking. As noted in the Introduction, these four words are set in boldface type throughout this book. I've done this purposely to help you be aware of how important they are and how deeply they infiltrate all areas of life.

As we **justify** and **rationalize** things, we try to make something that's not right sound right. We attempt to explain something in such a way as to avoid its true meaning, in order to make it appear more tolerable and acceptable. We tell ourselves that things have to be a certain way, even though that's not true. Sadly, against any hope of success, when operating under the influence of any of those four words, we create a world in which we feel helpless, and the problem with feeling helpless is that it won't put one inch of dirt in the hole that you're trying to fill. You'll just go around explaining to people that something wasn't your fault. You'll be unaccountable but also unsuccessful. Living with that kind of personal identity will leave you deeply unfulfilled and insecure at your core. Eventually, it causes long-term distress.

If you are blinded by a mentality of **blame** and **excuse**, and your reality doesn't match what you're telling yourself, you may feel so internally conflicted that you become resentful—until the problem is understood and addressed, which takes courage.

For some, the actual truth of a situation is so far removed from their consciousness that they cannot handle even slight criticism. Deflection is immediate. By deflecting responsibility often, the practice becomes effortless and automatic. No thought is required, only feeling. To change this practice, you will need to find a way to increase your level of confidence. It's confidence that will help you to overcome your problems and accomplish great things.

PERSONAL ACCOUNTABILITY IS YOUR SELF-CONFIDENCE

Embrace this tenet of philosophy, and your life will change forever. Here's how it works.

One day, you must decide that you are going to swallow the pill of personal accountability. It's a big pill. It goes down hard, and it hurts to swallow. But when you take it, it feels completely liberating. You begin to feel like this is the moment you've been waiting for, because now your brain no longer has to worry and work overtime coming up with reasons to **justify** or find **excuses** and **blame**. All it has to do is ask questions to find answers. It's simple enough.

Interestingly, you have one thing working against you, and oddly, it's a fight from within. Think of it this way: There are two people who live in your head. There's the you that you talk to all day long, the one you bounce questions and thoughts off. But there's another person who lives there too. We're going to call this person Lazy Brain.

Lazy Brain, if it were in human form, would like to sleep all day on a comfortable couch. Lazy Brain likes to put its feet up, kick back, and relax. It watches a huge television and likes the remote control to be right next to its hand, because heaven forbid if it would ever have to get up and get it from across the room. That would be too much work. Lazy Brain wants its head on a pillow with a drink nearby and an extra-long straw for maximum convenience. It does anything it can to remain as lazy as possible. Unfortunately, that voice lives in your head.

So, as we talk about Lazy Brain, let's also discuss a simple element: light.

If you're sitting in a room that is lit, get up and turn off the lights. This is the room's *default setting*. Notice how dim or dark this room would have naturally been before electric lights had been invented. When you turn the lights back on, you now see the room in what is a *designed setting*.

Somebody designed the lighting, and it significantly changed the condition, the environment, of the room. You can see better and more comfortably. But someone had to design that lighting in order for there to be an effective change. Now, equate this to your life.

In life, Lazy Brain is your default setting, the voice that never wants you to be responsible for anything. It hasn't even bothered to notice how it's resigned itself to helplessness. It just wants to accept things as they are, because it's easier. In your default setting, Lazy Brain tells you that *whatever happened in a poor outcome* "wasn't because of you." It is the voice in your head that suggests there's nothing you should spend any time on to fix. It **justifies** inaction by wallowing in pity and offers you an internal self-talk that decries how bad things always happen to you. Poor Lazy Brain! So helpless!

Letting others see you as a victim gets you noticed. Self-pity is a pseudo-empowerment that wallows in a problem but never the solution. The best thing is to fix the problem, so the exaggerated need for attention becomes redirected into healthy and productive actions, which are more fulfilling.

HOW TO CHANGE NEGATIVE THINKING INTO POSITIVE ACTION BY DESIGN

To change this pattern of internal influence, you will need to create a *design setting* for yourself. You can wake up Lazy Brain with the snap of your fingers. All you must do is ask yourself two essential questions: *What did I say or do that I shouldn't have?* and *What could I have said or done that I didn't?*

In any situation where you are being held accountable, instead of deflecting **blame**, making an **excuse** or a **rationalizing** thought, or coming up with a **justification** to be right, just ask yourself those two essential questions instead. You'll then begin the process of finding answers. Those answers are what you need to begin solving your problems, and by looking inward for ways to improve, you'll learn to depend on your own ability to help yourself. That is the only real way to grow your confidence.

If you avoid the responsibility of owning a problem, you'll never have the keys to fixing it. You'll just externalize it to some other force that's beyond your control and make yourself helpless. The truth is, most things in life *are* within your control—and it is important to believe that—and by taking personal accountability, you'll wake up Lazy Brain and put yourself in control.

INTERNAL BLAME VERSUS A CONSTRUCTIVE INTERNAL LOOK FOR ANSWERS

Blaming oneself is nothing more than internal **blame**, which is just as destructive as the external kind. In order to grow, we must take a *constructive* inward look and use some critical thinking skills to find answers. *Critical thinking* is the rational, unbiased analysis or evaluation of factual evidence.

Your thinking is influenced by your conscious and unconscious efforts to navigate through life. Anything you feel or experience can cause you to develop coping mechanisms to steer yourself toward comfort. That's natural. Even something as simple as your birth order, in relation to your siblings, could affect a need for attention that calls for comforting. The danger is when we begin developing patterns for coping that paralyze our growth. It's when we feel hopeless to take action that we lose our way to finding happiness. If this sounds strange, then great! Enlightened awareness—new thinking—is always the first step in finding answers.

For those who would be tempted to look for an easier and more passive approach to taking that inward look, or to hide from responsibility in a situation, consider your answer to this question: "If your house is burning, whom should you call, a reporter or a firefighter?"

The reporter is going to look at the fire and report about it: For example, "Somebody's right at the edge of the balcony. He is going to fall from the balcony railing . . . Oh no, he fell off the balcony; he hit the ground!" That's the reporter. The firefighter, however, creates change by taking an action, shouting, "Get out of my way! I'm going to put this fire out. Nobody's going to get hurt!"

Who is more important to effect a change in that outcome, the reporter or the firefighter? This is the sort of control we have in our own lives.

Instead of acting on the changes we need to make, too many of us are reporters. We talk about and **blame** the forces that we imagine are conspiring against us. We think circumstances are beyond our control. We tell ourselves that our situations won't allow us to be successful and that we can't get things done. We **justify** the helplessness of a situation, instead of focusing our efforts on solving our problems. Every time we think like that, we feed and encourage Lazy Brain. Ask yourself in any given situation, based on your actions, *Are you a reporter or a firefighter?*

Be a firefighter. Take control of your life, and find answers inside yourself. Own your challenges so you can become empowered to find the solutions you really need. That's the only way to build a strong confidence. Then things improve because of *you*.

WHAT YOU CAN DO TO IMPROVE IMMEDIATELY

First, make a conscious decision to stop making **excuses** for why something isn't your fault. Stop **rationalizing** why things didn't happen. Redirect your energy toward finding answers over **justifying** poor outcomes. End any idea that listening to Lazy Brain is somehow acceptable, and recognize that the negative voice in your head is destructive. Identify Lazy Brain as the enemy. Stop reporting what's going on in your life as though you're watching it from afar, and actively participate in the efforts to improve your life. Stop externalizing away the responsible role you play in your own successes and failures. Internalize your focus on finding answers from within.

Swallow the pill of personal accountability so there won't be any more need to wait for something to change before you do. Liberate yourself to be free from the burdens of having to come up with reasons to **justify** failures, so you can develop your sustainable problem-solving skills from within. Think positively in the fix instead of wallowing in what's wrong. This alone will free up a lot of space in the most creative faculties of your mind.

Successful people are active participants in their careers, and the same applies to life. The most accomplished people are active participants in their own lives. They sit front row center in pursuing their passion. With openness comes the confidence to find our purpose, to unlock our best selves, without inhibitions, so we can thrive.

You can grow your confidence to succeed, but you must first realize how **blame** and **excuses** hurt your efforts of discovering your best self. They are nothing more than poison to everything you try to accomplish. I would venture to guess that more than half the people I meet are regular **blamers** and **excuse**-makers and don't realize it. Misery loves company, and it's easy to get sucked into that mentality. What you must understand is, your confidence is on the line when you don't embrace growth and change.

What Employers Need to Know

Systemic deflection of responsibility breeds negativity. People who systemically justify failures will keep producing more of the same. Not only do they accomplish very little, but they are also dangerous to any work environment; they demonstrate to other employees how to justify whatever didn't work for them, too.

Anyone can change, of course, but people must first see the need to do so. That's why, in a business setting, it's dangerous to hire people who appear unwilling to take accountability for their outcomes. In the working world, time is ticking. Things need to get done. There is little time to spend with someone who **rationalizes** away a poor result. However, if the same person is truly open to development, it's possible for the person to grow and learn to become productive. The bottom line is, it's a personal choice that every individual has to make for themselves.

If you choose to hire someone who profiles as novice (or potential, which has similarities), the need to teach this foundational selling philosophy is obvious. *Philosophy is a love of wisdom, and a selling philosophy is the love of a selling wisdom.* We must remember that *every* personality type needs to develop itself into a clear state of virtue. The teachings of this essential tenet of philosophy apply not only to novice and potential profiles but to all other categories and personalities. Learning this critical tenet of philosophy, and then teaching it, are prerequisites for any hiring manager and every sales manager. Without them, you're only guessing at what you need to know.

If You Were Profiled as a *Novice*

If you were profiled as a *novice,* you must be willing to do the following:

1. Embrace all your training as gospel. Do not fail to follow the steps of your sales presentation exactly as it was taught to you. If you have questions, ask—but commit to following the steps of your process with precision.
2. Decide what success at selling could mean for you and others you love. Think about how your own life could be improved by making a healthy income. Think about those who depend on you, and let your level of care for them equal the effort you place on learning to follow process. Consider the people you can help by serving their needs. Think of how influential you can be by pointing out the needs your prospects might

not have considered. Think of the impact you can have on others by succeeding at selling. Make it your mission to excel.
3. Most novice and potential profiles who now succeed at selling have stated that they are different people than before they learned to sell in this way. Thus, make it your goal to grow into a different person—a stronger one who sees no limits on your ability to achieve whatever it is you put your mind to. The sky's the limit.
4. Go *all in* and place yourself in the hands of a process that you might sometimes disagree with or agree with in part. Agree to follow it without making changes.

If you cannot bring yourself to do all these things, I recommend that you not work at a company with a process-driven approach that you did not create.

Questions for Someone Who Profiled as a *Novice*

There are three sets of questions you should ask that have been designed for the specific profiles in this book. Ask the first two sets before you hire an applicant (global and specific interview questions). And ask yourself the third set (30-day review questions) 30 days after hiring. You can access the questions and the 30-day reviews at www.myleadprofile.com.

YELLOW

Personality: *Idealist*

1.0% of Yellow; 0.6% of all profiles

VIRTUE
Visionary

TRAITS USUALLY ASSOCIATED WITH THIS PERSONALITY
Fantasizing
Romantic
Hopefulness
Utopian
Entrepreneur-minded

VIRTUES HELPFUL TO SELLING
Seeing a person who does not own your product or service
as someone you can help

DEFICIENCY (THE OPPOSITE OF THIS PERSONALITY)
Unimaginative
Strictly practical
Easily accepting what is
Low energy and low effort
Sympathizes with prospects when they will not be moving forward
Too understanding; quick to acquiesce to helping someone
with less than what is actually needed
Philosophically immature; believes something is better
than nothing versus all-or-nothing psychology.

EXCESS (THIS PERSONALITY WHEN OUT OF CONTROL)

Challenges to Selling

Optimism based on hope, not strategy
Runs a risk of not being fully committed to process
Unrealistic in approach
Impractical

TRAITS SIMILAR TO IDEALIST'S

Demonstrative (when passionate)
Sensitive (when excessive)
Willful (when entrepreneurial)

MOST RELATABLE GREEN TRAIT

The most relatable Green trait is *demonstrative*.

WHAT YOU NEED TO FOCUS ON

Learn to set realistic expectations based on selling psychology, philosophy, principles, and protocols. Temper optimistic thinking that is not supported by those four Ps. Learn to support your company's vision, and adapt it as your own. Eventually, you could become a manager or an entrepreneur.

The *Idealist* Candidate

George's Story

I think most people who see a great product would want to have it. I am confident that after showing a potential customer what I have to offer, they'll jump at it. I carry business cards with me and give them away every chance I get.

I sometimes talk at chamber of commerce meetings about my product, and I can see the looks on the faces of the people watching. I'm really excited to continue spreading the word about what I sell. I've been giving out literature for people to check us out. I'm sure it's going to take off really soon!

About the *Idealist*

Idealism is inspiring. It motivates artists, musicians, and other creative and visionary types from all over. Entrepreneurs feel it when they become stimulated with ideas that can change the world, or at least *their* world. Idealists make our lives less predictable, more interesting, more enchanting, and more creative. Without idealism, passion for new thinking could not exist, and people who think differently would be edged out, leaving their creativity sitting on the drawing board.

IDEALISM CHALLENGES THE PRACTICAL

Yes, some degree of idealism is important, but for idealist salespeople, there are a few challenges. For one, idealism is often at odds with what is practical, and selling systems are based on a practical psychology that's built on the known realities of buying and selling. Creativity can interrupt the flow of a preplanned process (like a sales presentation) if acted upon in real time. To be successful at selling, idealists should internalize the fact that there is a time and a place for creativity, but it's never in the middle of a process-driven sales presentation.

Idealists, however, are the kind of creative thinkers who can perhaps design selling systems that work. Many selling systems are outdated in today's rapidly changing world. When these creative personalities are tasked to write up-to-date selling procedures, given their faculty for vision, some might be considered among the top-selling strategists. They are the *practical idealists,* which is perhaps an oxymoron, a contradiction of terms, like a *little giant.* They are real, but rare.

PERSONALIZATION AND INDIVIDUALIZATION ARE NOT THE SAME THING

An *idealist* salesperson who is both creative and process-driven is using both sides of their brain, the creative right and the methodical left. Theoretically, each side represents different things, and idealists tend to be right-brained, more creative. But while they use their left brain to follow structure and suppress their need to create during a sales presentation, they can benefit by using their creativity to *personalize* the delivery. In the case of selling, personalization is about using your unique personality to create connection and rapport. It can make communication more interesting.

Personalization is great, so long as it is only about letting your unique personality shine through while following the sales process. Individualizing the process itself, however, is to change it, making the outcome far less predictable. That's when creativity can interfere with consistent results.

EXCESSIVE, IMPRACTICAL IDEALISTS

To some, an *impractical idealist* seems to live in an imaginary realm. Granted, it's a multifaceted world where both certainty and possibility coexist; poetry and idealism live in the same land as predictability and reason. But there is often a wide chasm between how things really are and what the impractical idealist believes things to be or could be.

It can be said that without imagination, life would be boring. Who wants to live in a world without imagination or new possibilities? Let's also apply our maturity to be able to see things the way they actually are, without disparaging the idea about how things could be better.

The *excessive idealist* is highly impractical, and this person likely leans into being willful. The two personality traits together can create an obstinance that would be hard to reason with, especially if the opposing view is practical and merely logical. An impractical idealist doesn't often make a good process-driven salesperson. Remember, there are lots of reasons to fail at selling, and we must notice when a personality presents any kind of challenge to what we know to be necessary to successful selling.

If You Were Profiled as an *Idealist*

If you were profiled as an *idealist*, you must be willing to do the following:

1. Accept the principles, protocols, psychology, and philosophy of selling wisdom. There are certain realities you will need to embrace, or your road to understanding will be unnecessarily complicated and undoubtedly blocked.
2. Avoid romanticizing how you would like prospects to behave. The science of selling has been in existence for a long time. If you follow the things that are already known to successful people, and allow them to teach you, you will fast-track your way to the top. Just because you'd like customers to have certain buying habits doesn't mean they will. Listen to those who've gone before you. There is a lot of wisdom to be gained. Don't slow your development with skepticism or with romantic notions about how things should be. Wisely learn how things really are.
3. Avoid individualizing your approach to selling. Don't change the steps of the sale or the details of the steps your company

supports. Avoid becoming enchanted with online entertainment selling figures, who may be creative and flamboyant but will derail you from your company's particular selling process. Personalize your approach via your unique personality. Customers buy from those they like. Be you, and be the best process-trained salesperson you can be.
4. Go *all in* and place yourself in the hands of a process that you might sometimes disagree with or agree with in part. Agree to follow it without making changes.

If you cannot bring yourself to do all these things, I recommend that you not work at a company with a process-driven approach that you did not create.

Questions for Someone with an *Idealist* Personality

There are three sets of questions you should ask that have been designed for the specific profiles in this book. Ask the first two sets before you hire an applicant (global and specific interview questions). And ask yourself the third set (30-day review questions) 30 days after hiring. You can access the questions and the 30-day reviews at www.myleadprofile.com.

Green Personalities: Introduction to the Five Stages

Green personalities have natural proclivities to work in the field of selling, and 14% of the people we've studied had some Green in their personality profiles. Green symbolizes *go*, a green light. However, it's important to note that every Green trait requires achieving a balance, because while these traits are, in and of themselves, natural for selling, they aren't a guarantee that someone with a Green personality profile will succeed. Nor does it mean that you need Green traits to be considered for a sales position, or that everyone with those traits is a good hire.

Again, every Green trait requires achieving a balance. Balance is not found when someone operates in a state of deficiency, lacking awareness or motivation or exhibiting laziness or cowardice. Nor is balance present when a Green personality exhibits behaviors that are excessive. When out of control, these personalities will cause chaos to ensue all around them. In selling, when balance is not achieved, Green personalities can become downright destructive to their customers, to themselves, and to a business.

Awareness Comes First

How do you reel in salespeople who have excessive personality traits? They must be taught how to turn their excessive or deficient behaviors into virtue.

Awareness comes first. For people to make changes, they need to understand what is happening. It requires great courage and a willingness on their part to even want to address the certain personality-related issues they face. Some Green personalities, when out of control, feel that they can do no wrong and see no problem with their behavior. Salespeople with *excessive* Green behavior traits will point out that they are selling regularly as proof they're on the right track. For the novice sales manager, it might seem like a convincing argument; after all, isn't selling the salesperson's objective? On the other hand, the more growth-oriented leader will note the dangers of working with someone who performs with a mindset that's infected with excess. And if you think *infected* is a strong word, I wish I could think of an even stronger one to make my point.

The Destruction of Good Company Culture

A company's culture should reflect its owners' beliefs and values. If it does not, the company is rudderless and cannot grow. Excessive Green personalities can be very destructive to a company culture. Just because someone can sell well doesn't give the person the right to destroy a company's culture. Excessive Green personalities are known for following their *own* way of selling, which means they aren't operating on *your* process. Since they have a natural selling personality, they can be very successful at making sales, and they might have an office filled with trophies that validate their amazing numbers. They might even make more money than everyone else on your sales team, but if they are successful, and their colleagues see that they aren't following your process, why wouldn't your staff want to do the same? Allowing hypocrisy in your organization will cause an entire sales team to collapse.

Excessive Green personalities have nontransferable selling styles. Just as the word suggests, *nontransferable* means they aren't relatable to anyone but the person who sells that way. In other words, you can't teach someone how to think exactly like you do. Since non-process-driven salespeople sell on instinct, they are baffled to understand why others can't just sell as they do. After all, their thinking is, if someone goes on a sales call with them, they must have seen the obvious way the sale was put together. Excessive Green personality types will never come to terms with why others can't just do the same, and for this reason they don't make good sales managers. Too many companies confuse someone who can sell with someone who can manage, yet they rarely ever share the same skill set.

Since the excessive personality will see how other salespeople just can't do what they do, they begin to think, "I'm superior and better than everyone else." This creates narcissism—a monster whose only purpose is to stop anyone from being as good as they are. It's hard to work at a company where someone is walking around with a God complex, and that's toxic for any organization.

Excessive Green personalities who are out of control are highly manipulative. If you are running a sales organization, consider this: Is it enough to have only one or two on your sales staff sell like crazy if it's at the expense of everyone else? Not if you are trying to grow a sales team and build a business. Excessive Green personalities will turn others away from following your process by pointing out that they sell by *not* listening to you. They'll intimidate and play with the fragile egos of new recruits and demean your system as something that's for beginners. They'll beat their chests and assume the importance of a sales champion while telling the members of the management team that they support them and care about retention, when it's the exact opposite. And when you find out *how* they're making sales, you will be shocked and appalled.

There are some who are so competitive and out of control, they'll reintroduce former drug-addicted salespeople who are in recovery to their deadly kryptonite, competitively selling alongside them, just because of a perceived threat to their crown. They can be completely unconcerned with the well-being of another person, and their big egos have them seeing other promising salespeople as "the competition" that must be destroyed, sometimes going to any extent to get them out of their way. Yes, it can get that out of control!

Some excessive Greens will go as far as to tell prospects about human tragedies, such as how they lost their spouse to cancer, just to garner sympathy. None of it is true, and unbeknownst to the prospect, this is a mere ploy to acquire sympathy for a *highly* manipulative salesperson.

And sometimes excessive Greens will even give hope to lonely prospects, implying that there might be a chance for romance. Or telling a potential customer, formerly in the military, that they too have served their country when they haven't. It seems there are no limits to what these highly manipulative Green personalities will do when thinking in excess. Never forget, if you are an owner, they represent your company. They represent you! And if you keep them, they'll kill your business.

In the Big Picture, Virtue and Process Will Beat Instinct

When Green personalities are in control, *working in virtue*, they see process as the key to success, a systematic constancy-to-purpose prescription that can be taught to others. Process, working in virtue, makes Green personalities strong and very successful.

No matter what personality or category people show on the LEAD spectrum, if the personality or category is not honed to virtue, it will eventually serve as a block to keep people from faithfully following a process, and they'll eventually go rogue. It will be the reason why people couldn't manage to get their selling career off the ground or why their selling career derailed when there was so much promise at the start.

Virtuous selling requires balance, and deficient and excessive behaviors need to be tamed to achieve that balance. Deficiencies lack belief and understanding, making what is important not urgent. Perhaps out of ego or boredom, excessive personalities rush through a process, without respecting its inherent wisdom. In contrast, *virtue* is a well-built core belief in one's process and acting upon it.

The Five Green Personality Profiles: A Road Map

There are five Green personality profiles. From most to least common, they are:

1. Demonstrative (9.0% of all profiles)
2. Advantageous (2.3% of all profiles)
3. Serious (1.5% of all profiles)
4. Influencer (0.43% of all profiles)
5. Persistent (0.31% of all profiles)

Based on our studies, if your company is regularly investing in talent acquisition, it will take an average of nine applicants to find one with Green personality traits. It will take more than 300 to find just one who is at the top but likely in need of some realignment in mindset. That's why it's so important not only to look for salespeople who profile as Green but also to develop others from the Yellow and Orange personality profiles. You cannot grow a sales organization without those other colors. And the good news about hiring and training from colors other than Green: With the assistance of the LEAD profile and this book, you will hire fewer people who have selling habits that are already established and might be poorly developed and difficult to change.

Our research shows that while about 14% of the people we've profiled were shown to have traits in the Green, roughly 62% are Yellow, and 12% Orange. If you are looking for process-driven salespeople, the remaining 13%, who are profiled in the Red, can be summarily dismissed. That illustrates why it is so important to be able to hone the skills we've discussed in this book—the skills to "read" applicants for their potential and groom them for development with more than just your gut feelings. You need the right information.

The five Green personality profiles in the chapters that follow aren't just profiles. They are the road map to mastering virtue and mastering sales. From *demonstrative* (Green Stage 1) through *persistent* (Green Stage 5), these are the stages that *every* personality type must work toward mastering, and they must be mastered in their correct order. They progress in a specific way, and each stage is built on the previous one. Each salesperson must be dialed in to think in virtue and not be allowed to become and remain deficient or excessive and out of control. When someone masters all five stages properly, there is *nothing* more powerful to achieve when learning to sell professionally.

Adapting the Green Stages for Various Industries

Because the principles behind the Green stages are a progressive climb to the apex of mastery, the same ideas can be used in a multitude of selling professions. There are some vocations that do not require learning all five of the Green stages. If you were a stock trader, for example, you would need only Green Stage 2, advantageous; Green Stage 3, serious; and Green Stage 5, persistent. If you aren't working in a position that requires influencing another person, you wouldn't need Green Stage 1, demonstrative, or Green Stage 4, influencer. And similarly, if you are in another field, you can apply an adjusted knowledge as a guide and adapt it by remodeling the wisdom of Green Stage 3, serious, as it relates to your industry. Direct selling, however, requires all five stages to be mastered as outlined below and discussed in detail later in the chapter.

THE FIVE STAGES OF GREEN

Stage 1—Demonstrative

Possessing the ability to captivate

Easy to remember: Captivate, connect, communicate

Stage 2—Advantageous

Opportunistic, capitalizing on a prospect's perceived interest

Knowing enough to make a sale when perceived interest is detected but not necessarily skilled enough to influence a best-case outcome, maybe not satiating the complete scope of the opportunity

Easy to remember: Something is better than nothing, settling

Stage 3—Serious (Selling Maturity)

MINDSET LOGICAL: BECOMING KNOWLEDGEABLE

Possessing a willingness to govern self, using an agreed-upon set of metrics and a transferable systematic approach

Having a well-developed sense of judgment based on proven, transferable practices

Well versed in known philosophy, psychology, protocols, and procedures related to selling in your industry

Enjoying the ability to build on what is known with passion for continued growth; a true process salesperson

Easy to remember: Intelligence, information, insight

Stage 4—Influencer

Persuasive, possessing the ability to get others to see the things they didn't see before, uncovering needs that might not be recognized by a prospect, thus expanding the opportunity to serve someone

Easy to remember: Effect, elevate, encourage, expand, enthusiasm, energy, exhilarate, excite

Stage 5—Persistent

MINDSET EMOTIONAL COMMITMENT: BECOMING UNSTOPPABLE

Intensity

Fully using a carefully crafted process with maturity and judgment to create power and follow-through as a means for achieving uncommon quality, permanent purpose, and excellence

Easy to remember: Constancy, ceaselessness, contribute, consistent

Now that you've been formally introduced to the five Green stages, get ready to explore each one in detail. Chapter 4 covers Green Stages 1 and 2, Chapter 5 focuses on Green Stage 3, and our final chapter, Chapter 6, discusses Green Stages 4 and 5.

CHAPTER 4

Green Personalities: Stages 1 and 2

GREEN STAGE 1

Personality: *Demonstrative*

66.1% of Green; 9.0% of all profiles

VIRTUE
Possessing the ability to captivate

TRAITS USUALLY ASSOCIATED WITH THIS PERSONALITY
Charm
Uplifting attitude
Enthusiasm
Contagious personality
Respectfulness

VIRTUES HELPFUL TO SELLING
Appealing

DEFICIENCY (THE OPPOSITE OF THIS PERSONALITY)

Reserved
Unnoticed
Introverted

EXCESS (THIS PERSONALITY WHEN OUT OF CONTROL)

Challenges to Selling

Needing to be liked at too high a level
Overpromising behaviors, causing chaos
Unreliable
Virtue signaling
Fears of criticism (sometimes hidden)

WHAT YOU NEED TO FOCUS ON

Focus on mastering the skills to captivate—to be outwardly excited and/or command respect, preferably both. Get your prospects to feel warm about you. Let them sense your genuine care for doing right by them. Next, cultivate these skills to identify opportunities, which can be capitalized on.

The *Demonstrative* Candidate

Jessie's Story

My parents are both great people. They divorced when I was a kid. Middle school is a tough enough time in life, but dealing with insecurities brought on by divorce was an even more daunting task for me.

My address changed when I was 12 years old, and that meant I had to go to a new school and meet all new classmates. Imagine the cliques that were already cemented around me as I tried to figure out how to fit in. I was the odd kid out.

After being rejected and ignored, I finally made a few new friends. I thought that if I would be the nicest kid around, they'd have to like me. I guess I overpromised the kids I hung out with, just so I could earn their friendships. I became the guy that told everyone what they wanted to hear. Feeling guilty over my parents' divorce—since some of what they argued about was me—I was in a mental space to not risk any more rejection.

As I grew into adulthood, I've been criticized for not delivering on some of the promises I make. I know it's a fair criticism. I am also quick to repair arguments when they happen. My wife always tells me that I avoid conflict. I guess I probably do. I really dislike chaos and drama. It's so unnecessary. I like to keep the peace and make people happy. Life is short.

> ### James's Story
>
> My father was an out-of-control tyrant. He left when I was in eleventh grade and, soon after, never spoke to me or my siblings again. It's as if we never existed. I've been very protective of my mom ever since. I've always felt that I needed to keep things feeling right in my house. I used humor and light-heartedness to bring a sense of normalcy to my family.
>
> One time, in late winter when I was in tenth grade (before my father left), I came home 5 minutes after my curfew, which was 10 p.m. My father grounded me for the rest of the school year. I cannot, for the life of me, understand why he was the way he was. Very difficult, uncaring, unfeeling.
>
> I see my role as the peacekeeper of my household. I know my father screwed up my ability to be stronger and stand my ground, which would have gotten me hit when he was around. I've made many promises. I try to live up to them, but if I'm being honest, I know I don't always do what I promise. It feels right in the moment while making the promise, but sometimes I just can't deliver. I just try to be a good person. I do avoid conflict, but it's better than the opposite.

About the *Demonstrative*

The *demonstrative* personality captivates a prospect during a sales presentation. There are two distinct styles of delivery that captivate: the highly respected and the enthusiastic. If you possess both styles, you'll really ace the first level of Green.

The highly respected style of the demonstrative personality is less common. It can be thought of as like a doctor's demeanor. Doctors aren't known for waving their arms in the air with enthusiasm. They are considered the kind of personality who can deliver serious news, very respected, with bifocals perched on the edge of their nose. By simply looking up and talking with an unquestionable authority, they will immediately convey their trustworthiness and expertise. It is captivating. Highly respected demonstrative salespeople captivate prospects by the same heightened level of seriousness and professionalism they possess. And it works.

More often, however, demonstrative people have enthusiastic personalities. They are friendly, charming, vibrant, upbeat, and widely accepted by others as fun to be around. They are not usually reserved and unnoticed. They don't speak like dispassionate professors, nor are they lecturers in their style of delivery. They are, in most cases, more like the life of the party. One would assume that they would be perfect for selling. Who wouldn't want to buy something from someone like that? In reality however, when they are acting in excess, that's not how it actually works.

WORKING WITH DEMONSTRATIVE PERSONALITIES

Excessively demonstrative personalities tend to keep many of their thoughts private. When presented with challenging training, they might smile their way through whatever makes them feel uncomfortable but be far from accepting of it. They'll easily dismiss the importance of learning adaptive behaviors, thinking they probably won't need them. Since they aren't necessarily vocal about their innermost feelings, a trainer can be flying blind while trying to help demonstrative personalities overcome obstacles. It's difficult to train people who don't share their feelings honestly, and it's those feelings that will block them from following a process they themselves didn't write. In fact, even a process they would write would be filled with regular exceptions and high pragmatism instead of faithfulness to systematic behaviors. When it becomes noticed and they are confronted, they'll likely make it feel okay by making you like them at such a heightened level. It may not seem so in the moment, but it's a form of manipulation.

To work effectively with demonstrative personalities, avoid catering to them in an effort to draw out their innermost feelings. Rather, set the tone of your relationship to one that is comfortable for speaking freely. However, you must also avoid opening the door to a lot of complaints and problems. It's a fine line. Your relationship with a demonstrative salesperson will be compromised if you become the sounding board for problem-dwelling complaints. Draw the line between respecting expected professional behaviors and legitimately gaining the person's trust. Serious-minded (mature) managers know the importance of this line.

When in excess, demonstrative people can also be manipulative (as noted briefly above). When you think of the word *manipulative*, it almost sounds a bit evil. Manipulative people take advantage of others for their own benefit. However, manipulation can also mean a less-than-honest approach in the way someone deals with difficult issues, which may not be evil, only disingenuous. Many excessively demonstrative personalities use a lot of energy to be upbeat. They want to make others happy. It's unrealistic to think that someone can naturally have an everyday personality that is so excessively happy-go-lucky. One would think that an easygoing person is generally a positive one. It can be shocking to learn what realities the person might be holding inside.

Excessively demonstrative salespeople can see their job as a role they play—thinking of selling as having to put on a selling persona—and some might over-personalize their approach. I've heard prospects reflect on sales presentations given by excessively demonstrative personalities and remark, "I know everything about the salesperson's personal life." . . . Yet they didn't buy from them. Those encounters lack effectiveness when the balance is lost. Yes, prospects should like you, but you are there to serve them. You must always remember, it's not so much about you. It's always about the prospects.

Excessively demonstrative personalities are overcompensating for something; otherwise they wouldn't need to be liked at such a heightened level. Sometimes things are the exact opposite of what they appear to be. When needing to be liked that strongly, a person would have to hold feelings of insecurity that are greater than average.

If elevated, those feelings could lead to some unusual behaviors that are coping and defense mechanisms. For instance, someone could feel the need to level another person, if that other person is perceived as a threat, by diminishing the person in the eyes of a third party. As if relationships work like a teeter-totter, excessive demonstratives might attempt to bring someone else down in order to raise themselves up.

Being excessively demonstrative is an unnatural disposition. If you examine what causes a person to become excessively demonstrative, it is mostly attributed to a need for acceptance. Not to overplay the idea, this doesn't mean it is all-consuming, just present. Fear of rejection is powerful. A heightened fear of rejection can come from a variety of less obvious places, and it can be present in people who you would never think in a million years are insecure—people with model good looks and seemingly perfect demeanors, for example; yet something inside them is desperately restless. Most people wouldn't connect beauty with a fear of rejection, and one would probably think it's present much less in people gifted with stunning appearances. However, it happens. Perhaps they are rejected less often, which makes them unaccustomed to handling it.

Infrequent rejection can exaggerate an occasional rejection in someone's mind while to most others, that small level of occasional rejection would seem optimal. But to the person who is not used to being rebuffed, a slight rejection can be a point of raw sensitivity, and therefore heightened. I've witnessed salespeople with great appearances crying because they aren't selling as they had expected. In selling, rejection happens, and basic sales training tells us not to take any of it personally. Prospects do not reject salespeople *personally*.

In addition, excessively demonstrative personalities are notorious over-promisers, and that's when the need to be liked interferes with selling. Over-promisers who do not live up to their words are on a collision course with truth. It's tiring trying to be everything to everyone, and it's unrealistic. After all, it's a role requiring a person to always be at the center of optimistic expression, a façade that simply cannot be sustained indefinitely. That is when demonstrative people eventually manipulate the appearance of their own reality to maintain the expectations others have of them. They'll show an exterior happiness, but inside they feel the opposite. It's understandable for a prospect to get irritated or mad at demonstratives who overpromise, since, though they tell the prospect everything the prospect wants to hear, they fail to deliver.

Since they are so agreeable, excessively demonstrative personalities can also give the appearance of being followers. People have a need for being heard, and the demonstrative personality provides a listening ear. Excessive demonstratives mean no harm; it's just that they make most of their decisions emotionally, and they have a strong desire to please others. But since a person cannot possibly live up to being everything to everyone, an excessive demonstrative will likely let you down.

Let's also bring some attention to the responsibility of the other party who is in a relationship with a people-pleasing demonstrative personality. Some people encourage demonstrative over-promisers to get real and tell the truth, but when they do, they are chastised for it. Sometimes people don't want your truth; they want you to agree with *their* truth. This is a paradox that keeps the demonstrative person from being more honest.

If it is understood that someone is demonstrative, isn't the party who takes advantage of the demonstrative's good nature and desire to please somewhat culpable when a demonstrative fails to deliver? If you know someone operates with a certain predictable personality trait, as we all do, does it make any sense to be surprised when the person acts as you predicted? If a person keeps trusting the word of an overpromising demonstrative person, knowing the over-promiser is likely to underdeliver, both parties are set up to fail, leaving the demonstrative person to take all the **blame**.

Consider what this means for training them: If people tell you what you want to hear but don't act in accordance with what they say, they wouldn't be ready-made for working a process-driven selling system. That is, unless they change their thinking. In a selling situation, becoming *advantageous* is the next stage on the Green path of growth—

Green Stage 2. Green Stage 2 focuses the demonstrative person on opportunity for a win-win arrangement with a prospect.

The question in selling is this: Is the demonstrative person willing to stop overpromising to make a sale or to step up and correct a prospect who suffers from mistaken thinking? Excessive demonstratives will compromise results for what they perceive as relationships. This means they might fail to persist when trying to close sales. They fear risking the friendly, accepting relationship they've built with a prospect. In selling, there are many problems with this mindset. First, the salesperson is likely to change the sales process to individualize it—even over-personalizing it by projecting fears—and make it more about a personal connection than about the product or service the salesperson is offering. While it's true that prospects are more likely to buy from someone they like, it's also easier for a prospect to tell a friend that you need a little more time to think over an offer. By over-personalizing the sale, the demonstrative personality relates to the prospect's reasons for not moving forward today and accepts the **excuse**.

Wanting to be liked at too high a level can also manifest itself through virtue signaling. The thinking becomes "I am a good person if I give you the space you need to think over my offer and get back to me." Unfortunately, much of the time, when given the opportunity to call a company back, a sale will instead go to a competing company that sent the best-equipped "closer," regardless of whether it had the best product or offered the highest value. Closers know how to close sales, and they can run circles around excessively demonstrative salespeople who are more casual about think-overs.

You should never have to choose between supporting a relationship with a potential customer and providing your product or service to the customer. Both things should be virtuous. The thought of having to choose between them is a false choice.

For sales managers. Like all other salespeople, demonstratives will become frustrated when they are not succeeding. Most problems are directly related to an inability of people to accept personal accountability for their actions. Humility is a hard virtue to learn, but it's the most important one to possess in order to grow.

A sales manager must hold the professional line and redirect the salesperson's mindset to the strict adherence to process and keep the salesperson accountable for following it honestly. If the manager is too open and becomes the kind of person the salesperson is comfortable complaining to, the demonstrative person will eventually "own" the manager. *If the demonstrative person feels free to express constant negativity to you, the sales manager, the person will not make it in selling at your company.* When this happens, a demonstrative starts to tumble out of control. Don't let it get to that point, or you'll be wasting good potential talent. Teach the demonstrative personality to engineer an outcome—something predesigned by way of process protocols that deliver regular, sustainable, repeatable, and predictable results.

UNDERSTANDING THE DEMONSTRATIVE

Being demonstrative might have come about from an experience. Something like living with an impossible parent, one who could never be satisfied, or having a family broken up by divorce. That's enough to start someone on the path of people-pleasing at a very high level. It could be furthered through the development of coping mechanisms from our formative years that helped us to rock the boat less and fit in better.

However, if salespeople cannot ask for an order by building a process-driven case to a selling climax, they will not maximize their true potential. Typically, the descending sales career finds its way to making **excuses** about how the opportunity just wasn't right. When salespeople give up, the **justifications** for leaving their position win out, often manifesting into a transference of responsibility where the salespeople will not work their demonstrative qualities into a winning virtue. They will instead **blame** everything and everyone but themselves for failing to produce. The best you'll get at that stage is only false modesty, still placing the bulk of the **blame** on outside forces to preserve an ego.

Personalities who are both willful and demonstrative can go either way. That is why it is so imperative for any sales management team to understand the dynamics of what is at play. These ideas are the foundational ideas behind the LEAD Personality Profile Program for selling.

While known for having energetic, uplifting, and contagious personalities, demonstrative personalities are hard to read, making these personalities a true dichotomy. Often, in the beginning, these uplifting personalities are more interested in you, the sales manager, feeling good about the training. They play to you, and they will be less open about their own needs. And when coupled with other complicated personality traits, like willfulness, it makes working with an excessive demonstrative person all the more challenging. (Luckily, LEAD helps you sort it all out.)

In an interview, if the right questions aren't asked, the demonstrative personality can easily and falsely impress an unskilled interviewer, getting the interviewer to believe that the demonstrative candidate will be the most incredible person to work in the sales department. So outgoing and charismatic, surely the person will do well. Sometimes that can be the farthest thing from reality, but the responsibility of what comes from the interview is on both the candidate and the hiring manager.

Interviewing itself should not be an assumed skill. When a company gives someone a manager's role, it's too often assumed the person will know how to conduct a good interview. Interviewing is important—which is why we offer you both the Six Global Interview Questions and the interview questions specific to each personality at www.myleadprofile.com. A demonstrative person can be so delightful, that a hiring manager can be charmed in an interview and might succumb to the person's pleasing nature. Then, slowly, procedural transgressions are casually overlooked. This is dangerous to a person's development, and even more so to the company when others see that *not* following your system is a matter of getting in good with the boss.

It's easy to confuse a demonstrative person for someone with transparency. Try hard not to conflate agreeability with openness. Saying you are open does not necessarily make it so. Genuine openness is the most important and one of the least common traits to find in anyone. It involves honest trust, which tells you a little something about how to manage; and in order for people to be truly open, they need to feel safe to share what they actually think and feel. No manager should hammer a salesperson into submission. They should understand what is actually going on and help to correct misconceptions over time.

How the Demonstrative Can Be Successful

Demonstrative qualities are the most common of all Green traits. With 9% of all people showing some demonstrative competency, it is far from rare, but it might take you, on average, 10 interviews to find someone possessing a significant amount of it. Demonstrative people can make good field marketers, show and event marketers, and retail and business-to-business salespeople, as well as one-call sellers. Most demonstrative people are warmer than the average person, so it stands to reason that others enjoy their company.

Salespeople of all industries benefit from being demonstrative, so long as their personalities are controlled by virtue and avoid excess. Being demonstrative might get you in the door of an opportunity, but it's not all that's needed to sell consistently. To become successful at selling, you'll need to master all the other Green selling stages.

When people profile as either Yellow or Orange, or both, their first goal—while dialing their natural personality into a state of virtue—must be focused on mastering the first two Green stages. It starts with learning to become demonstrative, and since it's the most common, for some it's the easiest to learn.

A sales trainer should note just how outgoing a trainee is or isn't. Can the trainee captivate? That is the number-one question about the demonstrative person. Can this person open a prospect through conversation and put the prospect at ease by asking the right probative questions? If the trainee is too shy or too introverted, it's not likely to work.

A good needs assessment is placed at the beginning of a sales call for that very reason. When probing, is the salesperson careful not to put prospects on the defensive by asking questions the wrong way, thus spawning fight-or-flight scenarios? Do prospects feel that the salesperson is interested in them? Is that interest genuine? Even taking genuine interest in others is a skill that can be honed with the proper training. And it works! A person can be taught to care about others. These are just some of the secrets of learning the virtues of becoming demonstrative.

Demonstrative people can be seen as the spirit of an organization. This is true because of the energy and the positive bounce in their step. If these traits are mixed with a good sense of humor, demonstrative people can be a catalyst for others to let loose and enjoy the ride a lot more, too. While they have contagious personalities that are uplifting to others, are they the actual life of an organization? Many times, yes, but we must remember, *we work to accomplish something*. It could be multiple things that we focus on, but *accomplishment* must be at center stage. Having fun is great, and when work is fun, it can be far more enjoyable and keep employment-retention rates in the positive.

However, a cautionary note for business owners: Always look at metrics to tell a story. In order to manage someone in an honest and productive way, study the person's actual record of accomplishment, and learn the areas where the person needs help. Don't ignore signs of trouble and poor results; nor should you overlook cultural misfits. If you decide to see only what you want to see, it will hurt you. Unless you are running a philanthropical endeavor and don't care about profitability or accomplishment, there is more to running a successful sales office than the fun we all hope to have. Performance records must be measurable and measured each day, week, month, and year. You can even elect to measure results in periods, such as four weeks being one period. It is a method used for pulling thirteen periods instead of twelve months in a calendar year—all equal in time (28 days each), therefore perhaps more accurately comparative.

Encompassingsales.com, a marketing-based website for managing lead flow and sales scripts, also offers a variety of reports to help track the most important key indicators for your sales team. If you aren't quantifying the results of people's efforts, chances are you are overspending to get them. The bigger an organization gets, the more those numbers (even in fractions) have massive importance to the overall bottom line. You must know your numbers, hire to the best of your ability, and understand just how to develop those salespersons you choose to work with.

TRANSMUTING RESPECTFULNESS INTO HELPFULNESS

Growing up, most of us are taught to be kind, courteous, generous, and understanding, and not to impose our will on others. Those same principles apply to selling, but with a twist. Demonstrative people do not want to see themselves as pushy. They see pushiness as a form of disrespect, and they are correct. Being pushy isn't a good quality to possess; however, persistence is. To the untrained manager or salesperson, they can be easily confused.

This brings to light a new question regarding influence. If what you sell is truly in the best interest of your prospects, and knowing that if they continue to shop, they will likely fall into the hands of a smooth "closer"—perhaps someone with an inferior product who cares a great deal less about them than you do—shouldn't your persistence for helping them to get it right be the main driving force for selling to them and, thus, serving them?

If your answer is yes, what if your prospects don't see it the same way as you do? Should your persistence for helping them to get it right be any less the main driving force for serving their needs?

Demonstrative people, operating in excess, share something in common with Yellow respectful personalities. Both personalities must embrace the idea that respectfulness must be transmuted into an *action* of helping something improve. If left in excess, fear can be a strong detractor of persistence at a prospect's first or second objection. But which way helps prospects more? Obviously, if you know that your product or service is the right choice, serving your prospects would be in *their* best interest. So, how do you do it? You can't force people to buy something. You have to convince them to want it.

When working in virtue, demonstratives are naturals at working verbal and nonverbal messaging. They fall into a convincing *sphere of influence*: words, tonality, and body language.

According to psychology professor Albert Mehrabian, who developed the 7-38-55 rule, only 7% of our influence is derived from words alone, while 38% of influence comes from tonality and voice inflections. One can talk in a whispering tone or more loudly and can speak in staccato or legato in phrasing, and the tone can be varied in pitch and speed, based on how the influencer wants to convey a message. The same words used without a more influential tone would have dramatically less effect in nearly every case. That leaves the language of physiology with an amazing 55% importance to influence. And like the voice, body language has many nuances. Human beings can identify about 250,000 different facial expressions alone. Nonverbal communication gives your brain a lot to interpret. And unlike words, the brain encodes those nonverbal cues at lightning speed. Believe it or not, using words is the slowest form of nonspecific communication.

For example, suppose I looked out a window while sitting down, and said in a monotone voice, "There's a bird." You might think I'm a little crazy, but likely you would not pay much attention. If I say the same words but with a more passionate tone, "There's a **bird!**" I will garner a little stronger attention from you. But if I stood up, turned to you and pointed to the bird outside and motioned for you to come over, still using the same words with an even more passionate tone, "**There's a bird!**" you would get up and come to where I am, for I would have strongly influenced your attention. When words, tone, and nonverbal communications are in sync—the 7-38-55 rule—you're at your best to strongly influence others.

Cultivating your influence is critical to selling. If, however, you say everything with 7-38-55 all the time, your influence will be zero. It has to feel emotionally bought-in, not mechanical, in order for the meaning to flow to another person with influence. In other words, it has to *feel genuine*. By definition, if it's genuine, it must be real and therefore felt. Since selling is a transference of feeling, being genuine sells.

That's why many salespeople sound "salesy" when they over-comment about a prospect's boat, or the color of their living room, or some other personalized thing in a prospect's possession. It sounds too much like a selling technique than a true feeling.

Demonstrative people are personable, and it's usually intuitive for them. When respectful personalities fall short in their demonstrative capabilities but develop them, they could turn respect into a virtue by way of becoming more demonstrative. Then, they can learn to transmute their beliefs of what respect is—from a mere kind consideration into new ideas about *helping and serving others* through action.

ENERGY FLOW AND HOW TO MASTER DIRECTIONAL LEADERSHIP

Let's say you are at a concert. Your favorite band is playing. You scored great seats, and you are sitting front row center. The lights go down; the rumble is felt. Suddenly, the lights go up, and there's your favorite band, but something seems off. The band members are staring at their shoes, never looking up. They appear tired and bored. They look like they don't even want to be there. How would you feel? Most would say that they've been cheated. You may even want your money back. You didn't have fun. It just felt long and depressing, and you vow to never go see that band again.

Now, let's reset the stage. . . . Your favorite band is playing. You scored great seats, sitting front row center. The lights go down; the rumble is felt. Suddenly, the lights go up, and there's your favorite band rocking your world. The band is on fire, and the whole crowd is going crazy! How do you feel? Pretty great, right?

Consider this: What was *your* role in both cases?

You were in the same place in both scenarios, just standing there. Yet in one case, it was a miserable experience, and in the other, a fantastic one. The *only* difference was in the energy flow coming from the leading source.

We're all wired to feel what others show us *they* feel; we're all vicarious. When the flow of energy feels great, we are attracted to it. It's fun. But what if we are supposed to be the leading source, and the flow of our energy is great only when the receivers *acknowledge* our energy? That's when we then try to seek their acceptance or approval, which produces insecurity and doubt. And that stops us in our tracks.

For that reason, *the flow of energy needs to come from you, the leading source, and only from you, not from your prospects.* Make them feel what you feel. That's the secret to influence. Forget trying to read your prospects for an interest level—or you'll only be looking for their approval. Learn how to create the interest instead.

The person who holds the force of energy inspires the direction of the outcome. When in the presence of great energy flow, your prospects, being vicarious, will absorb feelings that flow from you. If you show it, they will know it. If it's real, they will feel it, and it will produce influence.

PROMISE LITTLE AND DELIVER A LOT, QUIETLY

Demonstrative and advantageous personalities are notorious over-promisers. For the demonstrative, the reason is they want to be liked. For the advantageous, it's more about fear of losing a found interest.

When demonstrative and advantageous personalities are caught up in the moment and offer more of themselves than they actually can deliver, they immaturely set themselves up for failure. In the moment, both of these personalities might believe they're going to follow through with their promises, but too often they don't. The net result creates anger and disappointment in those they let down. They then try to make it right by promising even more, only to raise expectations and dash them again. You would think they would eventually understand that they are creating this chaos themselves and would fix it by a simple change in behavior. Regrettably, needing to be liked at a high level is a difficult mental position to outgrow. Those who are people pleasers at a high level **rationalize** it as, "I was simply being kind." In selling, **justifying** overpromising must stop.

For those who have been overpromised and consistently let down by a demonstrative person, trust declines. The person's overpromising ways become less and less believable. The person's credibility is diminished, and dependability issues surface. This is all due to a lack of concern for how others feel. Unfortunately, sometimes excessively demonstrative personalities can have a lowered self-awareness, and it can be made more difficult if they have a lower-than-average emotional intelligence (EQ: self-awareness, self-management, social awareness, relationship management). You can have your EQ profiled by a number of qualified online opportunities. However, like all personality assessments, just remember—garbage in, garbage out. If you don't answer the profile questions honestly, it serves no purpose.

It's challenging if demonstrative people don't understand how they are being perceived. Eventually, the behaviors that cause these problems will translate into the excessively demonstratives privately feeling a tattered, lowered self-esteem, while publicly showing the opposite. Then comes the **excuse**-making, the lack of accountability, which leads to their potential not being actualized. Unfortunately, many go down this path, smiling on the outside while it's happening.

Correcting this is not difficult, provided these demonstrative people have the capacity to see the trouble they create for themselves, and have the willingness to make the changes needed to quit this troublesome pattern of behavior. It takes true courage and humility to change. A good modus operandi would be to adopt this simple classic adage: "Promise very little, and deliver a lot, quietly." It is mature to set the correct expectations for those to whom we sell our services. Overpromising is immature.

For example, if you sell a product that is custom-built, and you know the standard lead time from order to delivery is somewhere between four and six weeks, the demonstrative personality might optimistically tell customers that "it's usually ready within four weeks or so, maybe even sooner." No mention of the possible six weeks, and that's not even accounting for human error that can add more time to a standard process. Then, in four weeks, the customer calls the salesperson asking about the status of the order and is told that "it will be two more weeks." The prospect feels disappointed, because they were unnecessarily overpromised by a demonstrative salesperson. Look at the damage it creates. All of which was 100% unnecessary.

A more mature selling approach would be to recognize that four to six weeks could possibly extend beyond the norm in rare cases, so why not just plan for it? Tell your customer, "The product usually takes six to eight weeks to get in." That way, when the product arrives in four to six weeks, a positive call can be made to the customer, indicating you've delivered ahead of schedule and beyond your promise. This approach makes you a hero, not a zero, to your customer.

Unfortunately, excessively demonstrative salespeople don't usually think this way. They want to please at any cost. Do customers really care if the product comes in within four to eight weeks? My own experience tells me no. Usually they don't. However, they *will* care if you don't meet expectations that were set by you.

With all personality types, the goal is to unblock whatever is in the way of following process. For a demonstrative personality, the next step in development is learning to recognize opportunity by becoming advantageous, through Green Stage 2.

If You Were Profiled as *Demonstrative*

If you were profiled as *demonstrative*, you must be willing to do the following in order to advance to Green Stage 2, *advantageous*:

1. Learn to become the leading source of energy flow in a sales presentation. Do not look to read your prospect for existing interest. Keep your level of excitement genuine.
2. Learn to use all three elements in the sphere of influence—words, tonality, and body language—in an expressively genuine way, in order to become a master of creating influence.
3. Learn to avoid overpromising your prospects by not promising anything beyond standard protocols. Set expectations that are genuine (or slightly buffed), ones that are in line with your company's practices for delivery.
4. Go *all in* and place yourself in the hands of a process that you might sometimes disagree with or agree with in part. Agree to follow it without making changes.

When all four goals are accomplished, move on to Green Stage 2, advantageous.

Questions for Someone with a *Demonstrative* Personality

There are three sets of questions you should ask that have been designed for the specific profiles in this book. Ask the first two sets before you hire an applicant (global and specific interview questions). And ask yourself the third set (30-day review questions) 30 days after hiring. You can access the questions and the 30-day reviews at www.myleadprofile.com.

GREEN STAGE 2

Personality: *Advantageous*

17.2% of Green; 2.3% of all profiles

VIRTUE

Opportunistic

Capitalizing on a prospect's perceived interest

TRAITS USUALLY ASSOCIATED WITH THIS PERSONALITY

Luck

Time

Will to negotiate

VIRTUES HELPFUL TO SELLING

Base-level competency

Can fill a specific need

DEFICIENCY (THE OPPOSITE OF THIS PERSONALITY)

Fear to engage with prospects and close

EXCESS (THIS PERSONALITY WHEN OUT OF CONTROL)

Challenges to Selling

Arrogance

Quirkiness

Defensiveness

Individualized strong-willed opinions

Egocentric behaviors

Trouble with change

Compromised selling, off-process

Rejection of criticism
Fear of critique
Not forthcoming about feelings
Closed-minded
Sensitive
Takes orders instead of making orders through influence
Projects one's own fear of affordability onto the prospect
Fear of losing "found interest"

WHAT YOU NEED TO FOCUS ON

First, start by selling. Get your feet wet. Serve your customers. See the virtue in what you do. Admit that you don't have all the answers. Then, dive into the details of your selling process, and put process-driven answers into action. Develop the leadership skills you need to discover, and expand opportunities, maximizing the efforts to serve a prospect better. Don't look at the prospect as a dollar sign. Look at the prospect as a person you need to help as much as you can. Gain confidence. Cultivate a strong, genuine, trusted connection with prospects without compromising your company's interests. Avoid catering to quirky ideas from prospects, and don't offer any quirkiness of your own. Then, learn and apply the many benefits of selling maturity, influence, and persistence to what you already know.

The *Advantageous* Candidate

Ari's Story

I came to America when I was 15 years old, after my father died. I had to learn the language, which took time. Later, I became a chef and eventually a master chef. I have a passion for cooking. I know good food, and really enjoy a good meal cooked expertly.

I was kind of a tyrant when I worked in the kitchen. I gave my staff seconds to communicate with me. I threw things around and made sure everyone knew I was in charge.

Years later, I needed to shift gears. I became tired of working at a stove, and after hearing from so many about how I'd make a good salesperson, I decided to take a shot at it. I applied and was hired for a job at a sales organization, selling one-day baths. I was told about a process I needed to follow, but I couldn't help but notice that the one guy who was selling the most wasn't following that process. He had a boatload of trophies and made a lot more money than anyone else. He was someone who would say anything, whether true or not, to a prospect during his presentation. The prospects believed his nonsense, and I began to think that must be how it's done.

My cancellation rate was very high. I was pushy and kind of negative in my general outlook. I was doing whatever I had to do to sell. Which, for me at that time, meant lying, fabricating stories, literally making things up to artificially bond with my prospects. When I got to a close and felt I was losing my audience, I would inadvertently start panic selling. My cadence changed, and my speech grew faster. I would over-negotiate. I was in sheer panic, fearful that I was losing what I thought was a sure thing. I wasn't going to walk away empty-handed!

It wasn't until the company brought in a new selling system that I began to understand the value of process. The owner and I helped break in that new system by running some leads together. Process became about honesty, humility, openness, and hunger for success—which now meant doing the right things for people.

For the next 14 weeks, my selling was stronger than ever before, and I had zero (yes, *zero*) cancellations. When they got rid of that other toxic guy, we started talking about how to build a sales team based on aptitude, attitude, and culture. My selling is a 180-degree turnaround from where it was in my earlier career. Cancellations are rare, and my selling results are stable. I see opportunities and make sure I sell whenever the prospects are cooperative. My focus is now on learning to better influence my clients to get them involved and more interested.

About the *Advantageous*

Advantageous personalities are opportunistic. *Opportunism* is defined (by *Lexico*) as "The taking of opportunities as and when they arise, regardless of planning or principle." For someone new to selling, performing as this definition suggests would require becoming solidly adept in this basic selling skill. Thus, for every personality type, after mastering the virtues of demonstrative (Green Stage 1), becoming advantageous is the next goal. Basically, it gets you comfortable selling something.

Those individuals who profile as advantageous are enterprising and always on the lookout for potential opportunities with new prospects. Mostly, they make good salespeople. They are personable and good at networking; they troll for interest. Their Achilles' heel, however, is in how they limit a prospect's interest to only face value. Equally important is how they handle objections and deal with rejection.

Advantageous personalities must focus on developing a selling-mature judgment to help further expand a prospect's interest and to influence an increased need for the salesperson's services.

All salespeople want to make big sales and for the best terms possible, but that's not how they all act. Advantageous personalities take prospects' up-front interest a little too seriously before teaching the prospects what they still need to know so they can make the *right buying decisions*. This is reactive behavior, not proactive leadership, and presenting in this manner would align itself more to order-taking than influential selling.

When a salesperson is confronted with a retail objection—that is, a prospect's objection or concern early on in the presentation—like "I'm not buying anything today"... and takes it too seriously, it gives it a legitimacy that it doesn't yet deserve. It breathes life into something that might be meaningless. Many retail objections are simply basic thoughts that prospects share before they understand what's important. At this early stage in the presentation, the salesperson hasn't yet had a chance to enlighten a prospect, and the best thing the salesperson can do is to remain calm, nod to acknowledge, smile, and continue performing the process as it is supposed to be laid out. A well-written sales presentation, after all, should strategically knock out many concerns along the way.

Advancing the Advantageous Salesperson

The growth goal of an advantageous salesperson is to learn the virtues of the serious personality at Green Stage 3, and then to acquire the traits of the influencer at Green Stage 4. It is the influencer who will open the door to even more possibilities for helping a prospect. Without applying those two stages to the advancement of an advantageous personality, the salesperson will default to becoming a deal-making compromiser or order-taker, which is only natural without applied wisdom and experience.

But first, for an advantageous salesperson to advance, we must examine the driving force behind any mindset for selling. When your efforts are focused on helping someone to benefit from what you sell, you are not really concerned with selling. Think of the irony. You are reading a book about selling that is telling you not to concern yourself with selling.

Let's put it in the proper perspective. The only reason you are a salesperson is to help people. It's not to sell them things, especially things they don't need. By guiding your prospects into doing what is right, you'll be genuine in your role. Is this a selling tactic? No, it's not. It's simply doing right by your customers. It's acting with character, something you need in order to be proactive in your mission to serve and be virtuous. Even after the initial excitement has subsided, you must show commitment and dedication to those goals. Dedication has everything to do with character. If you won't dedicate and commit yourself to advancement, you are someone who only *talks* about advancement.

When you commit to selling on-process—the way selling is supposed to be done—you'll avoid compromising the size, scope, and terms of your offer. You'll concentrate on what is needed, which is oftentimes more than what your prospect initially considered. With mature judgment, and by using a closely followed process, you can permanently avoid the things that forever plague the advantageous among us—like promising too much or injecting unneeded quirkiness into the agreements you write. The key is to redirect the advantageous opportunist away from doing *anything it takes to get that order at all costs,* into simply focusing on serving the customer properly.

IT'S ALL ON THE TABLE

Good selling starts by putting on the table the maximum advantage for a prospect, and you arrive at a partial sale only after first exhausting the possibility of doing everything you should to help. Advantageous salespeople are philosophically more attuned to the tenet of "Something is better than nothing." However, "It's all or nothing" would hold a better and truly servant-minded conviction. When "Something is better than nothing" becomes your comfortable opening volley, your offer becomes a compromise prematurely, right out of the chute or soon after.

Some salespeople will settle for selling anything just to say they have something. Would you consider that to be a strong persistence? Would that sound more like the thinking of an opportunist or a persuader? Is it more like the habits of the advantageous or the influencer? If the goal is to become a master at the craft of selling, then you're going to have to come to terms with the idea that mastery involves a consistent preplanned strategy. It also takes using an extraordinarily well-developed instinct that comes from perfect practice, the reinforcing of the right thinking until it becomes a muscle memory. Even well after it's developed, it will require vigilance to keep it on track.

IT'S EITHER ON-PROCESS OR NOT

Philosophically, it's black and white. You are either on-process or off-process, and you should train yourself to never see a gray area. That gray area is dangerous to anyone with a definiteness of purpose. To gain clarity of mission, you'll need to form some very important foundational core beliefs. Those core beliefs (covered in depth in Green Stage 3, serious) cannot be formed if things aren't determined to be on- or off-process in absolute terms and without exception. Will there be exceptions? If the process says no to the exception, then it's no. If you allow exceptions into your core thinking, it won't be so clear and/or ready when you need it. Those beliefs need to harden into stone for them to become your unconscious way of thinking. Without establishing such core structure, you'll think too much, then react instinctively when you're pressed by a prospect during a sales presentation. You'll be on shaky ground of your own making. Following process makes it much easier.

The trouble with many people who are advantageous (as well as those who profile as Yellow willful) is that they have powerful opinions about how things should be. My advice is, if you want to improve your selling, *stop having an opinion. Just follow your company's selling process.* Unless you have perfect instincts—and you don't—the only way you are ever going to improve enough to have a successful selling career is by putting aside your opinions and whatever you think you know. Grow a sense of intuition through the experience you'll gain from following process—not the other way around.

If you follow your gut instinct, you will be tempted to shortcut your presentation when you see you are starting to lose a prospect. You'll second-guess the next procedural move because you are trying to gauge a prospect's reaction and change something on the fly to fit *what you feel*. This won't work in the bigger picture. The decision to stray from process is driven by emotion and instinct, not your selling process. If your process has more to cover, but you rush through it because you are being hurried along, then you're reacting to a feeling of *Let's get something*—as in, *anything—out of this*. It's opportunistic, but not influential, and your goal is to focus on advancing from an advantageous to an influencer.

Some salespeople will come right out and say, "I don't want to work that hard." You might get an A for honesty, but there is no way to become a great influencer if you're not trying as hard as you can to influence a buying decision by using the best odds—that is, by staying on-process.

You can easily **justify** or **rationalize** shortcutting your process by telling yourself that you were losing your prospect anyway. So, why not capitalize to a lesser degree and not walk away empty-handed? As I discussed previously under the Yellow novice personality, the most destructive words around which to form a personal identity are **blame, excuses, justifications,** and **rationalizations**. The problem isn't that you were losing your prospect. The problem is your prospect was bored by your presentation. Take accountability (which will help you to strengthen your confidence) and drill. This is where your hard work has to come in. Go back and revisit your training in an effort to get it closer to the way it was taught to you.

While some prospects just won't give a good presentation a fair listen, enough will, provided the presentation is actually good. First, check the delivery of your presentation for effectiveness. Are you making points in a way that has actual meaning for your audience? If not, fix that first. If you think your presentation is great, but the metrics don't agree, accept that the metrics tell the true story. Denial isn't productive; it's only ego. Kill the denial, and tame the ego.

Work to pinpoint exactly where in your presentation you've stopped performing on-process. Zero in on what triggers you to make changes on the fly, and stop it immediately. That's one of the great things about a step process. It's broken up into simple steps that together equal a powerful presentation. You can easily pinpoint the areas on which you need to concentrate.

The off-process lazy "pitch" happens when you just give prospects the information *they* are asking for. This is a poor way to do your job, because your prospects don't know the value of the points that you aren't making; however, *you* know. Delivering a good process-driven sales presentation is the key to solidifying important points that differentiate your offer from others. And *differentiation is a very important key to selling*.

A good sales presentation should be written to highlight any exclusive features of your product, the things people cannot get from anyone but you. The presentation should be delivered by a selling zealot who is 100% committed to the betterment of a customer. If you abandon these important tenets of presenting, your presentation will devolve into a price war with your competition. The better product won't win the sale if it's not differentiated enough to make the case. Prospects feel passion, and they can tell when it's real. Real sells. If it isn't there, then only price will matter.

The lazy pitch will be **justified** and **rationalized** by salespeople who see process-driven performance as more of a rough-guide, not a necessity, and they think they know better. Lazy presenters—salespeople who are not fully committed to process—always have some good-sounding reasons to justify going off track in the real time of a presentation. "This one was different because . . . ," then fill in the blank. Those arguments can be very convincing, and since they are used so often, they're polished. There is always a kernel of truth in every **justification,** which makes it tempting, but it is unproductive and never right. **Justifying** and **rationalizing** against faithfully following a process will kill a sales career.

How to Hurt Yourself When Selling

My window company offered a free estimate that was good for one full year. It was designed to relax the expectation of any pressure the prospects might anticipate. It alleviated the fear of being hard-closed. We also offered a small discount for choosing to go with us within 30 days, and ultimately a lower price if they signed up on the initial visit. Our system involved no pressure. Zero. I mean none at all. We had a process that was well written, and it worked amazingly, turning prospects into satisfied customers on a single visit. It had a very high net ratio as well. When performed with precision, we rarely saw any cancellations.

In the first step of our process, we discussed with our prospects the agenda of our visit. In the explanation, we would remind them that they would be given a price good for one full year, and we would fill them in on any incentives available. We agreed to do this *in exchange* for their giving us enough time to properly cover what we needed to show them, and that everyone involved in choosing colors, style, or pricing—the decision-makers—would be present.

Advantageous personalities capitalize on interest. When they *feel* something is there, they become energized, like a fisherman getting a few nibbles on a pole. The advantageous, in turn, instinctively try to protect that *found interest* by relaxing any concerns about buying anything on that first visit.

While our great process did remind prospects, when necessary, that they would be given a price good for one full year, the advantageous personality might mention it a number of times *unnecessarily* throughout a presentation. By over-reminding, they unwittingly diminish their own capacity to sell by underplaying the expectation of a sale, and the prospects might even perceive it as a kind of nervous fear. As well, some salespeople show their own fears through unintended nonverbal cues. Since people decode nonverbal communication through instinct, the salesperson's actions of over-calming the prospect can be read by a prospect as a nervousness, an apprehension about something.

Sensing even a slight nervousness can trigger a prospect to unconsciously question the value of the salesperson's offer. After all, why would someone selling something seem nervous if the product is so good? These thoughts pop into a prospect's mind at lightning speed. A prospect might interpret that uneasiness as an implied *unworthiness* of the product, company, and offer, and it may produce a red flag about doing business with that salesperson. This is where being advantageous becomes self-sabotage.

In order to master selling at Green Stage 5, persistent, we must first master Green Stage 3, serious (selling maturity) and Green Stage 4, influential. Using a more mature approach, you would not feel a need to over-calm a prospect's concerns about buying something on the initial visit. Influential personalities, for example, feel there is integrity in what they offer and know beyond the shadow of a doubt that their product/service is worth it. They themselves are convinced, and, therefore, their case is genuine. Once again, real sells.

Another fear that an advantageous personality faces is losing a sure thing. An example is the marketer who is asked by a manager to get appointments for this week and "Also try to get one for tonight." The advantageous personality might feel that tonight is short notice, and will **rationalize** that trying "to get one for tonight" would risk losing an opportunity over the added pressure of making it for the same day. Tomorrow would be just as good, the marketer thinks, and so never even attempts to make those last-minute appointments. An advantageous personality will factor in the possibility of losing the prospect by asking for too much, such as an appointment on such short notice, but influencers don't. Fear of losing an appointment is the problem, and if you get rid of that fear—which only lives in your head—opportunities will open up. Your mindset is your choice.

The Roles of Doubt, Fear, and Ego—the Differences Between an Advantageous and an Influencer

Advantageous personalities share similarities with influencers, but the two are different in how committed they are to circumventing a gut feeling and following a process. While advantageous people see small opportunities for the taking, influencers see process as the gateway to all things good. It's not that influencers do not feel the same things the advantageous feel. Certainly, they do, but they have trained themselves to be more loyal to what process says to do, instead of what their own feelings urge them to do.

Influencers who are working in virtue are proactive and see anyone who qualifies for their product or service as a completely viable prospect. They set the stage for their performance and are excellent presenters who can convince skeptical prospects by showing them that what they're proposing is in the prospects' best interest. The fact that they themselves are convinced helps them to convince others. They're not concerned about losing a sure thing, because they feel they discover the need themselves; then, through that discovery, they significantly enhance the prospects' interest level. If you help create the interest, you will be less concerned about losing it. This is new found interest that the prospect might not have known about until convinced by the influencer. In a sense, if you create the interest, you own it.

DOUBT

When advantageous salespeople perceive a prospect's predetermined interest, they sometimes do add to it, but only in small ways. Mostly in a noncommittal way, they'll only go through the motions of trying to influence a prospect of the benefits of a larger purchase, a larger investment, because they lack confidence that they can change a more challenging objector's mind. They'll use "mention selling" that gives it the old college try: "You know, we *could* do all the windows in the house today. What do you think? It could be good?" To *mention* or suggest something is not the same as selling it by way of process. This behavior is the manifestation of an insecurity. It makes for a less heartfelt and emotionalized presentation and, therefore, falls flat on influence. In the window business, putting just one more window into the mix doesn't make you an influencer, not when your overall average sale size is performing under the intended target.

It's easy to find examples of salespeople who fail to connect a prospect to an emotionalized state of goodwill. Just this morning, I ordered breakfast in a hurry at a famous drive-through chain. The person handing me my order said thank you, but it was obvious to me that he didn't mean it. The tone was so awful that I felt thanked by a machine. I went to that same drive-through earlier that summer and was so impressed by the caring tone of the cashier that I made note of her name (Heidi) and wanted her supervisors to know the outstanding job she was doing. Her tone was so legitimate that I actually felt appreciated. There's a big difference between these two simple everyday examples of emotionalizing and not emotionalizing efforts. The difference is in making a customer feel a genuine sense of care. Real care sells.

When lacking in belief, advantageous salespeople are often unaware of how they project their doubts. Yet human beings are highly attuned to picking up on vibes. Even slight doubt is easy to sense. Remembering that people are capable of detecting more than 250,000 different nuances of facial expression, it would be easy to imagine advantageous salespeople projecting some of those doubts without even knowing they're doing it. What you feel is what shows as real. For advantageous people to become influencers, they must believe in what they do and see it as virtuous. If you don't, why are you in sales? Being good at the creation of interest makes the influencer's selling efforts that much more valuable to any company.

FEAR

Let's go back to the replacement window business again. If replacing all the windows in a house could dramatically lower a person's energy bill, then why would a salesperson sell a partial job?

Did you answer, "Prospect affordability"? Why not see your role as identifying the need for your product/service, but let the lending institutions decide affordability? The banks aren't going to offer financing if they conclude someone cannot afford to invest in something. Therefore, salespeople should not play the role of a bank. The salesperson's job is to create interest in the offering, not to decide affordability, thus writing off a consumer. So, what else besides *perceived* affordability would dissuade a salesperson from simply following the process? The answer is *fear*. Fear that the prospect will reject a whole-house order as too big. But since the prospect has already expressed an interest in the first-floor windows, why not just capitalize on that? Advantageous people do, and influencers might eventually reduce their offer to the first floor but not before making a valiant effort to convince the prospect about what's in that person's best interest. And certainly not before following their selling steps in order.

Giving prospects what they want before they know what they need isn't helping them. It is true that influencers help more people than do advantageous salespeople. I know you're probably saying, "Aw, c'mon, the advantageous salesperson wants to help prospects, too!" Okay, sure. But then why aren't advantageous salespeople doing more to help them? The answer is *fear*.

Every living person is emotional, and fear is a strong emotion. It's something that all the great salespeople wrangle with and have to learn to overcome. What is the worst thing that can happen to you if you go for the whole house of windows? The prospect declines your offer. So what? If you were operating with a good process that didn't turn any prospects off during the presentation, you can always go to the partial offer later, if needed. Try it in reverse, and it's a lot harder. Larger offers left to marinate on the table become the comparative number that will make a partial look that much more enticing if needed later.

When prospects take the time to do the mental gymnastics of considering a larger offer, a larger deposit, a larger monthly investment, they become conditioned to that price. Many times, they are sold right there, provided your presentation was great. By the time you go to a partial consideration, which often isn't even needed, the comparatively lower offer, the lower deposit, and the lower monthly investment look so much more attractive in comparison. But only if there is a comparison to begin with. Just understand that that's part of well-known selling psychology that persuades a prospect to buy. And it should be a part of any selling system.

Advantageous salespeople don't want to rock a prospect's financial boat. This is especially true if these salespeople are not well-off themselves and struggling financially. They sometimes project their own sense of unaffordability to the people they see and create an issue that wasn't there.

Let's say a prospect would be much better off with an easier-to-reach gliding window above the kitchen sink, where bending over and lifting a double-hung-style window is difficult. But because it might cost more than the double-hung style, which window might the advantageous salesperson suggest? If trying to *help* a prospect, the salesperson would focus on doing what is right, like an influencer would. Advantageous salespeople struggle with choices like that, because they sense the prospect's interest and are fearful they can lose what seems like a sure thing. So, they sell the cheaper, less-helpful window.

Remember this: Any idea of price versus value lives in the head of the presenter. Fearing a problem of affordability, salespeople create the objection themselves. It's a classic projection. They try to decide for themselves what people can afford and what they can't. No matter what objection you hear from a prospect about affordability, you can never know for sure if it's true. Don't get the wrong idea. Never sell to a prospect who lives in an obvious state of destitution. But don't go around thinking you can size people up for affordability either. Never take advantage of anyone. Just never sell anyone short because of a gut feeling *you* have.

Also, never take advantage of anyone whatsoever, such as older folks, especially those who you suspect have compromised faculties, or those who rely on their adult kids to help them make buying decisions. As a salesperson, your job is to probe for situations that involve anything like that. You also do not want to write off seniors who clearly have their full faculties and are interested in what you offer. Some companies treat perfectly good senior prospects as over the hill and unworthy of bettering their lifestyles. Treat a prospect with respect; just never sell to someone with a compromised ability to make decisions.

Advantageous salespeople who learn to help their customers with the right choices, regardless of cost, learn to work as virtuous influencers. It takes selling maturity to do the right thing.

In addition, remember to never be the reason for the objection. Projecting any of your own fears can create *reverse-objections*. That means, your own fear places the thought of the objection on the table, and then it becomes the prospect's fear, although it never would have happened had you not done so. I've seen this happen when a sale should have been sewn up, and would have been had the salesperson performed on-process. Sometimes off-process is as simple as over-speaking by as little as *one sentence* in a close, where the salesperson should have been silent. That misplaced sentence in a critical moment can add a very slight issue for the prospect to consider when everything else was going perfectly. Precision is important in a step-selling process, which is why you need to constantly revisit your company's system to keep it sharp in your mind.

EGO

And as you go forward and work toward Green Stage 3, serious, remember that a surefire way to slow your progress is to be influenced by your ego. Ego is powerful, and the cure for a swollen ego is learning the value of humility. Being humble makes you a better student and more willing to listen to those who can play an important role in your development. *Openness is the only sure path to fast-tracking selling-maturity, influence, and growth.*

What do people say about those who abuse alcohol? They aren't going to get the help they need until *they* are ready. In order to improve, advantageous salespeople need to agree about their own need to improve.

Growth begins with awareness. It is important to chart activity on sales calls, to read proper metrics and work toward becoming business scholars of key indicator reports that show what is working and what needs work. The better a report conveys the right messaging, the better the advantageous—or any other personality—will understand what to do to improve. Don't question the importance of a report or defend yourself with **excuses** when presented with poor numbers about you. Don't protect your ego, but instead embrace the information it offers. To reject that is to reject intelligent improvement itself.

Ultimately and always, however, *sell only as yourself.* Advantageous personalities sometimes change their personas in an attempt to match the personality they think a particular prospect needs them to be. They might also have different approaches for women, men, nationalities, sexual orientations, races, or religions. By applying the virtue-building traits of Green stage 3, serious, the lesson learned is to sell as yourself. Be who you really are with every prospect, without overanalyzing who you think the prospect wants you to be. Then you can learn to become your best-trained, well-equipped self. Sell as *you*, but the best version of you there is, developed by following your selling process with virtue.

A Few Words for Managers

From a manager's standpoint, excessive advantageous personalities give noncommittal answers to important questions. Fearing criticism, they semantically avoid responsibility and argue against critique. They'll give you a partial point for something you are suggesting they should work on, but they'll split hairs about small differences, miss the big picture, and forgo a full buy-in of your evaluation. They feel the need to equalize the criticism with the counterweight of their opposing view, which is simply a sign of immaturity and of blocked openness. Sometimes a point is just a good point and doesn't need a counterweight argument. Defensiveness is a poor reaction to critique. Openness is prerequisite to growth. That is the reason many people do not advance past the point of being advantageous.

It is the responsibility of the sales management in any company to teach selling maturity—the mindset of knowledge, along with how to influence prospects and the undeniable value of persistence. Those are the very things that get advantageous salespeople onto a growing career.

Additionally, managers need to avoid delivering a less-skilled, *destructive* critique and provide the *constructive* kind—even though sometimes telling people what they need to hear isn't comfortable.

Managers need to care about the people they lead. If they don't, it will be noticed, and they'll have a really hard time building a team that sticks. No one will tolerate working for a manager who is insensitive to the team's needs. Managers can be correct in the information they convey, but their message may not *feel right* unless it takes into consideration the feelings of the people they are speaking with. Managers must preserve the dignity of those they lead. If you are trying to influence someone, but what you're saying is falling on deaf ears, your influence will be as insignificant as a tree falling in the woods with no one around.

That said, a message should not be left undelivered because of the feelings of an employee who is not open. If you are hiring and training with the right materials, and you are consistent in your approach to coaching and running your company, if you have built trust within your team and actually care, then process is process, and it shouldn't be disregarded by an unwilling player.

If you are a manager and are struggling with training an uncooperative individual, there are times when you'll simply have to agree to disagree and part ways. You cannot let lack of cooperation hurt your ability to run your business. Just remember to always show faith in those you lead. Never let others sense your doubts in their ability. Leaders inspire; they don't shame people. Shame is very damaging and can easily be detected through an inconsiderate tone. As society progresses, shame is less tolerated. People will leave employers if they sense any of it or if they detect a lack of honest care. Be careful and aware.

Nevertheless, never settle. Even though it doesn't always feel like it, there are plenty of good people out there. Don't settle on hiring or keeping the wrong salespeople just because they can bring in volume, or you'll risk your credibility and your growth. Remember that one salesperson with a bad attitude can destroy an entire team, no matter the sales volume that person brings in. It's not worth it. Focus on only hiring those with whom you can build a process-driven team. Don't settle for less.

Just a Few More Words About Advantageous Personalities

Advantageous personalities are less common than demonstrative types. Only 17.2% of those we've profiled as Green have it, while demonstratives make up 66.1% of all Green personalities. This demonstrates how every Green trait after demonstrative becomes more and more specialized.

Remember, you can hire qualified salespeople who profile with no Green traits. You just have to (1) develop their natural personality into a state of virtue, (2) introduce Green Stage 1, demonstrative, and (3) introduce Green Stage 2, advantageous. All three should be simultaneously focused on at the very beginning of a new hire.

While the advantageous person progresses by being focused on going up the Green stages to eventually becoming *persistent*, we need to recognize that being advantageous is a clear sign of selling potential.

That should *not* be dismissed as insignificant. It's a good sign, as long as the advantageous person is cooperative and not stubbornly obstinate with behaviors running in excess. Potential is so often unrealized by those who reject proper structure.

While the advantageous person's virtue is found in the ability to identify preordained opportunity, that particular virtue is not enough to sustain a thriving career in selling. Being able to spot opportunity is a good first step, but it doesn't address opening up and cultivating additional value once it's found.

A person who fails to develop beyond advantageous will have trouble committing to a selling philosophy. Most have a negotiable set of core beliefs. Consequently, they might remain stuck in wishy-washy thinking that disallows a good process to fully form. Without faithfully following a good process, instinct would be your only guiding law of action, and you will eventually fail.

If You Were Profiled as *Advantageous*

If you were profiled as *advantageous,* you must be willing to do the following in order to advance to Green Stage 3, serious (selling maturity):

1. Internalize that your job is not to feel out a prospect for interest. Your job is to create it. Your role isn't to gauge the effectiveness of your process by how a particular prospect takes to it. It is to follow your process and lead/direct the way. You must be the one leading the presentation of your company and product, and ultimately the closing steps. Don't default that responsibility to your prospect.
2. Admit that you don't know as much as you thought you did. If you know everything, and you convince yourself you are at the top, the only place left to go is down. Stay hungry for critique. Don't be defensive when being reviewed. Critique is an important part of your development.

3. Follow your process *completely*. Don't compromise on the size, scope, or details of your offer, unless you are at the part of your presentation where the process says it's okay, having exhausted all other system-oriented viable possibilities first.
4. Go *all in* and place yourself in the hands of a process that you might sometimes disagree with or agree with in part. Agree to follow it without making changes.

When all four goals are accomplished, move on to Green Stage 3, serious.

Questions for Someone with an *Advantageous* Personality

There are three sets of questions you should ask that have been designed for the specific profiles in this book. Ask the first two sets before you hire an applicant (global and specific interview questions). And ask yourself the third set (30-day review questions) 30 days after hiring. You can access the questions and the 30-day reviews at www.myleadprofile.com.

CHAPTER 5

Green Personalities: Stage 3

GREEN STAGE 3

Personality: *Serious (Selling Maturity)* and with the Mindset of Knowledge

11.3% of Green; 1.5% of all profiles

MINDSET LOGICAL
Becoming knowledgeable

VIRTUES

Having a well-developed sense of judgment that's based on proven, transferable practices and performing duties with loyalty to that judgment

Being well versed in the known philosophy, psychology, protocols, and procedures related to selling

Enjoying the ability to build on what is known with a passion for continued growth: a true process salesperson

TRAITS USUALLY ASSOCIATED WITH THIS PERSONALITY
Wisdom
Understanding
Maturity
Knowledge
Level-headed

VIRTUES HELPFUL TO SELLING

Seriousness that became selling maturity

Strategic with clarity and vision

Possessing a learned wisdom to stay the course on process

Well versed in realities of known, well-established
facts and ideas that propel consistent forward momentum

Acts with acceptance of known, well-established
facts and ideas, without exception

Listens open-mindedly to ideas and takes
in productive criticism without defensiveness

Exercises good judgment that doesn't need to be justified later

Possesses a hunger to learn, to develop a better-informed judgment

Process-driven and less instinctual, leading to
smooth and favorable outcomes

Critical thinker grounded in foundational selling protocols

Productive thinker with strong core-belief values

True believer in a constancy-to-purpose approach to selling

DEFICIENCY (THE OPPOSITE OF THIS PERSONALITY)

Advantageous behaviors unattached to process

Immaturity

Less urgent in nature

Expedient
Uncommitted to process
Lacking specific goals
Instinctual in approach
Impressionable to quick ideas inspired by gut feelings

EXCESS (THIS PERSONALITY WHEN OUT OF CONTROL)
Challenges to Selling
Closed-minded to listening and learning more
Impulsive behaviors
Impressionable and susceptible to quick ideas
and easily persuaded by gravitational pulls from instinct

WHAT YOU NEED TO FOCUS ON

Internalize every aspect of mature selling philosophy and psychology. Understand and assume all things known to be true about the industry you are in. Apply knowledge from selling maturity to every move you make, even in the face of the hardest instinctive pulls that question process. Choose process every single time. Work from a disposition that is based in character. Develop an unshakable adherence to process while remaining open to, and in search of, meaningful growth. Know the difference between quick ideas that are erratic (the shiny objects) and core beliefs that are well founded and deeply established, and act with loyalty to core beliefs.

The *Serious* (Selling Maturity) Candidate

Bill's Story

My father was my cheerleader in my formative years. When I was young, he tried to embolden himself by attending a Dale Carnegie course. He had also read many empowering self-help books. I was probably 9 or 10 when he sat me down and told me, "You can do anything you put your mind to." It had a lasting effect on me.

I was 11 years old when my father suddenly passed away. My mother and brother and I were all lost. I was the youngest. Through financial struggles and hardships, my mother found her way to raising two boys. It wasn't easy.

I do remember one day when school was getting out for the summer, and I was going to look for a full-time job. I told my mother of my intentions. She asked me how much I thought I would make a week. I gave her an answer. Her response was, "You're not going to make that kind of money!" I felt at that time that she was showing a lack of belief in me; the opposite of what my father tried to instill. I told her that I would earn that money. She looked like she didn't really believe me.

I now had two things going on inside me. The first being, I needed to show my mother that I was better than she thought I was, to prove I was good enough. The second was to live up to the confidence my late father had in me. I had something to prove and something to uphold.

I did earn that money. I showed my mother my paycheck, and it surprised her. Her reaction almost made me feel that she was only challenging me for my own good.

All my life, I've been on an overachieving mission. In a way, I suppose I was trying to pack a lot of success in what could be a short life. I used to have a fear about dying young.

> I think big, although I've struggled in the past about not having the proper follow-through to see some of those ideas to the end. But I have created a number of businesses from scratch. I have a number of accomplishments that I am proud of. Although I'm getting better, I guess I still feel the need to prove my worth as a part of my mental programming from growing up as I described.

About the *Serious* (Selling Maturity)

Former U.S. Supreme Court Justice Potter Stewart, speaking about obscenity, once said that he couldn't really describe obscenity, but "I know it when I see it." I feel the same way about selling maturity. It can show up in many different ways, but I always know when I am in the presence of someone possessing it. I know it when I see it. Mature salespeople know it, too.

Selling maturity provides the keys to advanced thinking and gives you the detailed knowledge needed to go from being advantageous to being an influencer. Green Stage 3, serious, is broken up into three parts:

- Developing your core-belief thinking
- Developing sound judgment based on core-belief thinking
- Growing with an open mindset and transferable practices

Each part will build on the other and hone your thinking.

Part 1: Developing Self-Determination and Self-Governance

Developing Your Core-Belief Thinking

This section is vitally important in helping you to achieve success because, in order to persevere, you must first believe you have control over your ability to do so. Some of what is covered here deals in the little nuances that salespeople can sometimes miss. It is frequently little things that add up to bigger ones because of how they relate to our overall decision-making, which, in turn, contributes to the building of a mindset.

In order to absorb the important content, you must completely believe that you have the power to effect change. If not, you'll never quite make it, and we'll see you in 25 years when you figure it out on your own after wasting a quarter century. If you think I'm kidding, I'm not. Before moving forward, promise to be open.

Selling is 100% about mindset. According to Sean McPheat, managing director of MTD Sales Training Specialists, mindset is defined as "A fixed mental attitude or disposition that predetermines a person's responses to and interpretations of situations." Thus, selling with frequency begets even more selling. Slumping works in the same way, too. In each circumstance, whether sales are made with steady frequency or whether they elude the salesperson, the prospects are typically unknown to one another, and their only common denominator is having met with the same salesperson.

That is why all salespeople need a productive core-belief system. Self-determination requires a feeling of expectation, that you, the salesperson, must understand. It is your mindset that has brought you to where you are now. And when successful, it has allowed you to thrive there. It is also, in large part, the reason you've slumped from time to time.

How could selling something to one prospect create a snowball effect for more sales to follow? Selling begets more selling, and slumping begets more slumping. It's all in the way you manage your mindset about success and failure and what you believe is within your control and what you think is beyond it. In the big picture, it is never really about the prospect. It has always been about the frame of mind of the salesperson.

Manage your emotions. *Case in point:* You are issued a morning sales appointment in a town that is 45 minutes north of your departure point. You drive all the way there only to find that no one is home. You then drive back to where you started. Just as you get back, someone from your office calls to tell you they have confirmed a backup appointment in the same town you just left. You feel aggravated because you just came from that town, and now you have to drive all the way back, another 45 minutes. Would it have felt better if the backup appointment was 45 minutes south of where you are? Mentally, yes. Logically, no. It's the exact amount of driving in either direction. This is a good example of how we must manage our emotions. You cannot let any circumstance dictate your emotions, and you must make your objective your only guide. The facts are simple: You were on the schedule to run appointments, backups are a part of the plan, and you were issued a backup; just go. Choose to be happy that you have a probable opportunity to go to, and don't let a circumstance cloud your emotions and judgment. Emotions are what connects us to what is possible and what we think is impossible. It's all perspective.

Prevent making an emotional soup. Just think about how a customer feels when you show up late for an appointment. The customer may not vocalize it, but you can bet the customer noticed. Then, when your crew shows up a little late on the same job, the prospect connects your tardiness with the crew's. And then, if something slight goes wrong, it will add to the ingredients of your customer's growing emotional soup. Each ingredient alone would not taint the soup, but when added together, they make a toxic brew.

Emotions can turn little things into bigger ones when compounded. Soups like those cause anger, resentment, even wildly dangerous thinking for people who see the last ingredient as the straw that broke the camel's back. Think about how important it is for you to not only manage your own emotions but help others manage theirs, too. Emotions are magnificently empowering but can be powerfully destructive as well.

Identify fixed and growth mindsets. What people believe about their ability is a key factor of mindset. There are two known mindset dispositions that produce different efforts and, hence, different end results. The first is known as a *fixed mindset*. People with a fixed mindset believe that we are preordained with a certain level of ability and that we cannot change that. The other is a *growth mindset*. Believers in a growth mindset think they can bring about outcomes based on effort and hard work. A growth mindset lets people believe that they hold a certain control over their own abilities. This way of thinking is predominantly found in more successful people. It creates a drive and a persistence that together tend to produce results.

Fixed-mindset personalities are more likely to gauge themselves on how well they've done. On the other hand, growth-mindset personalities are inspired by information on how they could do better. The key difference is in what the two mindsets believe about their ability to effect meaningful change.

Fixed-mindset people see results as realities that tell a fixed picture. Growth-mindset people do not waste time considering things they cannot control, but in the face of setbacks, they immediately channel their energies into concentrating on things they can do to improve a situation. These two mindsets are what separates problem-solvers and problem-dwellers. Growing your selling maturity adds a seriousness to your mindset. Finding a productive balance of attitude and good judgment means learning to become a more intelligent thinker. If you think having maturity like this is innate, think again. You weren't born with this kind of wisdom, but it can be acquired.

Developing Selling Maturity

Selling maturity has its roots in simple maturity. Mature salespeople who educate themselves to become successful focus on a number of core areas.

1. FINDING BALANCE IN THE TONE OF THE PRESENTATION

In selling, your style of delivery is a make-or-break proposition. You can refine your approach to appeal to more people. Some salespeople are blunt and pushy, while others are ineffective and pushovers: two ends of the extreme. There is no need to offend anyone by acting in a way that is turbulent when working with a prospect. That's just manipulation and intimidation. Your points will be better received if they are delivered in control, in a balanced way. Ignoring your need for balance is a neglect of personal responsibility, a deficiency. Recognize the need for balance, and apply a well-developed tone to your presentation skills.

Finding balance is a virtuous goal in life, but it is not enough for a life in sales. Balance must converge with other important virtues to achieve dependable results.

2. CREATING DEEPER WANTS THROUGH EMOTIONALIZED POINTS

Influence is about persuasiveness. When you influence the power of reasoning in a prospect, you persuade the prospect to take your advice and move in your direction. Influence adds the magic of emotion to your purpose when selling, and the emotionalized points you make create deeper wants in a prospect. When your prospect feels the emotion coming from you, you're more likely to make a new customer. Balanced tonality converged with emotionalized influence creates a persuasiveness that will be better received. Balance and influence alone, however, are still not enough to sustain longevity in a career in selling.

3. WORKING A PROCESS THROUGH A CONSTANCY-TO-PURPOSE APPROACH

Next, we must add *process* to the mix. Process is a planned strategy to say what needs to be said, and to show what needs to be shown in a way that considers all relevant factors and obstacles. You must be knowledgeable about your products and services—so much so that, in order to become a master at selling, you will have to bring out the best features in your offer and know how to get the benefits to register both emotionally and logically with your prospect.

Mastery is about more than just making points; it's making them so they will be well received. The techniques that help make this happen must be understood and acted upon with precision. It takes the best psychology of influence (see Mehrabian's 7-38-55 rule on page 163) and balanced presentation skills to communicate in ways that will be better received. When you marry those two things to the exact sales process, you become more efficient. Being able to perform a presentation for a new prospect with the same enthusiasm you had for your first presentation, perhaps 20 years earlier, is the sign of a true pro. It all sounds logical, but there's still more that is needed for a successful career at selling to develop and go the distance.

4. ADDING IN PERSISTENCE, A ROCK-SOLID CORE-BELIEF COMMITMENT TO VISION AND ACTION

In addition to balanced tonality (becoming better received), influence (communication with emotion), and process (using the exact materials that have been found to be the most effective at closing sales), we need persistence. Persistence is having a rock-solid, core-belief commitment to vision and action.

Any process will, at times, be challenged by circumstances. Salespeople are on the front lines. They are the ones dealing with a wide variety of prospects. Muddying the water is the fact that salespeople are human beings and can relate to the things that derail process. It sounds rather complicated, but it's actually very simple. If salespeople allow balanced tonality, emotionalized-influence, or process to be circumvented by situations that challenge their ability to use what they have, they'll be right back to selling by way of instinct, and far less effective.

Persistence means a lot of things. Most importantly, here it means having core intestinal fortitude to stay concentrated on the processes related to delivering your presentation.

Salespeople must be more committed to process than they are to selling itself. If you get your process down, selling will take care of itself.

Having a faithfulness to process means a myriad of things, which include:

- Being true to delivering the steps of a sales presentation as intended
- Having the knowledge to anticipate objections and handling them
- Cultivating the mindset needed to turn imperfect opportunity into gold
- Being energized enough to persist in the face of objections
- Practicing the humility needed to work with negative prospects
- Building a state of mind with the determination to focus on a single-minded objective
- Possessing the power of dedication to never quit
- Having the judgment that allows a methodical approach to triumph over feelings or intuitions
- Displaying wisdom to disallow any and all exceptions to the standards listed above

Let's Get Serious (Selling Maturity)

Green Stage 3, serious (selling maturity), is perhaps the most thought-provoking stage to conquer. It takes more time to learn because it requires that you willingly accept, internalize, and apply a wide variety of information. You'll need to understand selling philosophy and selling psychology and learn how to apply them using a well-built set of core beliefs. You'll need to foster all of this, even though parts of it will, at first, feel counterintuitive to what you thought you knew. You must fight through your gut feelings and commit yourself to growth.

It can take an ordinary person a lifetime of experience to embody the wisdom of a selling-mature personality. And some never get there through experience alone.

There are only two ways to learn anything new. Which describes you?

1. Through experience itself, which takes time. This is the most common approach.
2. Through listening open-mindedly to the wisdom of others who can back up their talk with results. This is quicker to learn but requires *uncommon openness*; thus, this approach is less common.

Advancing Beyond Green Stage 2, Advantageous

I've seen countless numbers of salespeople cap at a lower level than their true potential because they failed to become serious, to become selling mature.

Everyone has an opinion about everything in these early days of the information age, where a simple internet search can produce answers to whatever we want to know instantaneously.

Thus, more than ever, people speak with a conviction on topics they know very little about. There are many *dabbling experts*. When it comes to selling, you can learn a lot from a book, and even more from a great trainer with a great process, but what neither can give is the actual experience—which leads to my next point. Even with experience under your belt, if you want to move to the next level, there is something more to consider: *You must understand how to apply a broad spectrum of wisdom correctly and open-mindedly to get the results you desire.*

For salespeople who have climbed to the Green Stages 1 and 2 and have become demonstrative and advantageous, it's a great start; but if you plateau there, you'll eventually tank. Staying there means you'll struggle more, leave opportunities on the table, and sell things for less than they're worth. You'll become overwhelmed more often and feel more defeated when you fail. There's even a good chance you'll jump ship and move on to another career. You'll eventually lose interest and treat your career with the same respect you'd give to discarded exercise equipment.

If you want to go the distance in selling, your need to grow is immutable, and the only way to make incredible changes in your life is to be totally in control of your thinking. You need to understand the power of self-determination and self-governance, which comes from the development of a strong core-belief system. Too many salespeople get stuck on advantageous (Green Stage 2). It's probably because you can indeed make a living at that level. However, you won't ever get too far ahead. Either you design what you want out of life, or you default to just getting by.

TRACK YOUR SALES USING THESE THREE "SELL" BLOCKS

Think of selling as a something you do with a specific core-belief mindset, and the more that mindset is refined and process-driven, the better it will perform. Consider selling as something that can be categorized in one of three types:

- **Sell Block 1.** Selling using all your process steps in order, starting with the most beneficial terms, the right deposits from customers, and the largest dollar volume, as laid out in your presentation. Fully working an all-or-nothing philosophy before going for less.
- **Sell Block 2.** Selling that resorts to a jump down from your offer to something that is prematurely compromised. It could

be going from a target sales volume number to whatever number a prospect says, before your original (larger) offer is given the proper time to marinate and be seriously considered. This is when a salesperson jumps at money, a something-is-better-than-nothing philosophy.
- **Sell Block 3.** Selling that results in quirky and off-process deal-making. This is the least effective method of selling. It lacks confidence in process and in oneself.

Which one do you identify with most?

What to do with this information. Track your sales honestly, and determine which sell block your sales fall under. If the majority of your sales are in Sell Block 1, then you are process-driven and on the right track.

If your sales are mostly in Sell Block 2, you'll need to work on slowing down your price rollout and connecting with your prospect in your product demonstration. Remember, the best close is a masterful presentation.

If your sales are mostly in Sell Block 3, you are stuck. To grow, you must become process-driven and devote yourself to learning Green Stage 3, serious (selling maturity).

SELF-DETERMINATION: DO YOU HAVE A NEED TO GET AHEAD?

On December 16, 2019, a GOBankingRates savings survey reported that 69% of Americans had less than $1,000 in a savings account, average household savings were at $16,420, and 22% of Americans had less than $5,000 saved for retirement. In addition, 54% of Americans between the ages of 45 and 54 had no savings at all. These statistics should worry you. They tell you that if you don't do something to get ahead, you are going to wind up poor, or at the very least, you'll have far fewer choices in life. You won't have enough money for the things you need, such as a home, transportation, and college tuition, let alone anything you might desire, like vacations or a luxury. Even the poorest among us have dreams, but if you obtain those things without a change in your income, you'll go into debt, which can be massive. Is that really the life you want?

After hearing those statistics, ask yourself, *Do you have a* need *to get ahead?* If you do, then you'll have to drop your opinions and put down your ego in order to admit that there's still a lot more to learn. You can no longer be your own boss. *Your new boss is process.* Even if you sell with some frequency right now, you can be better. Don't be nervous if that sounds harsh, because it's true and valuable. If you don't become truly broadminded and grab hold of your own fate right now, you'll stand no chance at all at getting ahead.

Our program was written to give a salesperson a faster track to reaching selling excellence than through experience alone. However, it's not meant for people who will pick and choose the parts they like just to feed their sense of comfort or hubristic opinions. You must be willing to confront why you're hesitant to do what is necessary to become great. In order to develop yourself into a better and more equipped you, it requires a *full buy-in* to your process of selling in order to advance in a program like this. Without real discipline, there can be no effective self-determination or self-governance.

The LEAD program is a program of awareness, about who you are and what likely challenges you will face because of who you are. It wasn't designed, however, to be your only means of becoming great at selling. LEAD should intersect with other good mentors, sales trainers, and practices that can be used to elevate your entire selling life. There are many pieces to this puzzle, and available today are some excellent selling tools that—if worked in conjunction with our focus on mastering the five Green stages—can launch a salesperson into an amazing career, one that is not only financially rewarding but spiritually rewarding, as well.

EXPEDIENCY VERSUS PROCESS

When working in virtue, influencers (Green Stage 4) have good self-discipline and keep their eyes on properly played end-game strategies, the practices that bring sales presentations to properly closed sales. Inappropriate actions of the excessive advantageous personalities (Green Stage 2) will too quickly compromise the terms of an agreement, such as by not asking for a respectable deposit for the contracts they write. Or by needlessly giving the store away with extra-special finance terms, or by entertaining quirky customer requests that unnecessarily bite into a company's profits. The advantageous do all this instead of standing up to a prospect about the value of an offer. Hence, they allow these deviations from process in, and they wind up with the hardest-complaining customers. By entertaining quirkiness, they cultivate it.

Instead, use good judgment. Influencers appreciate the importance of maintaining the right gross profit margin in the jobs they sell. They remember that the companies writing their paychecks do need to be profitable. Advantageous personalities, on the other hand, don't want to risk losing a sale by asking for too much. But what is too much? Is following your process too much? Of course not! If you're not strong-minded enough to do so, you're guaranteeing your limitations. By lacking enough self-discipline and without being fully committed to process, a salesperson will settle for average, which will result in *just getting by*.

Always advancing, serious people understand the realities of their industry, and they don't make impulsive moves that conflict with their process. That is why Green Stage 3, serious (selling maturity), is about acquiring knowledge. You must learn to keep a leader-like grasp on telling prospects what they can and cannot do, rather than overpromising something compromised out of fear. Give honest answers to prospects. They will respect you for it. Consumers appreciate that kind of stand-up honesty from a salesperson, and it creates an asset of trust. If people don't want to do business with you because they cannot get an unreasonable request met, you likely shouldn't want them as customers.

Due to a lack of self-awareness, some advantageous personalities see themselves as influencers. How are they different? Influencers, who work in a state of virtue, are developing their selling maturity. They study more, ask for help, and apply what they learn, *actively* participating in the growth of their career. Influencers working in virtue are not lazy. They are willing to put into action more drive, more determination, and more intensity, passion, and care, and they seem genuinely interested in improving. They don't think they know it all, and they do not see failure as an option.

Lacking in selling maturity makes a person less driven by process. It leads to pointless compromise and a fearful approach to decision-making. By entertaining whimsical or odd ideas, you'll concede the integrity of a sale. Behaviors like these come about when salespeople do not spend the time to build the right core beliefs, and instead default their decision-making to instinct.

What Exactly Is Selling Maturity?

Selling maturity can be described as *determined thinking with a specific approach to selling, a process based on tenets of good philosophy and good protocols*. It requires judgment that's built on process-driven knowledge and, as well, requires the development of a strong core-belief system, all of which come with time, experience, and an open-mindedness to taking in the right information from good sales trainers.

You really must know your materials and your process. You cannot bluff your way through learning the craft of selling without compromising your results. Further, process salespeople will learn the steps of their process and work it in a specific order. This includes understanding the need to fact-find the reasons for any close that's been rejected. Process salespeople will learn to isolate the true objection, not just treat every rejection as a matter of affordability, as amateurs are quick to do. Sometimes it's not about money. Once an objection is properly isolated, it needs to be established as *the only thing* that's preventing a prospect from moving forward. Then, process-driven steps are taken to solve that roadblock and close successfully. *Understand, failure in selling or mastery in selling is 100% your choice.*

Of course, having a sales trainer who is a concise communicator is always beneficial. Sales managers who operate using the LEAD program will have a far greater advantage due to the deliberate structure it brings. The five Green stages provide clarity and direction to fast-tracking your selling success, and they bring a meticulousness to the process of development.

But first and foremost, developing your selling maturity requires you to move away from ideas that are highly individualized to your own way of thinking. Without **excuses**, dedicate yourself to faithfully working an organized process all the way through to a successful conclusion. If your thinking doesn't follow the process, don't follow your thinking.

HUMILITY

In order to develop at Green Stage 3, serious (selling maturity), you must demonstrate and exemplify a strong sense of humility. Don't be stubborn. You don't know everything. Embody honesty in your approach with everyone you meet. You must also remain open to learning, no matter how much you think you already know, and feel a hunger to be great. It's what drives you.

I've critiqued a number of salespeople in my career. Those who were truly open learned from the experience. In a truly honest relationship with a salesperson, even the trainer is open to learning, and there's a bond there. I've also attempted to critique others who've defended themselves against my appraisal because they weren't mentally strong enough to handle it—no matter how gentle my approach.

Egotism can be described as *an undue sense of self-importance. Feeling you are always right, and others are wrong when they disagree with you.* Egotism is always at odds with humility. Being humble is a necessary ingredient for unblocking whatever stands in your way of becoming process-driven, and it's one of the four Hs, the other three being honest, hone-able, and hungry.

One telltale sign of a lack of humility is when salespeople try to mitigate the amount of critique they receive by attempting to be a little less wrong, instead of taking full responsibility. When it comes to their own accountability, less-mature individuals feel a need to split the difference. But to agree with only parts of someone's critique and to allow a half acceptance of other parts—just to support an ego—is to defend against an evaluation that's potentially valuable. Ego thus blocks progress. It's a sign of being closed-minded and immature.

Being open-minded requires maturity. Mistakes are how people learn. They are a great teacher, as long as we reflect on and understand their lessons and choose to grow from them. It's 100% mindset.

SAGE THINKING

Do you have unique opinions about things, and yet your results do not match the expertise you preach? Do you sometimes complicate a process with individualized twists and turns? Are you open-minded enough to examine whether you do? If you're planning to go the distance, you'd better be honest about your own self-evaluation.

How good is your post-demo analysis? Does it protect you, or does it cause you to return to your selling process when you have strayed? Are you aware when you have drifted off-process? Are you looking for metrics to prove you right or to learn where you can improve?

Are you the kind of person who sometimes makes leaps in logic? Are you connecting dots that make sense to your gut instinct because you believe you're intuitively gifted and insightful, but to others it seems like 2 + 2 = 3? If so, you're immaturely complicating things. Accept this as a drawback, and work to eliminate it from your way of thinking.

Brilliance is found in taking a complicated structure and making it easy to understand for a prospect. That's the gift that process brings to you. Almost every organized process will work, some better than others. However, a process won't work if you're only half following it. Making individualized judgments about certain aspects of a process, picking and choosing whatever feeds your latest need for comfort or importance, and/or trying to connect dots that are based in opinion not procedure: These things will destroy your ability to learn the right way. Process will eat your opinions for breakfast. Even if you lose an occasional sale because you are on-process, you will lose your entire way if you're not.

Process salespeople, *working in virtue,* will be confident enough to admit when they are off, because they know it's the only way to make needed corrections. It requires the ability to govern your mindset through honesty, without ego, even in front of others. It's not a show; it's simply reality. Others can learn a lot more from your slip-ups than they will by listening to the **justification** of off-system behaviors.

In selling, advantageous people are given a need and can fill it. Influencers discover a need and expand it. It takes the strong habits of serious personalities to understand the difference. Agesilaus, a Spartan statesman, once said, "It isn't positions which lend distinction, but those who enhance positions."

HONESTY

In order to develop selling maturity, you must be:

- **Honest with yourself.** If you cannot face reality and act accordingly, you will remain stuck where you are. Self-deception is the easiest kind to fix, and the hardest for some to admit.
- **Honest with others.** Your word is your bond. It's up to you to give it credibility. When credibility is lost, it is very difficult to regain. Treat your word as precious. Remember to be credible and to show care for the people you work with, manage, and sell to. If you violate your principles, it will be noticed by others, and your expert advice will be taken as seriously as an 800-pound person offering expertise on dieting. It doesn't work.
- **Honest about the outcome and true circumstances when resulting a lead.** Avoid self-serving reporting of a lead to preserve your ego. It is a block to progress and therefore dan-

gerous. Avoid revisionism when discussing a post-analysis of a lead. Focus on improving, instead of your ego. And never game your company's system and processes.

- **Honest about not trying to make an off-process situation look on-process.** You must be completely open and honest, or you'll sacrifice your credibility.
- **Honest about failing to appropriately follow process.** We all make mistakes. Repeated poor decisions are avoidable when you are willing to have a mea culpa and change behavior. Acknowledgment comes first.
- **Honest about owning up to your own responsibility when being critiqued.** Even in front of others, there is no need to preserve your ego. When confident enough with yourself, you can be critiqued in front of anyone, and it won't hurt your ego. Your standing isn't for show; it's supposed to be an honest reflection of your efforts, a baseline from which to improve. If you aren't honest, then you're making it a game. Don't make a game out of something as important as your career.

YOURSELF, IN VIRTUE

Selling maturity requires salespeople to present their product or service in a self-assured, procedural way. When salespeople perform off-process in a more instinctual manner, they will be *reinventing themselves for each prospect they see*. This is not only unstable and unsustainable; it's also mentally exhausting. It lacks core-belief thinking and is totally unacceptable behavior in professional selling; yet many salespeople are exactly like that. It is, essentially, a con job. *Selling in virtue is honest and trustworthy, not maniacal and phony.*

A mature salesperson always listens to prospects but does not cater to their requests if what they ask conflicts with any corrective thinking that should be applied when they get it wrong and need correcting. When a serious (Green Stage 3) presentation is professionally delivered in virtue, salespeople will be seen as more genuine by those they intend to serve. It happens because it's real, and whatever is real cuts through the clutter we bring to our selling approach. *Being real is a grounded attitude, and it sells because it translates into trustworthiness.*

When working in virtue, salespeople learn to become themselves. The goal is to become the best-developed version of yourself you can be. That's the *only* person you'll ever need to be. Plus, it works perfectly enough of the time—when coupled with a great process-driven delivery and a good personality—to help even new salespeople prosper.

When salespeople become good with themselves, they set the tone of their sales presentations with a steady ease. They aren't checking the mood of their prospect and trying to be what they perceive is needed. They stay themselves. Leaders are confident. They do not require a reinvention of who they are in each new setting. That's something only insecure salespeople do. It's the behavior of people who are unsure about who they are and therefore haven't developed a productive enough set of core standards and beliefs. Wishy-washy personas don't amount to building much influence with prospects either, aside from the easy, lay-down sales or order-taking, which require very little influence.

From a customer's point of view, a confident sales presenter is a respected expert and a trusted assistant buyer. When you emanate trustworthiness, you'll be both. Trust sells.

In addition, learn to work in virtue as yourself and with imperfect circumstances. Your skill level will depict how well you can bring more challenging situations through to a systematic presentation and a successful close. Learning to adapt to situations and making process work will make a world of difference in how *you* view prospects, and your ability to adapt will impact your belief system and mindset. With the right understanding, you'll recognize more opportunities in many circumstances, without the need to place **blame** on what you might want to call a *lousy lead*. The key is to walk imperfect circumstances step by step through your process and to do whatever your process tells you to do at all times.

NO ONE-TIME EXCEPTIONS

Selling maturity is the bridge between Green Stage 2 and Green Stage 4, between being advantageous and becoming an influencer. Simply put, that means learning *not* to rely on your gut instinct as your guide, which can easily be wrong and highly subjective, despite what you may think. Instead, work only from a set of principles, protocols, and steps—which we have been referring to throughout this book as your company's selling *process*.

Selling maturity means that, at your core, you will disallow even the one-time exceptions that challenge your process.

If an advantageous person makes a sale or two by ignoring process—in whole or in part—there is an excellent chance the person will struggle a lot more to become an influencer who works in virtue. It is hard to see it *in the moment*, but a principled approach should never be conceded just to make a sale. In the end, you will lose more sales by ignoring your process than you will ever make allowing in the exceptions.

Believe it or not, it's a fact that it takes only one exception to blow up how you think. And if it happens to work successfully, it will cause even more damage to process-driven thinking, because your mindset will always hold a possibility that exceptions can work. Your conviction will be damaged, and your brain will cut new neuropathways to a more intuitive way of thinking that will challenge the process-driven approach. You must never allow a one-time exception to win out. Your brain needs to hardwire selling maturity as your one and only mindset. This is about much more than a concept. It is about the reworking and hardwiring of your brain's physiology.

The Signs of Selling Immaturity

Most salespeople who are short on serious (Green Stage 3) fundamentals are unaware they're missing anything. Most likely, it's because they were never taught the value of some important basic and sound principles.

Here are some signs of selling immaturity:

- **Not using forms that were designed as a part of the selling process.** Substituting important and professional forms with a simple notepad instead. And not understanding the value of the form. Kindergarten scribble does not look professional. Napkins and scrap paper aren't a substitution for official company forms.
- **Showing signs of lacking commitment to following process.** Not completing daily reports and handing in information to your office on time. If you aren't taking deadlines seriously, what else are you choosing not to take seriously? It's like making your bed every day. It's not about the bed; it's about the discipline.
- **Shortcutting or cutting out parts of your sales presentation.** Justifying the idea that *this* one is different. In reality, situations vary, but the essence of following a process is a matter of learning to maneuver through obstacles and getting back to process. That's the only way to firmly develop an actual skill.
- **Hurrying through a sales presentation because a prospect is bored and doesn't want to hear your important information.** Keep in mind that customer dissatisfaction is largely a factor of uninformed consumers making erroneous choices. Educate your prospects so you can help them. If prospects refuse to listen, explain to them why it is important to hear what you are covering, so they don't make a regrettable mistake. If a prospect refuses to go through the proper process, you can simply tell them that it's not always a love connection, and perhaps they should call another company. Sometimes, that gets them to sit through a demo, and sometimes it means you'll leave. Either way, it's the proper approach to selling.

- **Not being responsive or engaged enough in your sales career, with respect to your dealings with customers, colleagues, subordinates, managers, and owners.** For example, having a noticeable connection to your cell phone, and yet people can't reach you. Managers will decide where it matters in the end, but they certainly should make note of it.
- **Giving special discounts or special pricing to customers when it is not part of your selling-process.** Making intentional pricing errors to give a prospect a price you are not authorized to give, then hoping your company forgives the "error" and pays you a full commission. Rules and protocols should be followed closely on what is and what is not acceptable to give away. It's only through fear or egotism that a salesperson feels the need to jockey around pricing for customers. It is a sign of weakness and general immaturity.
- **Making up or changing parts of a presentation without proper authorization.** Straying away from the company process for selling—adding in a little extra here and dropping a little part there—then not realizing how you've changed the process by doing so. It creates a situation where you no longer have a benchmark that is well-enough understood to measure against your performance. That's one way that salespeople stay stuck in being advantageous.
- **Projecting fears about pricing, finance terms, or interest rates.** Often creating your own problems through projection—and even slight projection is projection. Not realizing you are creating those problems just adds to them. Be open and self-aware.
- **Summarizing important constructed dialogue.** Putting important wording in a paraphrase when the process calls for certain company wording in some places. Then, being unaware of how your message might have watered down key presentation points.

- **Using any form of deception to justify not following your company's protocols and processes.** Remember, we get really good at the things we practice. Let's not make deception one of them. It's funny how some salespeople who won't stand up to a prospect have no problem standing up and **justifying** their off-system behaviors to the companies that sign their paychecks.
- **Overpromising to the people in your life.** You are trying to be everything to everyone without missing a beat, resulting in compromised accomplishments where truthfulness would have delivered better outcomes. Then, not realizing it, and continuing to do it. Stuck in a nonproducing loop.

Turning Seriousness into Selling Maturity

In the world of selling, seriousness must be transmuted into selling maturity.

To develop Green Stage 3, serious (selling maturity), you must:

- Study the craft of selling like you're on a mission . . . because you should be.
- Learn all the ins and outs about performing a process. Ask questions to your sales trainers, and develop a curious mind.
- Make a commitment to following your process, no matter what **excuse** you could use against it.
- Have and maintain a desire to succeed at a high level without compromise, despite occasional setbacks. You choose whether you will just scrape by or get ahead.
- Be determined to achieve and not fail, never giving up. You fail *only* if you give up.
- Develop a core-belief system that is completely aligned with the selling process you are using. No exceptions are allowed with core-belief thinking. You must follow process, not gut.

- Focus on self-reviewing where you ignored process, even inadvertently. Be mindful and honest about it, especially to yourself.
- Take personal accountability for all successful and unsuccessful outcomes. If it wasn't you when it didn't work, then it wasn't you when it did.
- Be open to critique, no matter what it's about or whom it's given in front of. Put down your ego, and be real.
- Exercise good judgment about not taking an easy and premature win that disregards process. One successful exception is all it takes to derail a salesperson from a proven process. If it leads to considering more exceptions, it will limit if not kill your selling career. It's always a bad trade.
- Replace ego by building a true confidence. Let reality be your truth, and let the truth be your reality about learning to be your best. Don't shade what's real. Be open and honest in self-reflection.
- And if learned at the highest level, show the maturity to develop in yourself a genuine servant's heart.

Always remember, all these things listed above are mere words until they are emotionally internalized and acted upon with genuineness. By summoning your personal allegiance to process and by pushing forth a self-governing will to believe that you can effect change, you'll display your mature and serious abilities in the way you care for your customers. You must also *feel* that sense of care, which cannot be faked. If you don't care for your customers, you cannot be a virtuous salesperson.

Part 2: Developing Sound Judgment Based on Core-Belief Thinking

What you know and what you act upon are two different things. Understanding the importance of certain core beliefs in selling will have tremendous impact on your selling career if you follow through and apply the knowledge.

The 92 Undeniable Core-Belief Statements for Selling-Mature Salespeople

You can adapt some of these statements of core-beliefs to your own specific industry.

MY PROCESS SHOWS THESE CORE-BELIEF STATEMENTS TO BE TRUE:

1. Following my process means my NSLI rate (my net sales dollar volume divided by the number of leads issued to me) will be X dollars or higher. If it is too low for my industry, I'll check my metrics of canceled contracts versus finance declines. Each should have its own level of acceptability and target goals. I'll find which is affecting my NSLI and do everything in my power to correct it.

    My NSLI number is far more important than a closing percentage. I will learn the proper NSLI for my industry. That number will tell me if I am truly profitable or not.

    (To learn how to calculate an NSLI, see "What Numbers to Track and Why" beginning on page 258.)

2. Following my process means my demo rate will be $X\%$ or higher. I will learn the proper demo rate for my industry.

3. Following my process means my net sales rate will be $X\%$ or more of my gross sales. Lost sales breakdown is $X\%$ cancel rate and $X\%$ finance rejection rate. I will learn the numbers that apply to my industry.

4. Following my process means my average gross sale will be X dollars or more. I will learn the numbers that apply to my industry.
5. Following my process means I will earn a healthy income. I will learn what the potential income numbers are that apply to my industry.
6. Following my process means I will have a minimum X% opportunity rate. I will learn the numbers that apply to my industry.
7. Following my process means I will cover X% of the leads I am issued. I will learn the numbers that apply to my industry.
8. Following my process means I will bring clarity to a prospect's mind. I recognize that a confused mind says no.
9. Following my process means I will work to get referrals from each lead I am issued. I am committed to an all-out effort to gain leads through referrals, job signs, or other means. I recognize that leads are the lifeblood of my selling career. I will not solely rely on the marketing department of my company to provide all my opportunities needed to be successful. I will commit myself to act and not just talk, and I will be active in my pursuit of excellence. As a habit, after every sales presentation, I will ask everyone I see for referrals in a specific manner.

For example, if I sell to my prospect, and the payment (investment) is X dollars per month, then before I leave, I will say the following: "Now, that we're all wrapped up, let's take five minutes before I go, to help you a little more. If there were some way to make your first X number of months of payment just fall out of the sky, you'd probably be pretty happy about that, right?"

I assume my new customers, in this case a couple, would agree.

"Okay, both of you take out your cell phones. Let's see what people you know who own a home like yours, who *may* benefit from something like what we just did for you. No guarantees, and my company will not be pushy in any way when contacting people you know. Here's the best part—we pay X dollars for each referral that culminates in a sale. Typically, we'll see X number of sales from every X names given (modify for your specific product/company). So, both of you, open your individual phones and go to your contacts. Start with 'A,' and let's see who might be helped by this. Each sale will pay you X dollars, so if you had three (which is common), that's X dollars for you, which you could use for around X number of months of your first payments on your new windows. Mary, who is in your A's? John, whom do you have?"

Referrals come with a high level of trust. The best way to meet someone is through a personalized introduction, whenever possible. This approach is after the sale or after the demo/no sale. Referrals are valuable. I'll try this approach.

10. Following my process means I will never separate myself *as an individual* from my company. We are as one. If I do, I know it will sow the seeds of doubt about doing business with me. I will never be the company apologist. I will always back my company's policies, programs, and protocols 100%.

11. Following my process means I know that if my prospects become customers, they will have a great experience working with my company.

12. Following my process means I will not sell to my prospects; I will serve them. I sell to serve, not just to sell. I will not sell things that are not needed. If I sell to help, I will serve my customers in a virtuous way. I will maximize the extent to which I will serve my prospects at all times. As an example, in the case of selling windows, that means if certain existing windows test well, new ones might not be needed. The same thinking applies in reverse to windows that a prospect doesn't think need to be replaced but test poorly.

13. Following my process means (for one-call selling) if I do not serve my prospect's needs on the initial visit, I believe that another company will come in and "close the prospect." And I will lose the opportunity to serve someone. I firmly believe that if another company wins the business of my prospect, that company will not handle the prospect as well as our company would have.
14. Following my process means I will not ballpark prices. I will work the proper sequence of the company's presentation. I recognize that doing it the right way is necessary in order to achieve the maximum understanding of the benefits I am offering to my prospect. No one gets a price before a masterful presentation. Never!
15. Following my process means I will have all the decision-makers present for my presentation. If not, I will *only* go as far as step X, then reschedule the appointment to have all decision-makers present. All the decision-makers need to be present so they can all be fully informed of the benefits and facts surrounding my offer. Otherwise, the prospects will not know how to properly invest in my offer. I am responsible for teaching my prospects how to buy what I offer. This is not something I leave to chance.
16. Following my process means I will earn the right to ask for the order by performing a masterful presentation.
17. Following my process means I will not judge any prospect for worthiness as a buyer or for a perceived lack of financial ability to purchase. I will let the banks decide affordability. I will recognize my role as a salesperson—as someone who creates the *desire* for my product—and let my company's finance department decide a customer's creditworthiness.
18. Following my process means I will spend X amount of time, on average, from start to finish presenting to a prospect. I will not shortcut my presentation.

19. Following my process means I will not stereotype any prospect by nationality, race, religion, gender, sexual orientation, or any other division that can be labeled. I will not eliminate a prospect from my help by way of prejudging. I will treat every prospect with respect and dignity. I will not attempt to size up my prospects or prejudge any situation.

20. Following my process means getting the appropriate deposits from my customers and recognizing that deposits are a good sign of their commitment to a project.

21. Following my process means if I sell based on rescission—the prospect's right to cancel—or if I get a signed contract only to hold a discount, I can expect a cancellation to follow.

22. Following my process means if I don't button up my sale, I might lose it to a possibly well-intentioned but interfering and less-knowledgeable third party, such as a family member, friend, or coworker, who will give an uneducated opinion without sitting through my value-oriented presentation. I will always button up my sale to safeguard against it being canceled.

23. Following my process means I will call my prospects by their first names and not use Mr., Ms., or Mrs. A first name puts us both on a more level ground and will help my prospect build respect for my advice. I recognize that people like to hear their own names. It connects me better with my prospect.

24. Following my process means I will dress properly for an appointment. I won't overdress, in a suit (such as with an in-home presentation). And I won't underdress, in a t-shirt, nonfitted untucked shirt, sweat clothes, blue jeans, or sneakers (with respect to in-home presentations). I will dress respectfully in a business-casual style, in khakis or clean black jeans and a tucked-in shirt or a fitted untucked shirt. This will vary based on industry and changing times, of course. But clothing is not an afterthought, it's a considered preparation.

25. Following my process means I will always respect my office protocols. I will hand in my reports and paperwork on time and show respect for my coworkers.
26. Following my process means I won't look for reasons to leave from an appointment because the winds of interest aren't blowing in my direction. I will stave off any gut feelings I have about something that seems lacking as an opportunity. If all decision-makers are present, despite resistance, I will stay and perform a presentation that's system-oriented and process-driven and work hard to *create* interest.
27. Following my process means always being on time. Up to 15 minutes early is fine. But I will *never* arrive at an appointment even one minute late. I must demonstrate to my prospects that I am a professional and that they can count on me. People use correlation thinking when making judgments. A prospect may feel that if the company is on time to the appointment, then they will probably be on time when fulfilling a work order. That's how people think.

    Sidenote: Sometimes being 15 minutes early means you arrive before another company does—this can occur when prospects overbook whom they have coming out. If you're there before the competition, you stand a much better chance of presenting your case than they do.
28. Following my process means feeding my mind with beneficial information—mental nourishment for encouragement—as much as possible. Being a road warrior, I'll have a lot of windshield time. I will make use of that time by listening to audio recordings from the great masters of selling. For example, anything by Zig Ziglar, who wrote the playbook that the selling industry still uses. I will enlighten my perspective and keep it sharp. I won't do this to impress other people. I'll do it to enlighten myself.

29. Following my process means I look at failure as a teacher and see it as a positive influence on the redirection of my efforts. Failure is the ultimate teacher whose lessons can be positively impactful to any growing mind. Tom Watson Sr. of IBM said, "If you want to succeed, double your failure rate."
30. Following my process means not following my *personal* instincts when I have a doubt, but only following my professional process.
31. Following my process means avoiding quirkiness in my contracts. I won't complicate the work I do by adding extras that throw off the rhythm of our company's delivery process. For example, I won't individualize sales to a point where the customer needs to speak directly to me when the job is being installed. In actuality, the installation shouldn't involve a salesperson. This only happens when a job is sold from a salesperson who over-individualized their approach.
32. Following my process means I recognize and respect that a company must speak with one voice. I recognize that the people in my company must work together as an ensemble cast. Giving out my personal phone number to customers sometimes complicates issues by my trying to handle things I shouldn't. Resolutions are better suited for the department that's tasked to handle those things, such as financing, installation, and service. I will direct all customers to call our office and speak to the specialists who can perform their own duties without interference from my well-intentioned self.
33. Following my process means I need to be captivating while serving. Captivating could mean in a demonstrative fashion, such as hands moving, enthusiasm, excitement shown through physiology, body language. It could also mean to captivate a prospect by being a very trusted, well-respected presenter, like a doctor who looks over bifocals to discuss a serious matter. I will be mindful that passion and respect lead to trust.

34. Following my process means mentoring my fellow salespeople whenever possible. To share the wisdom that I've learned and look to expand it in others wherever I can help.

35. Following my process means helping people. Of course, this means helping prospects to become customers. It also means helping everyone around me in any way I can. Filling a coffeepot with water, holding open a door, letting someone else go first because I sense that the person is in a greater hurry. Helping is a way of life. It is not an act to make a sale. I will cultivate the quality of benevolence in who I am.

36. Following my process means presenting in my own skin, as me, and not trying to be someone else. It means perfecting and delivering my process-driven presentation in the way it was intended to be delivered and doing so as me. I will look to be the best-trained and prepared me that I can be. I will dial my natural personality into a state of virtue and master all five of the Green personality traits. There is no one else exactly like me, so I have a responsibility to be the best me I can be.

37. Following my process means I will manage my ups and down by not mentally spending commissions from my sales before I am paid. In the event of a cancellation or a finance rejection, a salesperson runs the risk of being deflated and flattened by a negative surprise at the loss of a sale. I'll sell it, celebrate it for an hour, then forget about it. I'll move right on to the next prospect and serve that one. Having a number of sales in the queue makes dead sales less tragic to a mindset. It's part of the selling business. I'll just know that it happens and condition my mindset to deal with it productively and professionally. But I will follow process so I am not the cause of any cancellation.

38. Following my process means I will be aware of when I stray from my company's selling system. I will be vigilant about

recognizing that I've wandered away from my process and proactively reread through my training materials to reset myself. I will show active desire to find my way back. I will ask my management and colleagues for help to get me back on track. I will not become defensive about a need to improve. I will not let my ego get in the way of my success.

39. Following my process means keeping my word to everyone. In doing so, I will refrain from overpromising myself or my time to others. And I will control my time so that it does not interfere with my other responsibilities. Mastering selling maturity requires developing and applying good judgment. This is an area that many salespeople fail to master, and it costs many of them their careers.

40. Following my process means keeping my demonstration kit and samples in tip-top shape. I will be prepared at every stop to use spotless equipment that I will properly maintain. This is another example of prospect/salesperson correlation thinking. From the prospect's perspective, if my samples are dirty, the installation might be dirty, too. Poorly kept demo materials show a lack of concern for neatness and a lack in self-management.

41. Following my process means I will give my prospects the full first-visit discount, even if they were ready to buy from me at a price that is higher. I will be honest with my customers and not play with price. My integrity is paramount to my being. It is never for sale. When a prospect senses my level of integrity, it adds to my persuasive powers. And to know it is genuine makes it feel that much stronger at my core.

42. Following my process means I will be an *active* participant in my career. Anything less is a dereliction of duty. Passivity has no place in a mission as important as my career.

43. Following my process means that I do not use discount coupons or pricing in a way that does not conform to com-

pany expectations. I will not throw in extras that I am not supposed to, nor will I ever overcharge anyone.

44. Following my process means I will represent the four H's*: honest, humble, honeable, and hungry. This defines a growing culture. Everyone in a healthy organization needs to fit this description, or the work environment will be toxic.

45. Following my process means never sharing grievances or complaints with anyone who is lower than my level or at my level. I will never bring dissension into the ranks. I will contribute my part to keeping our culture strong.

46. Following my process means being 100% committed to performing on-process to the best of my ability. I will not ignore my company's process, nor breeze past the parts I don't like, nor change the process without the consent of my sales management. I understand that process means working the entire system, not just the parts I agree with or like best.

47. Following my process means my company celebrates every single sale. If there are issues with how I made a sale, they are discussed afterward with me in a cool-down queue. Companies should praise behaviors they want to see more of and discourage or reject behaviors they deem unacceptable, and my company's critique is based on where the salespeople are in their careers. The level of being *off* is more understandable for a rookie than it might be for a seasoned rep.

48. Following my process means that my selling mind must be pure from distraction. If I am not fully in agreement with some aspect of our company's process, or if I harbor certain limiting fears, I won't fool myself into believing I am hiding it from my prospects. What is real to me will show up in the way I conduct myself. Thoughts are things, and they are real. For instance, if I fear price, it *will* show to my prospect.

---

*The four H's is a philosophy credited to former business owner Robert Quillen.

The prospect may not have feared price, but my projection of that fear elicits a doubt in the person's mind. Since I sell a quality product, if I fear price, my prospect will detect it and think, "If your product is so good, why are you afraid of what it costs?" I will not allow my efforts to be seen as having questionable value. The counterweight to any price objection is value. If the value exceeds the price, the price will be perceived as well worth it. The opposite is true, too.

Note: A similar thinking applies to managers who say one thing and do another. Never get caught in thinking that it is okay to do something different than what you are teaching a salesperson. If there are differences between what you say and what you do, you are not fully committed to following your company's process yourself. Fix that!

49. Following my process means to understand that whatever I look for, I will find. I will focus on the things that make me stronger. I will be careful to choose wisely about whatever I am willing to seek out, tinker with, let in *just a little*, play with, have commitment to, or ignore. Playing around with my process is messing with my mind, and it will take me off my process 100%.

50. Following my process means giving my very best performance every single time. When salespeople get bored from repeating the exact same presentation over and over again, they're naturally inclined to make changes. It's where human nature conflicts with performing on-process, but making changes breaks with the concept of *constancy to purpose* and will cause unpredictable results. Boredom should be ignored, and that's why I will be purposeful. I'm sure the actors in the Broadway show *Cats*, which was performed 7,485 times in 18 years, must have felt slightly bored or tired by doing the same thing the exact same way every single time. Yet I'm sure they didn't change their scripted lines out of boredom.

Professionalism requires repetition. I'll find other ways of alleviating boredom in my spare time, but I will perform my sales presentation on-process.

51. Following my process means meeting and exceeding expectations by working both ends of a problem. For instance, when a lead time of a delivered product is discussed with a customer, I'll add some buffer time to the expectation. If the true lead time is three to four weeks, I'll use five to seven weeks. Then I'll go back and encourage my office to move more quickly. I'll ask whether I can have the product delivered within three weeks. Both ends of the problem should be worked to maximize an ideal outcome, and setting the right expectations will lead to happier customers. Therefore, I will manage expectations that allow for some wiggle room. I will avoid overpromising and underdelivering. I will be a hero, not a zero in the eyes of my customers.

52. Following my process means understanding the value of my own influence when handling *people who actually need my product but don't know it,* as compared with *people who think they need my product before even meeting me.* I am not doing my job if I do not provide prospects with *all their rightful options* when they do not already own my product. I will not limit the scope of my ability to help my prospects by predetermining what they want, until I have a chance to influence a decision for the right work on which to focus.

53. Following my process means I will show dedication, drive, determination, and desire to arrive at my growth plan. For example, I will become a great salesperson, great sales manager, great entrepreneur. I will not allow myself the luxury of being a slouch. I will get up and work on my goals, even when I don't feel like it. Especially when I don't feel like it! By the end of the day, I'll be glad to have those accomplishments. They will add to my feeling of completeness.

54. Following my process means I am helping my manager to fix me more easily if I were to drift away from my training. Without establishing a system-oriented baseline, there would be no standard for a critique. Like the alignment of a car, it goes out slowly and eventually needs correction. A presentation can either evolve or devolve, but the best predictable outcome comes from a constancy-to-purpose approach. I will always welcome my manager's opinions, and by following process, I will make it easier for my manager to analyze my presentation when I am off. I must remember that I can know what I know *and still* listen to my manager's professional assessment of my performance.

55. Following my process means I will never take advantage of anyone, ever.

56. Following my process means not entertaining crazy offers from prospects. Salespeople must stand up to crazy ideas from their prospects. Not only is it the right thing to do, but it shows a salesperson's command of knowledge, which helps the salesperson earn respect from a prospect. If a car sales rep, for instance, is selling a car at a dealership that averages $50,000, and a prospect makes an offer of $10,000, that salesperson should not breathe life into such a crazy offer. The sales rep should *not* bring it to a sales manager for consideration, or the rep will risk losing all credibility. Knowing what can and cannot be done is important. I must hold the line on what matters and never decrease the perceived value of my services. Standing the proper ground is one way to earn a prospect's respect.

57. Following my process means I will avoid the exhaustion of having to reinvent my approach for every new sales presentation. I'll master a process that works and consistently work it the same way each time.

58. Following my process means I will have already anticipated the objections I will encounter and have good responses

ready. I will continue my education by getting answers from my company and colleagues when I hear a new objection.

59. Following my process means I will become and remain a *true believer* in my company, my product, and my price. Never an apologist.

60. Following my process means I am engaged and responsive to the needs of my company and its managers and my subordinates, contemporaries, prospects, and customers. We live in a world of fast and instant communication. Avoidance behaviors are a tell-tale sign of disengagement.

61. Following my process means my presentation will be conversational, not confrontational. Selling, even one-call selling, should not involve any pressure whatsoever.

62. Following my process means I have committed to being on the fastest path to selling greatness.

63. Following my process means I will look to myself for answers when my results fall short. I will not turn to **blame** and **excuses**, but I will look to empower my efforts by taking responsibility for performing on-process.

64. Following my process means I recognize the importance of details. I will never leave any details undecided after making a sale. No signed contract should ever include any unresolved factors.

   This can include the features of a product. While selling windows, for instance, it might include the inclusion or exclusion of grids or their patterns, colors, or styles. If I leave a detail for later, customers will drive around town looking at other houses. They'll call friends, some of whom might have gotten new windows from another company. They'll compare prices but forget many of the details that mean quality. Customers may cancel orders because of a well-intentioned but less informed third-party.

All details must be decided at the time of sale and locked in, as *definitively decided* by the customer. It's my job to see to that. I appreciate the words of well-known American inventor and marketing personality Ron Popeil: "Ruthless attention to detail is a competitive advantage." I fully utilize the details of my company and product to sell the differentiating advantages my offer brings. Following my process means recognizing that details are not an afterthought. It gives meaning to what is important. Details matter. I will nail them all down at the point of sale.

65. Following my process means I will not add unnecessary stipulations to a contract. The product I sell must carry its own weight.

    For instance, I will avoid a need to reach a customer's specific financing requirements. I recognize that financing is only *how* something is paid for. It should not be *why* people invest in it. There are loans available to creditworthy customers. A salesperson's role is to sell the product. The product is permanent. The financing might later be replaced by another form of financing of the customer's choosing after the customer takes ownership.

    I understand that when a salesperson boxes in the agreement with individualized stipulations (unnecessary conditions), it limits the chance of a sale going through. Selling based on those sorts of ideas means my finance department is limited in the ways it can approve a sale. It might even hurt the chances of getting a customer financed if a special program isn't offered by the lending institutions we work with or introduce to our customers.

66. Following my process means making sure my prospect *feels* a need for our products. It is my job to strike an emotional chord—a feeling of connection—in helping my prospect become my customer. I remain conscious about my attitude

as I strive to be less transactional in my approach. I will avoid sounding like a professor in my delivery. My presentation must make an emotional connection with my prospect and not feel like a classroom lecture. If I speak too fast, I can adjust my rate of speech and stagger my sentences by inserting a pause here and there, even asking my prospect questions like, "Does that make sense to you?" If there are two prospects, ask them both separately. Connect to everyone. Ignore no one.

67. Following my process means I will live in a state of gratitude. Gratitude is the only known antidote to negativity. Allowing in negativity is a surefire way to decline in the world of selling. Allowing **blame, excuses, justifications**, or **rationalizations** to permeate a mind is a poison that interferes with accomplishing what I believe in. Gratitude is a positive mindset. Positivity is of key importance to anyone who works at a career in selling. Aristotle once said, "Pleasure in the job puts perfection in the work." Positivity allows us the feeling of happiness and pleasure.

68. Following my process means I make decisions with doing *what is right* on my side. There is never a need to argue from a weak position, if you believe in doing what is right and act upon those beliefs. I will work to align my core-belief system with the best of what I offer—in influence and brain power—toward my cause. Confucius said, "The superior man understands what is right; the inferior man understands what will sell."

69. Following my process means I am cooperative with the inside sales and marketing departments, which are notoriously at odds with outside sales sectors in business. I encourage measures to strengthen our mutual goals, such as partaking in the building of a solid SLA (service-level agreement) between outside sales and marketing. An SLA between the

departments creates a contract that holds each team accountable for meeting specific and agreed-upon expectations that align to the same goal, which is serving customers and driving revenue, the scoreboard of our helping others.

70. Following my process means offering my own innovative insight about how my company can move forward and stay relevant in a rapidly changing world. It is my responsibility to share ideas and, at the same time, to be gracious when my ideas are not utilized. I will respect my company's position when my ideas are not accepted.

71. Following my process means if I do not know something, I say, "I'm not sure. Let me find out and get back to you," instead of faking an answer. Being honest is being real.

72. Following my process means I understand that I will listen my way into more sales rather than talk. Plutarch, a Greek Middle Platonist philosopher, biographer, essayist, and priest at the Temple of Apollo, said, "Know how to listen, and you will profit even from those who talk badly."

73. Following my process means I have internalized and performed the six components of a masterful presentation.

    Four are about the product I sell: differentiation, exclusivity, passion, and WIIFM, which means *What's in it for me?* and focuses on how my product benefits the life of my customer.

    Two are about my style of delivery: tie-downs and trial closes. Tie-downs are endings to sentences of compliance, such as "wouldn't it," "shouldn't it," and "wouldn't you agree?" Trial closes are summary statements that kill off competition and set mini-commitments from my prospect about what I sell, after making a differentiating point.

74. Following my process means showing interest in other people: prospects, customers, and colleagues. Dale Carnegie, author of *How to Win Friends and Influence People*, said, "You can make

more friends in two months by becoming interested in other people than you can in two years by trying to get other people interested in you." I will take a genuine interest in my prospects and remember that it is my responsibility to make sure they *feel* my intention to help them. I recognize that conversational presentations feel warmer to prospects.

75. Following my process means that while I will always be respectful of my prospects, I will not credit their previous knowledge about the kind of product I sell. Thus, I will not skip parts of my presentation. My belief is that if I didn't say it, they don't know it for a fact. I will control the information I need to cover and stick to delivering my complete presentation each time. As the father of advertising David Ogilvy said, "The product you represent is depending on you, and if you allow yourself to take shortcuts or present a less than compelling argument, then you've failed."

76. Following my process means I will not fear price. Plato wisely stated, "A good decision is based on knowledge and not numbers." Customers who invest in quality are generally more satisfied and less problematic than those who only value a low price. Satisfaction is knowing you made the right decision. I will make a case that proves my offer is the right decision.

77. Following my process means never deviating away from my responsibility to deliver the proper results.

78. Following my process means respecting all my sales reports and tracking metrics. I will study the metrics I gather or am given, and I will make necessary changes to get and stay on my company's process for serving more people. I recognize that numbers always tell a story and that it is my responsibility to learn what that story is.

79. Following my process means I will remember to recharge my level of energy by taking time for myself and to relax at regular

intervals. I will reward myself for accomplishing my objectives. I will learn from my failures and rejoice in my triumphs.

80. Following my process means charging my devices and never running out of power in a presentation. If I use a computer, I will plug it in during my presentation as a caution against the battery running down. In addition, I will not leave any electronics in my car overnight. I will safeguard my equipment from theft and excessive heat and cold. I will carry extra batteries in case my battery-operated equipment dies. I will be prepared.

81. Following my process means keeping my car and my office or shop clean and neat. I will remember to project the cleanliness of a true professional. I will keep breath mints with me, I will use deodorant, and I will use a cologne or perfume that works as an attraction to my body chemistry. I will remember to use all the human senses to my advantage.

82. Following my process means I eat seafood four times a week. (This was put in here to see if you're reading this. You should read it all. Keep reading.)

83. Following my process means I will trust my prospect's non-verbal communication even more than what is verbally said. While my presentation needs to be delivered in a consistent manner, it is smart to notice if it is being embraced by my prospect. If not, I will work on my presentation to perfect it.

84. Following my process means thinking that what I do is purposeful. If there is no mission except to make money, then there will be too little passion to sustain me in the long run.

85. Following my process means I will ask each of my prospects who bought my product, "Why did you go with me today?" I will let them tell me why they decided to trust my guidance and expertise to satisfy their needs. I will strive—with respect to selling psychology—to learn and improve from the feedback of the people I serve.

86. Following my process means I will believe in myself. I will practice self-respect but avoid developing hubris, which leads to closed-mindedness and alienation of others.
87. Following my process means I recognize that I am a storyteller. I relate to my prospects with practical stories, ideas, metaphors, and analogies. Sixty-three percent of a selling audience will remember stories after a presentation, while only five percent will remember statistics.*
88. Following my process means I will speak to my prospects at a sixth-grade level, so they will understand everything I have to say. I will use bull's-eye communication by keeping what I say easy to comprehend!
89. Following my process means I am a leader in my sales presentation. Mary Kay Ash, founder of Mary Kay Cosmetics, gave the following advice: "Do not desire to fit in. Desire to lead." I won't pull back when my prospect is a low responder. I will not look to change what I do because of the flat attitude of a prospect. I will create a performance-rich atmosphere. I will design what I want it to feel like for my prospect. The prospect's experience is in my hands.
90. Following my process means I understand that to internalize my presentation and deliver it to the best of my ability will require repetition of thought and study. This never stops.
91. Following my process means I recognize that a goal is not a goal without a date. I will keep sales goals to specific start and end dates, so I can focus my collective energies of mind and body to achieving success as I plan it.
92. Following my process means I am guaranteeing my success unless I quit. That's why persistence is Green Stage 5.

Source: Chip Heath, Stanford University.

How to Stay On-Process

Brad Bishop, CEO of Green Machine Reflective Technology, LLC, was profiled through LEAD as serious (selling maturity). Brad has run many successful home improvement companies. He offers this advice about process: "If you go after selling in a lot of different ways, you will not be successful. The companies that fail do not have a selling process. Every big successful company has a good selling system, a procedure—the same order and sequence of events in every sales call. How do you fix someone who is broken if you don't know what they're doing? The order of sequence is vitally important."

DON'T BE RUSHED

By practicing selling maturity, you will keep your presentation from being rushed along by an impatient prospect. Any sales presentation must be performed confidently at a proper pace while building a pleasant connection. Never let prospects persuade you to skip parts you need to cover. If your presentation is well written, the prospects don't know the value of what they're asking you to omit. However, you do! If you're truly process-driven but have a weak moment and allow the shortcutting of your presentation, you'll always regret it later, when your prospects don't move forward with an order. Sleep well at night when you follow process precisely, for you will know you have done everything in your power to persevere. If you are honest with yourself, you will be restless at night when you compromise your process, knowing there was a path you didn't take.

Tips for preventing being rushed along in a sales presentation. You can give an impression of a quickened pace by saying something like, "It sounds like you already know quite a bit, so I take it you're probably already familiar with this...," and then go on to explain the next thing your presentation is supposed to cover. You can also tell prospects that you'll give them the *Reader's Digest* version of your presentation and then go right ahead and cover everything. Just make it fun, and keep it interesting. If the prospects are enjoying themselves, they won't keep complaining or take out a stopwatch. If you skip parts, you are not treating your prospects with respect, even though it might seem the opposite to an uninformed salesperson. Not serving someone to the very best of your ability isn't respectful at all, it's cowardly. Make it fun, and cover everything in your presentation.

Time stands still when you're masterful. No sales presentation worth anything should be blown through quickly, due to a hurried prospect who became tired or bored. If that happens frequently, re-examine the impact of your presentation, and work on making it more dynamic and captivating. I've had newly recruited salespeople come with me on appointments. They sometimes tell me, "The prospects tried to interrupt your flow and push you along, but you just acknowledged their remarks and continued covering your presentation seamlessly." It's true. I keep my presentation focused and on track. With the right skill level and a single-minded approach that performs on-process, I will never be thought of as rude. It just takes enough practice to get it down in tone, cadence, and sociability.

After completing many sales presentations, I can report that I almost always hear at the end, "That presentation was outstanding!" Sometimes, prospects who become customers add in that it was a bit long. One even suggested that maybe my staff should inform people over the phone that it will take as much time as it took, but then she turned to her husband and said, "But then we probably wouldn't have agreed to it." Her husband then remarked, "No, we wouldn't have agreed to it, and we wouldn't be getting these incredible windows right now either! It's a good thing they didn't mention that!" They laughed about it. The best part was, all I did was follow my process. Nothing was individualized. There was nothing all that special about me, the presenter. The way I conduct my process approach is 100% transferable to anyone.

I would rather have an occasional customer tell me that my presentation was too long and buy from me, than to have one buy from me without a proper presentation. The latter comes with a high cancellation rate because a value-centric case was not well made. The sale is just taken as offered. Without you influencing why customers are signing to go with you, they won't be loyal to you. If you leave prospects to become customers on their own, they'll often cancel their order on their own, too. Without a proper reason to go with you, your product, and your offer today, any sale would degenerate into a *price-only* matter. There's no loyalty to a brand or a person. It's literally the lowest price wins. That's not a contest I would ever want to enter. Not because it isn't easy, but it wouldn't really serve people. It would just be taking their money for doing the least amount of work I could to earn it. That's not the reason I'm in sales.

One-call selling does not mean pressure. Any sales presentation should feel like a meeting of the minds. Where two or more people find a common purpose—the prospect's project—and work together to turn it into reality. If performed skillfully, it is a calm, no-pressure get-together to discuss improving the life of the consumer in some way. My field has always required a one-call close. Many untrained salespeople automatically and incorrectly assume it must involve pressure. Great sales presentations are written to be conversational, which should not involve pressure at all.

It takes a certain amount of time to make a substantial case and to lay out pricing options and enticing discounts that can make a real difference. Especially when selling higher-ticket items. A sales presenter should not jump at a hard close at any point. Closing cannot feel to a prospect like a gotcha game but rather the offering of a great solution to a real problem. You must not be seen as a salesperson but as a *solution provider*. That is the connection that must be made. Jumping at a quick close is asking for a cancellation.

A spontaneous quick-thinking close means more cancellations. Mature salespeople do not jump at isolating objections prematurely—before the proper place in a process sale—and attempt to satisfy an objection with a quick-thinking close. Quick closing is what lazy salespeople do, and it comes with an increased chance of a canceled sale. A well-developed salesperson will close on point. The layout of which is performed at a preplanned place in a presentation, not when a customer gets bored and says, "Let's do this."

Your sales presentation must go through a series of steps, its process, before you can close. Each step needs to be completed and accepted by your prospect before moving to the next. Facts need to be understood, acknowledgments made, and points internalized by the prospect. Whatever activity is required for each step should never be rushed. With a well-developed judgment that's derived from core-belief thinking, process becomes your *only* guide. That can be a hard pill to swallow for those salespeople who trust their own judgment over what they would consider the blind following of a more systematic approach. Without consistent use of process, judgment is individualized. And since people cannot teach other people to think exactly as they do, selling at a master's level is taught through the faculty of procedure. The committed salesperson must cover every step, so the right outcome can be expected. Short of that, your success would be in the hands of Lady Luck.

Personalize, yes, but don't overdo it. Individualize, nope. If your sales keep coming up short—in pricing, commissions that fall short of expectations, compromised product volume, or technical problems on the job—or if you frequently seem to get that customer who needs to speak directly with you in the middle of a job because the person is disappointed by something not meeting a promise or an expectation, it's not an accident. It's because of something you are doing or not doing.

Don't get me wrong. You should definitely personalize your approach. Let your personality deliver the tone and influence as only you could. But don't individualize it. Individualizing means adding or subtracting something from the presentation as it was taught to you.

ADDRESS THE PROBLEM OF GETTING OWNED

If you've individualized your approach, you've gone rogue. It may have created what feels like a stronger bond at first, but it has made you *just a little too liked*. You became someone who's easy to enjoy and so nice and agreeable that your prospects feel that they sort of *own* you. You said you'll do a few extra things for them. You promised individualized attention when the work is being performed, something that's more than what your system protocols asked you to provide. And now you're on the hook. Overextending yourself like this can be decoded by your customer as fearful and produce an unwanted consequence.

Let your company and product hold all the virtue. Let the care you have for the prospect show as real. But don't push the limits of your approach to include putting yourself on a leash. It's unnecessary, and it can cause a prospect to respect you less in the end.

Let's take an example. In this instance, you are conducting an in-home sales presentation for replacement windows. The prospect is concerned about how much the frame of the window will cut down the glass area, because the new frames are a bit wider than the old frames. There are two ways this can go, two different approaches.

Case 1: The Chaotic Approach

Prospect: How much vinyl is your window going to have? I'm concerned that I'll be losing too much glass area with your windows.

You: It's only going to cut it down a little bit; it will be mostly glass area.

Prospect: (*Takes out a tape measure.*) Am I only going to lose this much? (*Pointing at two inches on the tape measure.*)

You: Yes. No more than that.

Prospect: Okay, I can live with that much, but no more.

You: It won't be more than that.

Case 2: The Orderly Approach

Prospect: How much vinyl is your window going to have? I'm concerned that I'll be losing too much glass area with your windows.

You: All windows that tilt in for easy cleaning will require the window to pivot down from a master frame. So, you'll lose a little glass. But the trade-off to get an easy-to-clean window is a pretty good trade for most people I work with. (*Offers an enlightened perspective to influence the thinking of a prospect.*)

Prospect: (*Takes out a tape measure.*) Am I only going to lose this much? (*Points at two inches on the tape measure.*)

You: It will cut it down a little, but I'm not certain it's exactly that much. It'll probably be a little more than that. Most people tell us the new linen-white color makes the room feel brighter and more spacious. (*Offers an enlightened perspective to influence the thinking of a prospect.*)

But I'm going from what many of our other customers tell us. Plus, you need a bit wider frame, but that's just so the window will tilt in for easy cleaning!

Prospect: Okay, I can live with the trade, as long as it doesn't feel like I'm missing too much glass area.

You: That's subject to personal opinion. I can only tell you that the cut-down in glass area certainly could be looked at as a small price to pay to have windows look this good, and as easy to clean as ours. (*Offers enlightened perspective and demonstrates the tilt-in feature again.*)

Prospect: Hmmm, I suppose you're right.

Breakdown Analysis

In the first example, the **salesperson** sees the objection about losing glass area as a concern that can cost the sale. Fearful to lose a noted interest, advantageous people are quick to alleviate the prospect's concerns by reassuring the prospect that the windows won't be losing much glass area. The salesperson even goes as far as to confirm the amount of loss that will occur—assuring them that the loss is no more than two inches. This is an immature way to answer that objection. When the windows are installed, the prospect is sure to take out the tape measure and compare the reality to the promise. If it's off by the slightest, the salesperson will be getting a call, followed by a difficult meeting where the prospect will attempt to prove the company did not deliver as promised, potentially looking for money off or even a full refund. If it sounds crazy, it's not. I've heard stories like this and worse. Disappointment comes from not meeting someone's expectation. Remember, it is you who sets those expectations.

Was it avoidable? Absolutely, but it requires selling maturity (Green Stage 3, serious). In the second scenario, the salesperson makes a point of not overpromising a certain amount of glass loss. That salesperson doesn't allow it to become an issue that will dominate the decision to buy. Rather, the salesperson wisely uses *maturity* to redirect the prospect's attention to the tilt-in feature and the new white color that will make the room feel more voluminous. Would the salesperson lose the sale by answering those concerns the orderly way? Not likely.

Serious salespeople are better at separating important information from unimportant little things. Sometimes advantageous personalities get caught up in small, technical details and entertain odd requests. They get sidetracked. It leads to unnecessary attention to minutiae. Then later, they'll spend an inordinate amount time trying to solve a problem they created themselves.

ADDRESSING THE PROSPECT WHO ALWAYS GETS THREE PRICES

All salespeople run into prospects who swear by the principle of getting three prices.

People need to eat, and they also need to sleep, but I assure you they don't need to get three prices. They *choose* to do that. Many prospects tell salespeople they are going to get three prices, but it's only to protect themselves from a high-pressure sales call. It's only a warning shot. Don't fear it.

The key to ensuring that your prospect isn't placed in a *fight-or-flight* situation is to avoid applying pressure. Your prospect needs to feel at ease, relaxed, knowing that you're not going to try to hard-close them. And the only way to overcome the prospect's *need* to shop is by your being highly prepared with a brilliant, systematic, and conversational presentation that appeals to a prospect's need for emotion and logic, providing the person with what is true. Great sales presentations, therefore, provide clarity of what's available in the marketplace. Being eminently prepared means that you know your industry, so you know all your competitors. Introducing your prospect to the truth about your competition is important. And it has to be the truth. Make sure you do your research about your competition in quality and price. Do not misrepresent your competition. Be honest.

Well-written sales presentations always include price conditioning, which, in part, means providing insight into your competitor's pricing. You won't lose business to another company's lower price unless you fail to meaningfully differentiate what your product offers against that of the other company. In the vast majority of cases, value will win over price, provided the value is seen as more impactful than a lower price. An true understanding of value is always the centerpiece of a masterful sales presentation.

Think of price and value as inextricably entangled in the minds of your customers. The two elements—price and value—sit on a teeter-totter together. *If price seems too high, then value seems too low. The same is true in reverse. If the value is seen as high, the price will not seem too high.*

People are not computers that are programmed to get three prices before proceeding. They are human beings who can be swayed, provided your presentation is designed to do so. And unlike computers, people will always factor in feelings that emotionalize their decision-making. When people feel they really want something badly enough, they'll move forward. They'll do it when they're persuaded that it is in their best interest. This is why the salesperson must be an agent of influence, not an agent of acceptance.

The three-prices concept sounds good, but it fails clients miserably. I can't tell you how many times our window company would meet a prospect who already had *some* windows replaced yet made terrible choices. Many had big regrets—and some would have regrets if they only knew they bought the worst product and sometimes overpaid for it, too. Getting three prices didn't help them, and the practice doesn't accomplish what it's intended to do—protect the prospect. Ultimately, people will move forward when they feel that a company appears to meet their needs to the exclusion of all other options. Those needs must be met in how a prospect sees your company, your product, and the value of your offer, not simply your price. If, in the end, a sale comes down to price only, the salesperson has failed to differentiate their offer by not underscoring the company, product, and value in an impactful enough way to the prospect.

In addition, you can tamp down the prospect's focus on getting three prices if your pricing structure incentivizes moving forward on an initial visit. You just need to have the right sales presentation and to follow it without exception. My company always had a very high closing average against competition; yet our prices were higher than most. Price had no bearing on hindering the making of sales, since our value exceeded the perception of price. That's successful selling, and how you do it is with the consistent use of process.

APPLY CLOSE ENHANCERS THAT WORK AFTER HEARING NO

Usually, when prospects say no at the close, they are indicating that they are not going to be deciding anything today and they'll think about the price you just gave them. Thus, I'd like to share with you two close enhancers that work in tandem. Each provides different benefits in helping you close the sale on the initial visit. Bear in mind that these enhancers are not designed to be a primary price rollout, and they are used only after you hear the first no at the close.

These strategies work only if you have performed a masterful presentation in virtue and with mature selling, and have therefore nailed down the following cases: First, ask if your prospect would feel confident working with your company based on your company's credentials. Get a yes, and the *company case* is made. Second, ask if your prospect would have your product installed if the product were made affordable. Get a yes, and the *product case* is made. Next, after these two important cases have been accepted and approved by your prospect, you'll move on to perform your standard price rollout.

Our window company gave a price that was good for one full year. We also gave a small discount for deciding to go with us within 30 days. Then, our process brought the price to a comparatively lower offer if the prospect decided to buy that day. All of which evolved over the course of three steps in our nine-step selling process. We weren't trying to close at the one-year or the 30-day price. Our first actual close was always at the same-day price.

After giving the same-day price, we remained silent. If you talk in this section, beyond setting up your same-day offer, this might be the reason why you don't sell. This is a sensitive moment. You must get uber-comfortable with remaining silent here. The old saying is, "He who speaks first, loses." However, since I believe it's always a win-win or a lose-lose, I'll only refer to that saying anecdotally, as a guideline.

If your prospects speak first and state that they aren't ready to move ahead, don't induce a fight-or-flight situation by applying pressure. Avoid that at all cost.

In this example, your prospects stated they weren't ready. Provided there are two prospects, use a positioning statement as something that *sets up the pins* for what you want the prospects to consider. You could say something as simple as, "We don't always make a love connection. That's all right. But for a lot of people . . . as long as you feel comfortable with our company, and you know our window is so much better than the others we compared it against, a lot of people generally feel that it's most beneficial to get it at its best possible opportunity, meaning its lowest possible price. By the way, would you mind if I use your bathroom?"

What you have to understand: Before you got to their home, most prospects (when there are two) had already made a pact with each other to *not* buy anything that day, no matter what. They are both bonded to that arrangement. When you leave to use the bathroom, you are providing an *unexpected* opportunity for the prospects to check that they are both happy with your offer. Incidentally, that's why I don't suggest using a *porch light close*, telling the prospects you are giving them a few minutes to talk. The *bathroom close* works better because that time is unexpected and gets the prospects to huddle on topic, not talk about what's for dinner tonight.

Once they've released each other from the bond of not buying that day, they'll breathe a sigh of relief knowing that no one will be sleeping on the couch if they move forward. When you come back from the bathroom (four or five minutes later), sit back down and remain silent. This may feel awkward at first, until you master sitting back down without saying a word. I can assure you, with practice, like me, you'll be masterful. About half the time, the prospects will ask a buying-signal question, such as "So, you're saying it takes eight to ten weeks to get the windows?" As long as they aren't starting by saying,

"Thanks for your time; leave us a card," you're still in the game. Now, you can proceed into making the sale.

It's easy to capitalize on buying-signal questions. First, answer the prospect's question with, "Yes, it takes eight to ten weeks to get the windows in." Then, you'll use the four best words to get it on the table. Those words are, "Let's say you say."

Here's how this works:

You begin: "Yes, it takes eight to ten weeks to get the windows in. *Let's say you say,* I love the window; your company sounds great; let's get it done. The first thing we do is to write up the agreement and get a credit app; then we'll bring your paperwork into our finance department. They'll get to work on it right away. You'll get a call as early as tomorrow during the day to go over what they are able to do for you. I assume you can take a call during the daytime?"

If the answer is yes, it is a buy-in from your soon-to-be customer. Now, you finish up the assumed sale by saying: "Okay, let me get the basic information I need [*reaching for an agreement*]. Now, I've been calling you Larry all night. Is your formal first name Lawrence?"

Start writing. The rest is selling history. Never, ever ask if it's a go. You must assume the sale at this stage. This technique could not be used if you continued talking when you heard no for the first time. Study the psychology of these moves. It's not complicated but highly effective.

Part 3: Growing with an Open Mindset and Transferable Practices

Despite obstacles in life, you'll find yourself where you put yourself. You cannot change where you came from, but you can change where you're going. It's a matter of practicing an openness and a willingness to learn how to grow, to evolve. Selling, after all, has had its own evolution, and change is at the very root of its nature. Successful selling uses well-informed practices that are transferable, teachable from one salesperson to another—but they continue to be carefully crafted to change with the times and the consumer.

The art of selling, in fact, has been a part of the human condition for as long as there have been humans. The earliest versions were likely very crude in approach, and while I obviously have no firsthand experience, I can picture how a caveman might have simply taken what he wanted. A club over the head might have been the only negotiation. While highly effective in a lawless world, it involved no influence, just blunt intimidation. Eventually, the expectation of being clubbed might have paved the path for preparation, as in preparing to give the counter-club. That's when the caveman probably began to realize that primitive society was on to him, and he needed to change his approach.

The term *snake oil salesman* came about around the time of the California Gold Rush. Claiming that oil would reduce inflammation from arthritis, bursitis, or sore muscles made it a popular remedy. Except, it didn't work. A poor attempt at marketing, it was missing one important element—the truth. Makers of the snake oil remedy were prosecuted in 1917 under the Pure Food and Drug Act of 1906 for selling what was really mineral oil, beef fat, red pepper, and turpentine.

Door-to-door selling has been a part of the American way of life that dates back to the time of covered wagons, and the twentieth century saw a boom in, for example, Mason Shoes, Fuller Brush, and J.R. Watkins liniment. Electrolux, Eureka, Kirby, and Hoover with their superior vacuum cleaners wrote many orders simply by knocking on a stranger's front door, and the 1960s was a time when selling encyclopedias became popular. Housewives would casually let into their homes the salespeople who arrived unannounced to sell their products.

Salesmanship is a developed artform that arose from a need to advance the persistent needs of people—both the buyers and the sellers—in ways that were designed to improve lives. Since early door-to-door consumers were naïve to the process, it was a booming way to sell these products with barely an objection. The company sent salespeople out, and they came back with orders.

But eventually, the rhythm began to change, and I can imagine the shock and dismay of the first salesperson who knocked on a door expecting an easy sale, when he heard the two words that stopped him dead in his tracks: "Not interested." I can envision his blank stare, not knowing what to say. Being conditioned to the idea that if someone answered the door, it almost assured a sale, this must have blown him away. No doubt, this deflated salesperson went back to his office, walked in to see the manager, and possibly resigned his position.

Very quickly, however, these men realized something particularly important to selling—that is, a little strategy goes a long way. After giving it a lot of thought, they finally found a way to counter the objection. They would calmly respond, "I can understand you may not be interested, but why don't I come in and vacuum your carpet for you?" They would simply *show* the consumer the product, and it worked! The product's advantages resonated with the prospect.

Selling was back in black, and sales kept rolling in when, all of a sudden, the consumer marketplace began objecting once again. This time, people used a new excuse: "I have no money." The unwitting salespeople were dumbfounded. How would they ever be able to sell to people who had no money? Back to the office they went. They worked feverishly through the night looking for ways to overcome the objection of someone with no money, until one of them looked at the other and said, "Hey! What if it isn't true?" The other strategist responded, "You mean, they're lying to us?" and a light bulb lit up.

The selling profession was progressing into a new phase, something called *selling psychology*.

Salespeople began to ask new questions like, "Why would they lie to us?" They discovered that human beings will, over time, find ways to avoid things they don't want to become involved with. And the question these salespeople kept asking was, "Why would consumers not want to involve themselves with a product that offered so many great features?" The answer was, "They need to be told why they should be involved."

Back out they went, knocking on more doors, meeting new people. They would hear, "I'm not interested," and overcome it long enough to continue talking. Then, they would hear, "I have no money," but they no longer believed it was guaranteed to be true. The salespeople of that day found a way to get their products in front of their selling audience. Vacuum salesmen, for example, talked about triple twisting rollers that worked at twice the speed of a cheap store-bought kind, and the encyclopedia sellers bragged about the book binding's double spine. However, it didn't work. So, back to the office they went with tails between their legs, wondering if the selling profession had seen its best days.

After a careful examination of their presentation, it finally dawned on them. They were talking about all the features, but how did these features benefit the consumer? Just talking about triple twisting rollers wasn't enough. What did it mean for the consumer? Triple twisting rollers meant a job would be more efficient, your rugs would be cleaner, and vacuuming would take less time, giving consumers more time to do the things they would rather be doing. Encyclopedias that were bound in a double spine would last longer and become books of knowledge that could be passed on to future generations, ensuring the intellect of your family's lineage. They tried it, and it worked. When product features resonated as true benefits to the prospects, they bought.

Selling essentially worked this way for a long time, and back and forth, the salespeople and the prospects learned how to outsmart one another from experience and wisdom—and then came the information superhighway. At first, it meant nothing much, but over time, sales organizations began understanding that the internet could hurt or help them. A nice website could attract customers, but poor reviews could hurt them.

Exaggerating salespeople could no longer flirt with dishonesty, since a consumer could look up the facts concerning anything online. Over time, this change led to new questions that created the need to better understand what consumers actually wanted. It made companies go deeper and ask more questions. It made them better. The information that they studied and learned informed salespeople how the consumer made buying decisions, what needed to be cleaned up and improved upon in manufacturing, how to create sales material that would be most widely accepted, and how to conduct a proper sales presentation so it would produce the best results more often. We learned rapidly in the information age. We had to! The selling profession needed to advance, to keep up or be left behind.

Today, we understand beyond a shadow of a doubt that a *constancy-to-purpose approach* is the best way to plan any selling strategy, and developing strategies that can be easily transferred to the right salespeople makes selling more assured. Rogue salespeople will struggle winging their approach that's based on instinct. Those committed to developing and using effective selling presentations and systems will have predictable, sustainable, and repeatable results. This is a new age. *Today's level of selling has evolved and demands that a well-equipped process of transferable practices must be followed for regular, steady success to occur.*

Transferable Practice: Appealing to the Prospect's Logical and Emotional Senses

To master Green Stage 3, serious, we must keep in mind that in order to maximize influencing another person, you must appeal to both their logical and emotional senses. If you are driving your points using facts with certainty and definiteness, you will be limited if you do not also include an emotional appeal. It is not enough to be right; you must also win over the prospect's mood and instinctive state of mind.

Don't dismiss a prospect's need for emotionally accepting a point. It's a mistake to consider someone's emotional acceptance as subservient to logic and reason. A logic-only reasoning will not be embraced without some pushback. We are emotional animals as well as logical ones, and emotions and logic matter equally and serve us in different capacities. If you were navigating a ship on the high seas in a massive storm, you would need to draw upon your logical senses. Yet what would put a logical person at the helm of that boat during a storm without an emotional passion for the adventure? You would build a house using a logically drafted set of blueprints; yet the choice of the exterior color would be decided emotionally. Mastering influence requires the understanding of how both senses are at play in the minds of those we wish to convince. It is not enough to be right. You must win your point completely, appealing to logic and emotion.

Transferable Practice: Delivering an Effective One-Call Sales Presentation

When going on a sales call, I'm sure that you, like me, would like to just go right up to the decision-makers and say, "We're going to do a great job for you! Just sign right here on the dotted line, and write a deposit check." That should take about a minute and a half. But if I were to do that, I would fail time and time again. A good presentation is successful in making a sale—not just taking an easy order, but creating a strong understanding that serves the prospect well—because it follows a series of effective steps. If it didn't work, we wouldn't do it. The structure below is for a classic step-selling presentation. There are nine steps, and *taken in order,* each one accomplishes a specific goal.

1. **Agenda commitment.** Setting the proper expectations for the sales call. Lay out for your prospect what you are going to do in your meeting. Make it feel easy and clear. Your prospects (*all* the decision-makers) need to stay with you throughout the presentation. If you get mild resistance, it's probably manageable if you are good at captivating your audience. If there's major resistance, you'll need to try to control your selling environment, getting all the decision-makers to stay with it. If it cannot be done, you cannot go past Step 4, The Company Story.
2. **Needs assessment.** Asking specific strategic questions to draw out the problems that need to be solved. The final question requires a commitment: "If there was a way to save money by starting the process sooner rather than later, I'm sure you'd want to know about it, right?" Get a commitment of yes from the prospect. A prospect will almost always say yes. It sets up a necessary pin for closing later in Step 8.
3. **Inspection.** Identifying needs and expanding on whatever the prospect might already believe is needed, where applicable. This step proves a need for your product/service by way of walking around (if it's a product for the home), measuring, testing, and envisioning creative ideas. How this is done will vary by product, service, and industry. This step will need to be modified for various industries. The point is to prove a need for what you sell and to show expertise and creative vision for the prospect's project.
4. **Company story.** Telling the story of your company. It should be compelling. It needs to differentiate why a prospect should choose to work with your company above all others. The prospect needs to answer yes to this last question in your company story: "Based on our credentials, would you feel confident working with our company?"

5. **Product presentation.** Demonstrating the value of your product or service. This should be spellbinding to the prospect. Point out whatever exclusive features you are offering, and differentiate your product/service from what other similar companies offer. You must know your competitors and speak truth about true differentiation. The final question, which requires a prospect to answer yes, is, "If made affordable, would you have this product/service installed/used in your home?"

6. **Commitment to value.** Confirming that the prospect sees the value of your product/service. You are not asking your prospect to buy anything here. You are discussing your price being good for one full year so you don't trigger any fight or flight in your prospect. Get commitment that the prospect feels your product or service is worth the price you are asking. Ask your prospect, for example, "When the time comes to replace your windows, can you see yourself investing X dollars, or are you thinking, 'Bill's a nice guy, but not for me, not in this house'?" A prospect must see the value in the product or service. If the prospect does not, certain techniques should be applied to raise the perception of value in the prospect's mind. A good sign of a masterful presentation is when the prospect answers yes, they see the value of your product/service without hesitation. You must get a commitment to the value of your product or service, or you have not completed this step and therefore cannot move on. This is a closing step. However, even if the prospect wants to buy, you're not closing here.

7. **Understanding of terms.** Introducing a price incentive, such as a special good-for-30-day price. The purpose of this step is to understand how the prospect would pay for your product/service *if* the prospect were to move forward in the next 30 days. If the prospect proposes to pay cash (no loan), just

ensure that the funds will be available within the next 30 days. If not, it would have to be, at least in part, financed. The following question should then be asked and answered: "If you were to take advantage of our 30-day incentive, how much would you be able to put down without taking any food off your table or changing your lifestyle in any way? Then I can show you what a monthly would look like." The purpose of this step is to know how a prospect would pay for your product or service. This is a closing step. However, even if the prospect wants to buy, you're not closing here.

8. **Initial-visit pricing.** This is the first time you are actually looking to close. Although Step 6 lays out a one-year price, and Step 7 lays out a 30-day price, if the prospect were to move forward today, the person would get a special *today* price. Every one-call-selling presentation gives a prospect a logical reason for doing business on the initial visit. If the prospect decided to move forward in Step 6 or 7, you would still give the Step 8 price for doing business today. That's honest. This is a closing step, and you are closing here.

9. **Post-sale button-up.** Following up. Every sale needs a button-up. It's a cool-down time. There are many kinds of button-ups, and the important components usually involve: protecting against third-party interference; testing to make sure that all prospects are 100% on board; bringing your new customers into the mindset of what they're likely to be feeling in the next 24 hours; and setting the expectations of the next steps in the process. Draw out any uncertainty here while you're still with them, or the first time they'll experience this uncertainty will be after you've left, leaving them without you to help them through those feelings.

Note: Certifications should be formally awarded to salespeople when they've achieved the following accomplishments:

- Understanding of the nine selling steps in classroom training
- Applied practical application of those nine steps in the selling field, along with both a mastery of their own personality traits dialed into virtue and a mastery of the demonstrative and advantageous stages in virtue
- Graduation to influencer
- Mastery of all five Green stages
- Eligibility for leadership/management
- Eligibility to own a dealership/franchise

Transferable Practice: Using and Interpreting Key Indicator Reports

It's important to let the numbers do the talking. Numbers tell a story. It's a sales manager's job to make sure their salespeople understand what the tracking numbers are saying. A company and its salespeople need a common respect for proper data. You'll need a set of key indicator reports that'll help you get and stay on track with the right numeric focus. The right information leads to good conversations between managers and salespeople. Logic must prevail, so reports are critical and should be computerized with the ability to look at numbers using date ranges, with updated information made available daily. Encompassingsales.com offers a platform that was created for the purpose of organizing lead activity, inter-departmental customer flow, and making available the critical reports that are needed to run a sales organization more effectively. This was developed by my company, and it's a powerful tool available for companies to use.

WHAT NUMBERS TO TRACK AND WHY

Key indicator reports will direct your efforts to grow. All accumulated information that is tracked should be *actionable*. There is no reason to gather numbers except to learn the story they tell and to alert us to changes that need to be made. They also inform us when we are doing well and should keep going in the same direction. (Continuing on a path is a course of action, too.) The numbers are your guide. These numbers need your attention and are considered along with the story you know from being at the company and in the thick of the physical work. Any growing sales organization must track a wide variety of metrics. These numbers should be looked at daily, weekly, monthly, and year-to-date, the results of which should be covered with all relevant players weekly.

Know the players, and know the metrics. Consider both to manage. Encompassingsales.com offers a wide variety of reporting tools to help you run your business or develop your sales career, so it can be tracked using reliable metrics. The basic tracking should include the following:

- **Requested appointments.** The number of appointments requested by a sales rep.

    Actionable: If your company is trying to grow, you can extrapolate the number of requested leads and run it through the other averages to see where the numbers would be. This number tells you if you have enough selling power on the street. This is good to track for a company, as well as an individual. Check it against your goals.

- **Supplied appointments.** The number of appointments a sales rep is supplied. To get the supplied percentage, divide supplied into requested.

    Actionable: How well is your marketing or inside sales staff doing to fill your schedule? What can be done to increase the supplied appointment rate?

- **Issued appointments.** The number of appointments issued to a sales rep. To get the issued percentage, divide issued into supplied.

    Actionable: Tracking this lets you know if you are over or under your ability to issue sales appointments to your group. This tells you whether to turn up or down your hiring efforts. There is usually a bit of a teeter-totter between marketing and sales hires for growing companies. Always hire talent as it becomes available, but concentrate on hiring for whichever department needs to catch up, in order to preserve balance with respect to investment and needs.

- **Covered appointments.** The number of appointments a sales rep covered. To get the covered percentage, divide covered into issued.

    Actionable: This number tells you if your sales staff is getting to the appointments they are issued. If coverage is a problem, find out why. It could be because your reps run late, which should be addressed immediately. Or it could be that they were selling or demoing their previous appointment, which is an acceptable reason for an appointment not being covered. Frown upon excuses but believe your staff unless proved otherwise.

- **Opportunities.** The percentage of opportunities a sales rep is given. To get the opportunity percentage, divide opportunities into covered.

    Actionable: Avoid too many gray-area results when reporting opportunities or when counting something as a no opportunity. Most no opportunities are clear-cut, such as the prospect not being home or missing a decision-maker for in-home sales presentations. Others are questionable, such as inconvenient time. Was is a bona fide inconvenient time-no opportunity because of a doctor's appointment, or was it something that came up not involving any urgency that the prospect is using as a reason that your appointment isn't good today? Some things are unfortunately true no opportunities, and other times, they can be worked into a demo if the salesperson can captivate the prospect properly. If we allow wiggle room, it will become the gray area that will interfere with performing with a definiteness of purpose.

- **Demos.** The percentage of appointments that were demoed by a sales rep. To get the demo percentage, divide demos into covered.

    Actionable: Once an appointment is considered an opportunity, the salesperson should proceed to demo it. Sometimes something will get in the way, like a prospect not understanding the time commitment needed for the demo. This is something that should have been vetted by the appointment-confirmation staff at your office. Stronger salespeople can readjust a prospect's thinking when performing as an influencer. Advantageous salespeople will acquiesce to the least confrontational will of the prospect. Tracking the demo rate gives you an understanding about how salespeople and your confirmation department are handling objections about time.

- **Gross number of sales.** The number of demos that resulted in a signed agreement. To get the closing rate on gross sales, divide gross number of sales into demos.

    Actionable: This number gives us a sales closing rate, which establishes a partial picture of the salesperson's ability to close sales. It is, however, only a partial snapshot of the salesperson's ability, since the number of sales is divided into demos. This will not show how many appointments could have demoed, since the salesperson has control over what they choose to demo. A far more important story is told when looking at the NSLI rate (explained below).

- **Gross dollars sold.** The total dollar volume of all signed agreements.

    Actionable: Knowing the gross dollar volume is an important factor in studying a salesperson's average sale amount.

- **Average gross sale amount.** The average dollar volume of gross sales. To get the average gross sale volume, divide gross dollars sold into gross number of sales.

Actionable: If the average sales volume is lower than the company's target, it is a possible sign that excessive advantageous behaviors are forming (such as an order-taking mentality)—making deals instead of making a case. When a salesperson settles for the order a customer gives and doesn't increase it to the maximized volume, the salesperson should apply the skills learned in Green Stage 3, serious. Learn to influence the need for the product/service, and you'll influence the average gross dollar volume, too. Customers will usually trust a respected salesperson for spelling out the scope of what they need.

- **Net number of sales.** The total number of sales that were approved for doing business. For example, those that did not cancel and that were approved for financing or cash, credit card, or check.

  Actionable: A salesperson who follows a strong selling presentation on-process will lose fewer sales to cancellation. Finance rejections are not the responsibility of the salesperson. However, if a salesperson continually has a disproportionate number of finance rejects, chances are, the salesperson is selling mostly to people who agree to buy more easily; hence, the credit issues. Train salespeople to make cases with people who don't say yes to everything. Each industry should have an expected number of net sales from gross sales. My company's selling presentation made for 85% net.

- Net dollars sold. The total dollar volume of all approved net sales (adjusted after bank fees).

  Actionable: This number is tracked for the same reason we track the gross dollars sold, except this time it's net.

- **Average net sale amount.** The average dollar volume of a net sale. To get the average net sale volume, divide net dollars sold into net number of sales.

Actionable: This is tracked for the same reason we track the average gross sales amount, except this is the average net sales amount.

- **NSLI (net sales volume per leads issued).** This is the profitability indicator. To get NSLI, divide net dollars sold into the number of appointments a sales rep was issued.

  Actionable: This number is the strongest leading indicator of whether a salesperson is profitable to a company. Know your industry numbers. Here is how you set a product NSLI:

  Take 1 issued appointment x .80 opportunity rate x .40 closing on opportunities x average sale $12,842.48 x .85 retention rate (after cancels and finance rejections) total = $3,493.15 (NSLI).

  This example was used for my company (pricing will vary), related to the replacement window industry. You will have to determine those percentages and numbers on your own. There are some simple and powerful uses for this number. It could tell you (as in the example above) that every time a salesperson starts their car and goes to an issued appointment, the salesperson will bring $3,493.15 in sales volume to your company. It is also used as a simple way to anticipate sales commissions for salespeople. If you pay salespeople 10% on average, they can look at this number and know that every time they are issued an appointment, they are averaging $349.31 in sales commissions, whether the appointment was an opportunity or not. This is advanced mindset training.

- **Net rate.** The percentage of sales that are approved for ordering products/services from all contracts written. To get net rate (aka *stick rate*), divide number of net sales into number of gross sales.

Actionable: Great selling presentations are designed to limit cancellations. If you have none, you are probably selling mostly or only to people who are easy to sell (lay-downs). Believe me, you'll have some cancellations, no matter how good you are. In my industry, we targeted cancellations to be 5% of gross sales. Finance rejections will vary, based on the average-size ticket and to whom and where you are focusing your marketing efforts. We aimed for no more than 10% finance rejections in Connecticut. Therefore, we targeted an 85% net rate. If it is too high, separate the cancellations from the finance rejections, and compare the two. If it is too low (on the cancellation side), you are likely leaving opportunities on the table. If it is too high (on the cancellation side), you are likely selling off-process. Please note: You can be 100% on your process, but your process may need re-engineering, too. If so, you can email us at info@encompassingsales.com for assistance.

Transferable Practice: Applying the Four Levels of Development

Your life won't take direction unless you tell it where to go. You have the power to change almost anything. Through learning and applying a paradigm called the *four levels of development*, you'll discover how to form new gut instincts to help structure your emotional core to accept change by design. This concept offers a framework for working through anything you consciously want to improve in your life. It's valuable in selling and in life.

By following this vision for development, you will learn to break ranks with old intuitive patterns and the coping mechanisms that you may have established along the way—ones that no longer serve any purpose for you. In this model, you will learn to develop brand-new intuitions that create better and more meaningful unconscious thought, a new standard for growth and fulfillment. Intuition can be developed through experience and learned knowledge. Following a process is how you get there.

LEVEL 1: THE UNCONSCIOUS INCOMPETENT

You will first enter anything new without knowing what you do not know.

We all start off as *unconsciously incompetent*. When we use the word *incompetent*, we'll use it only as it relates to having a faithfulness to a system or process. You should take no offense at being called incompetent at this stage. It's nothing personal.

As you begin on an unfamiliar journey of learning, you will have plenty of intuitions (vibes) about what you think you're experiencing. These intuitions don't hold much value for you at this early stage. They are gut feelings based on previous experience, so they are old intuitions. The way you feel is influenced additionally by coping mechanisms you've established throughout your life. Some of your old intuition and coping mechanisms may no longer serve any real purpose, and if they are outdated, they might be part of what is holding you back from advancing. It is important to identify what you're feeling and give it a proper, honest examination.

For example: When a child grows up in a family where the parents divorced early on, that child may have experienced a great deal of uncertainty in early life. Perhaps life involved transferring schools in the most formative years, when other children can be unkind to a newcomer. Experiencing that reception requires this child to find ways to assimilate to a new group of classmates. Naturally, a need to be liked is elevated, and this presents a potentially difficult adjustment for any child to make.

Soon, the child, having a strong need to be liked, finds ways to be accepted, including overpromising. Then, years later, this now-adult person wants to develop a career in sales but carries the coping mechanism of overpromising (a learned intuition) into that new occupation. And this salesperson will have to interact with prospects who are going to have objections that need to be overcome in order for a sale to be made.

Someone in this position might react to prospect objections in a way that is geared toward being liked by the prospect, thus falling short in overcoming the objection as it relates to making a sale. The old coping mechanism places the emphasis on being liked over making a product/service sale. If a salesperson is afraid to go further and challenge a prospect with the corrective thinking that's needed to make a sale, it will threaten the salesperson's chance of finding success in that career.

This example shows the power of early programming. The coping mechanism that was developed early on in grade school was needed at one stage in life, but in the adult years, this behavior no longer serves a useful purpose and only stirs up an unfounded fear. This is a good example of an outdated learned intuition. In the four levels of development, we call this a *gravitational pull*. Any old intuition we experience that conflicts with learning a new system should be consciously dismissed as irrelevant for now.

Old coping mechanisms can be controlled as you become more confident, and you'll be less afraid to address the issues you hold deep inside.

Summary of Level 1

At Level 1, you enter into new developmental situations not knowing what you don't know. Yet you'll carry your old intuitions with you. It is vitally important to ignore old intuitions, at least initially. Stay open-minded to learning. Big-picture thinking is needed here.

LEVEL 2: THE CONSCIOUS INCOMPETENT

Level 2 is where you begin considering a new idea. Learning something new can be a real challenge, and this is the stage in which some people leave their sales or marketing jobs, effectively giving up on themselves. It's where many people get in their own way and kill their own development. In a predominantly commission-based sales position, Level 2 is where your income plummets.

This is where you choose to be a *conscious incompetent*. Conscious incompetents listen to their old intuition and see it as a safe place. Familiarity is embraced, and you gravitate to your comfort zone. Level 2 is where Lazy Brain lives. (We learned about Lazy Brain under "About the Novice" in Chapter 3, page 126.)

Here at Level 2, you are introduced to a system for change, and you begin to understand it better. However, you're tempted to change it to fit what's more comfortable for you, instead of following it as it is laid out. Unfortunately, in order to grow, you'll need to embrace being uncomfortable on this journey. Sticking with what you already know only keeps you where you are, at best.

A little off-process is 100% off-process. Let's say the idea was to become nutritionally fit, and you are offered a new system that has a good reputation. You are told that in order for the new system to produce the results you want, you'll need to eat all the food on the table in front of you. If you are considering your comfort level, you might think, "I'll eat the broccoli, but I won't eat the spinach. I'll eat the tomatoes, but I won't eat the cauliflower." But being half on a system means being completely off *that* system. If you make choices that feed your comfort zone, or if you ignore a process because you think you know better, you will forfeit an important opportunity to grow. If you think you know enough and get sloppy about faithfully following a proven process in detail, you'll eventually fall to the hands of fate, instead of directing a clear path to your goals. Then, you could be successful only if you're lucky. If relying on luck is your strategy, and you find reasons to challenge your process, you will ultimately fail to reach your goals.

Challenges to growth in Level 2. *Imagined fears will keep you from growing.* People become set in their ways, and many are afraid to make a move. They're focused on what *could* happen if they fail. Unfortunately, this means they'll miss out on opportunities that come from having a willingness to take chances at success. What's the worst thing that could happen? Still, many people are afraid to interrupt the familiar pattern of their lives. Life becomes a repetition of predictable activities, and some people live life like a programmed robot. You can probably set a clock by watching their routines.

Negative self-talk has an impact. Even though it's easy to dismiss conceptually, what you tell yourself has dramatic impact on how you feel about something. I remember having a string of appointments that were canceling over a four-day period. By the time it got to the third day, I would tell myself that something is wrong with the leads, and yet it turned out to be complete happenstance. The leads had been issued randomly. The prospects didn't know each other. Still, it started to grow a little negativity in my mind. I began telling myself that the leads were no good. Then, when I covered one that didn't cancel, I was in a jaded state for no reason other than I had conditioned my thinking to sour.

Unfortunately, some people identify with the negative side of a consideration first, before considering a positive one. Sometimes people complain that everything in life is rigged and that there's no way forward, an **excuse**. Even if it were true, people can persevere through anything they make important enough to get through, by persistently following a system to do it. There will always be naysayers who will find it easier to reinforce negative beliefs, but to what benefit? Is anyone better off for thinking like that?

When thoughts of helplessness are left unguided and get inside a person's core, those thoughts become intuitive and keep the negativity alive. Worrisome thoughts become a subconscious block to thoughts that are more empowering.

Your self-talk has to match your solution, not your problem. You are your own worst enemy if you stay at Level 2. The good news is that if you muster the power within yourself to rise to the challenge of accepting change as empowering, you can solve problems that might have once felt limiting. Be your own biggest supporter. If you don't bet on yourself, who should?

Identify your gravitational pulls. Old, outgrown intuitions are the gravitational pulls that seduce you to reach for comfort over growth. It's like when your body craves sugar, it needs that fix. Your mind works the same way. Outgrown intuitions play tricks on you. Your mind will try to convince you that a job is wrong or that a company is bad, just so you'll have **justification** for leaving a job that pushes you to embrace whatever changes you are afraid to confront.

At Level 2, think through the gut feelings (fears) you're experiencing that prevent you from fully following a system's directives. Those intuitions are blocking your path forward. As you consciously cut ties that bind you to your old way of thinking, you'll start the process of creating replacement intuitions at Level 3.

Level 2 is the most dangerous of all the four levels of development. Level 2 is where the negative voice in your head speaks the loudest. It questions whether you really need to change at all. You must be mentally strong and willing to fight through the temptation of remaining complacent. No matter what it is that you desire, if the need is real and the will is strong, it *can* be done.

Summary of Level 2

People stuck at Level 2 will not grow. When confronted with new ideas or a new process that will lead to growth, they will feed their comfort levels instead of embracing change. Being stuck at Level 2 means you'll fear the unknown and make **excuses** to stay with what is familiar. In a sales setting, Level 2 thinking generates a plummeting income.

LEVEL 3: THE CONSCIOUS COMPETENT

In a commission-related scenario, Level 3 is where your income skyrockets.

Level 3 thinking is the nemesis of Level 2. It is the most challenging level, because it tests your will to be strong and requires of you your greatest leap of faith—a nonwavering commitment to the system you are choosing to follow. At this stage, you must make a *conscious* decision to cut ties with long-established limiting feelings—your built-in desire for familiarity and comfort—by working to create replacement intuitions.

We all have the ability to make choices. *Consciously* decide: How strong is your need for change? For those who are determined to master all five stages of Green, Level 3 is a baptism by fire. Level 3 is the most uncomfortable level in the four levels of development. Little changes and big changes alike have to pass through Level 3 to become changes that take significant root.

Those who are not a natural fit for selling, yet desire to become effective salespeople, have the hardest time at Level 3. Some won't have the determination or discipline strong enough to make it here. **Excuses** will surface. Yet without a Level 3 accomplishment, a person might as well quit selling and move on to another career.

Any unnatural and adaptive behavior practiced at a high level becomes a Level 3 accomplishment. Level 3 can be very de-energizing for those who are the most uncomfortable, but if there is a strong enough push through the awkwardness, nothing is impossible to change. That's the power of the challenge.

The goal is not to cause discomfort, but to master a productive comfort by design. If you don't want to change anything about yourself, if you don't want to improve, raise your bar, or get ahead, then stay where you are. If it brings you comfort that makes you happy, that's fantastic. But for people who are on a mission in life to grow, it requires change. To change, we must do something different from what we've been doing. Therefore, the things that make us comfortable, the things we are most familiar with, are some of the things that must change. The mission isn't to walk around through life looking to be uncomfortable. The goal is a comfort, a productive comfort. So, the question is, what kind of comfort do *you* need to be productive?

Have you listened to people who tell you why they can't do things? Have you heard some **excuses** that sounded shallow? Fearful? And when mentioned, did they touch a nerve? Those who are the most fearful or the laziest have the strongest knee-jerk reactions to being called out. They are firmly planted in their own comfort zone. But is that comfort zone at a mastery level of productivity, or one that's preventing a better end result?

You must decide what it is you want. In the world of selling, that might be to develop a level of selling proficiency that makes you highly successful. The goals, then, are to find what areas need improvement and to push through and make advances by following the four levels of development.

How does it feel to master a productive level of comfort? Let's say you are called into a meeting. The person leading this meeting is sitting behind a desk and has an assumed air of importance. To sit behind that desk gives one a feeling of control, a feeling of relaxation, a sense of confidence being in the driver's seat because the person is not in the "being-questioned" chair. The person is in the "questioning" chair. It's a comfortable place to sit.

Now, imagine you have mastered the five stages of Green. You're at the top of the selling apex, where you can make a great income quickly. You're going to your sales appointment with that same sense of comfort. Feeling that you are at ease doing and saying the things that create the sale, especially in the face of objections where corrective thinking will sometimes need to be applied. You become so relaxed about applying corrective thinking that it becomes second nature to you—intuitive. How much comfort is there at that level of mastery?

Level 3 is where those changes are defined and addressed, and new ideas are applied. *That's where the growth is.*

At Level 3, you have to choose to listen to the logic of what you know you need, over the emotional fear that challenges you from making those very changes. Interestingly, however, Level 3 does factor in the use of emotions, in that it requires a full emotional buy-in, in order for it to work. Pushing through that fear by courageously confronting what needs to be addressed will at first seem difficult, but it eventually becomes a lot easier. This is in part because our brains are wired with the concepts of freeze, fight or flight, and fright. When the brain feels fear, it places the body on a readied mode to notice it (freeze), to argue (fight) or to run from it (flight), or to ignore it and hope it goes away (fright). By confronting a fear enough times, the brain starts to realize there is no real threat, and feelings of fear subside. When the physical stimulation your brain was sending—the message to ready yourself for a fearful situation—ends, it becomes easier to accept change. When you push through working in this way, it becomes who you are and how you think.

Realize the incredible value of counterintuitive thinking. The most intense change that you will ever make will come from embracing counterintuitive thinking. Level 3 requires it. When you open yourself up to change, you must be ready to act in a manner that feels strange at first. Your experiences, up till now, have prepared you for what you should anticipate on the road ahead; yet those expectations are based on the road you've already traveled. In order to get to a new place, you must take a new road.

While Level 2 thinking means that you are not using the information from a new system to benefit you correctly, Level 3 is a place where you'll follow a new system *completely* and give it a *blind faith*. You'll allow it to lead you.

Level 3 thinking does not allow the luxury of *any* exceptions to the rule, and it's strict about adherence to a system of operation. Avoid allowing any of your preformed judgments to sway the process. And you must decide what will be your thought process about learning. There are three paths you can take:

1. You can decide to pay the high tuition of enrolling in the school of hard knocks. You can question everything and make decisions that fit your comfort zone. It's where you pay a "dumb" tax, so to speak. You can focus on peripheral considerations and over-consider less important questions. You

can put yourself in charge of what you need to know before you know what it is. This path is a spaghetti entanglement of self-doubt that leads to uncertainty and insecurity about the way forward. It's Level 2 thinking.

2. Your curious mind might want to watch a lot of motivational videos and read motivational books, which are great for the mind, and yet you might still pay little attention to the people who are training you on the specifics of your exact quest. If you are fortunate enough to be trained by people who walk their talk about system procedures, who show regular positive results, you have a great advantage in learning; it is a gift. If you are trying to form your own philosophy by listening to great motivators, that is fine. However, if it becomes the means with which to turn away from those who sell what you are learning to sell, it is merely a **justification** for having to individualize your own approach. Some are resistant to learning from others. It usually makes for a longer path to greatness. Some never get there at all.

3. You can choose the path where you simply put your faith in the hands of the training process and allow it to lead you straight up. Rise to the challenge of testing the boundaries of your comfort zone, and break through. Trust the process instead of questioning it too much. Thus proving, the shortest distance between two points is a straight line. This is Level 3 thinking.

Counterintuitive is a growth-thinking paradigm. A system is a structure that's designed to make something happen on a consistent basis. Any system that's designed for your development, and that you agree to follow, should be considered your sole guide. It is important to be mindful that old intuitions have deep roots in your subconscious thinking. They will keep resurfacing. Level 3 discipline is a lifelong process that requires a consciousness of effort to stay the course. Keep in mind that your beliefs live in your subconscious mind, and all ideas that challenge you have to pass through the subconscious mind, which wants to prevent change. Therefore, change requires a strong will.

For instance, when you hear you are at fault for something, it is unnatural to feel happy about it. By learning to be *counterintuitive*, we consciously change our intuition to one of being grateful for the information, not upset. Avoid feeling attacked, but feel inspired to know that you can change only what's in your jurisdiction. Empowering yourself to see this information as liberating, not upsetting, requires counterintuitive thinking.

Your comfort zones stop you from growing. A comfort zone is a place of limited size, a small space of contentment that lacks energy, a confined area in your mind where you remain as you are, without much to keep you excited or interested. A comfort zone is like an island in an ocean. It's a tiny place where nothing grows. It might be comfortable, but it's complacent. It's where you exist without really living, a place where there's no need to venture out.

Nothing ventured, unfortunately, means nothing gained. If you want to grow beyond your comfort zone, by definition, you'll need to embrace being uncomfortable at first, and you'll have to work counterintuitively against your intuition that's old, default-based, and untrained. Whatever you tell yourself—whatever makes feeding your comfort zone possible—must change. It's about getting good at taking in critiques about yourself in an honest way.

As you learn to adopt the thinking that makes you uncomfortable now, it eventually will become, through practice, your newly designed intuition. Over time, you'll become proficient at whatever you faithfully practice, and you'll form a new muscle memory that will kick in. It takes work, and you must want it badly enough.

All major change requires a logical acceptance for an emotional buy-in to occur. The first look at something new is always seen through the prism of logic. You first ask yourself whether something makes sense. If it does, it can then become emotionally embraced, where you feel it;

and when something is accepted emotionally, it becomes a core belief. It's then natural and comes forth with almost no effort. Then, you can truly convey your feelings to others.

A mechanical change is a start, but an emotional buy-in of that change is where the power is. Once it's felt, it's a core belief.

Summary of Level 3
Level 3 thinking seeks to cut ties with old and outdated intuitions in order to make way for the development of new ones. Level 3 thinkers welcome change. They accept that they will need to be uncomfortable in order to embrace unfamiliar ideas. In a commission-based sales opportunity, people who practice a new system at a Level 3 can set their incomes skyrocketing.

LEVEL 4: THE UNCONSCIOUS COMPETENT

Practicing Level 3 with discipline and dedication will bring you to Level 4. As it is with anything we practice with great discipline, it eventually becomes a reflex, a muscle memory. Have you ever watched someone learn how to ride a bicycle for the first time? It takes a lot of concentration, remembering to focus on pedaling, steering, and balancing. But what happens when Level 4 is practiced enough? Like the expression, "It's like riding a bike."

Yet, unlike riding a bike, when you develop new intuitions that challenge your gravitational pulls, you must be conscious not to let them slip back to where they once were. Old gravitational pulls will forever remain powerful; that means that Level 4 is always closely aligned with Level 3 but with less need of conscious effort.

Summary of Level 4
Level 4 is actually Level 3 that's been so well practiced that it no longer requires constant and conscious thought. The mastering of this accomplishment means that new intuitions are learned and embraced, and a new model for development is solidly in place in your mindset.

Just be careful not to take down your guard for too long, or your old thinking will eventually resurface. Like weeds coming back through the planks of a deck, you must remain watchful to cut them back at the roots every time they show up. Sustainability requires vigilance.

Choose what you are going to be unconsciously competent about. If you leave it to default, your unconscious competence will be in the areas you are the best at. This can include making **excuses**, using avoidance behaviors, **blaming** others, needing to be right all the time, finding it difficult to accept constructive criticism, and more. So much about successful selling is about the foundational pillars of life itself. There are many parallels: doing the right things, making the right choices, serving. Direct your attention to learning the five Green stages that develop your selling maturity and talent, and you will find yourself in a career that can be enormously satisfying monetarily and spiritually.

A QUICK REVIEW OF THE FOUR LEVELS OF DEVELOPMENT

You form your old intuitions at Level 1 through life experiences and by default. Your old intuitions are your old emotions at Level 2. You create your new intuitions—changes you want to make—at Level 3 by design. And your new intuitions are your new emotions at Level 4. The four levels are illustrated in Figure 4.1.

Transferable Practice: Making Key Decisions on Hiring and Growth

It is true that every company needs to hire the right people to grow its sales organization, and hiring the wrong ones is detrimental to growth. Therefore, for each hire, you need to see progression, a steady improvement in the application of transferable practices and with an open mindset. If progression is not there, you'll be stuck in place, not growing.

Sometimes, however, a hiring decision isn't always straightforward and simple. If you decide to move forward with an uncertain hire, make sure there are defined benchmarks in place that test for what is working

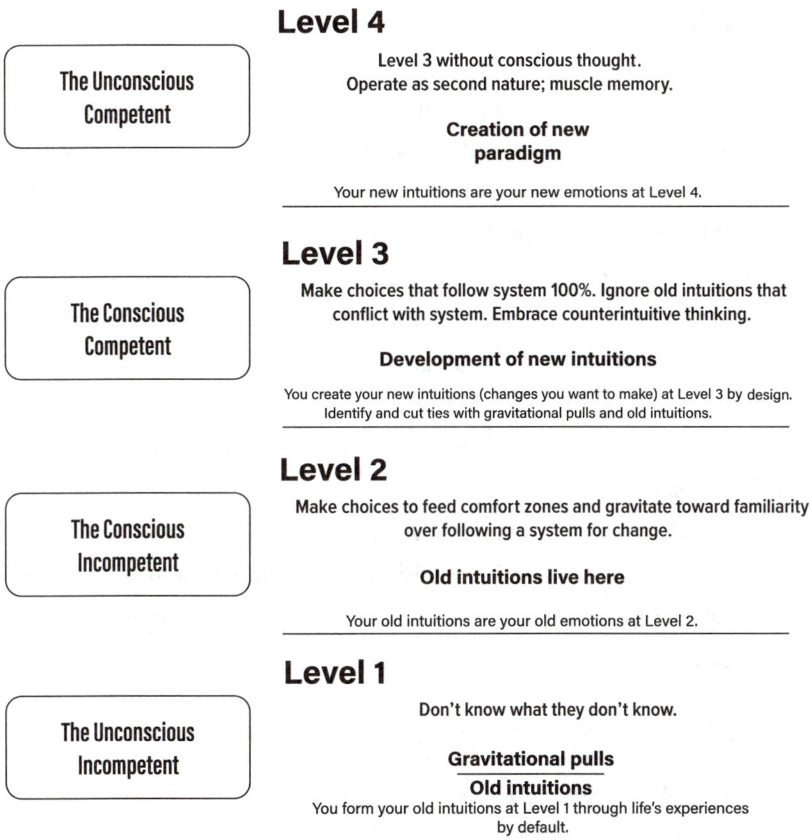

Level 4

The Unconscious Competent

Level 3 without conscious thought.
Operate as second nature; muscle memory.

Creation of new paradigm

Your new intuitions are your new emotions at Level 4.

Level 3

The Conscious Competent

Make choices that follow system 100%. Ignore old intuitions that conflict with system. Embrace counterintuitive thinking.

Development of new intuitions

You create your new intuitions (changes you want to make) at Level 3 by design. Identify and cut ties with gravitational pulls and old intuitions.

Level 2

The Conscious Incompetent

Make choices to feed comfort zones and gravitate toward familiarity over following a system for change.

Old intuitions live here

Your old intuitions are your old emotions at Level 2.

Level 1

The Unconscious Incompetent

Don't know what they don't know.

Gravitational pulls
Old intuitions

You form your old intuitions at Level 1 through life's experiences by default.

FIGURE 4.1 The four levels of development

and what is not. Use the LEAD Personality Profile Program for selling to help delineate whom you are working with, what to look for, how to proceed productively (found at www.myleadprofile.com).

As with anything else that must be learned, a selling process requires understanding. This can be complicated when a person has even a slight learning disability. Unfortunately, sometimes people are embarrassed and less forthcoming about admitting they have difficulty learning, which is a shame. We all have different ways of learning. Some do better by studying, others by watching. You can have a great selling process but still have a difficult time teaching it to someone who is having trouble absorbing it. This may take a great deal of a trainer's time, and it can slow down the training process for others if taught in a group setting.

The benchmarks you apply in this case shouldn't be any tougher than what is required of anyone else you hire, but you need to watch for progress. Pay close attention to how much is being learned and understood or missed. See if the absorption rate falls into the reasonable amount of time that it should take.

Use good judgment when confronted with situations like this. Decide for yourself, but never ignore any unfortunate factors your heart may want you to overlook. Avoid idealizing that one-off salesperson no one else can train because your sense of self-importance lets you think that you can.

Granted, some people take a bit longer, but there must be a measured period of time that is considered reasonable, or unreasonable. Use a cost-benefit analysis to face reality, and act accordingly. Be smart about your time.

CONDUCT A PRELIMINARY ONLINE VIDEO INTERVIEW

To effectively screen candidates, it's advisable to conduct an online video interview first, before asking an individual to come into your office for a formal one—where you'll use the Six Global Interview Questions and the interview questions specific to each personality type. Via video, you'll get a chance to experience the candidates in their own setting. I recommend you use the guide below to help you navigate through this prefatory discussion and probe the candidates with the right focus.

ONLINE INTERVIEW

Name: _____

Phone: _____

Email: _____

Date: _____ / _____ / _____

Experience: Probe previous experience.

Note: It's not that experience is necessarily needed. We just want to see how the candidate has dealt with past situations, to learn how the person thinks.

_____
_____
_____
_____

Mindset: Problem-solver or problem-dweller?

_____
_____
_____
_____

Persistence Level: Does the person appear to have a driven personality?

_____
_____
_____
_____

Accountability: How has the person been held accountable in past roles similar to this?

_____
_____
_____
_____

Expectations:

Of the job: Discuss responsibilities.
_____
_____
_____
_____

Of the financial: Discuss the person's desire to earn. How much is the person looking to make per year?
_____
_____
_____
_____

Work Availability: Are there are any days of the week or times when the person is unavailable?
_____
_____
_____
_____

Date Available to Start: _____

Impression:
- ☐ Exceptional
- ☐ Reasonable
- ☐ Not a fit

Again, remember, if you choose to invite this candidate to your office for a formal interview, be sure to use the Six Global Interview Questions and the interview questions specific to each personality type they profile as, to determine whether this candidate is a good match for your company, its culture, and its future growth.

APPLY KEY OBJECTIVES AND OBSERVATIONS TO BASIC TRAINING

Once a candidate is hired, the training begins. This means the two of you (assuming you will be doing the training) will be running sales calls together. Below are three key training objectives that every trainer should take to heart and carefully observe:

1. **Communicate clearly.** Is the trainee communicating at a sixth-grade level? Is the trainee easy to understand when making points, or are prospects getting a little lost?
2. **Have a command of the materials.** Does the trainee appear to have a command of the materials? A salesperson needs to be careful to not just "parrot" words—but understand the meaning of those words.
3. **Demonstrate enthusiasm.** Does the salesperson show a good level of enthusiasm? Enthusiasm is a transferable quality from salesperson to prospect. Appealing to a prospect's emotion will help make stronger bonds and more sales right out of the gate.

PREVENT A FREE FALL

After the initial training and time in the field, the next phase of growth is a reinforcement of process being correctly applied. Build steadiness. Don't let a salesperson decline into free fall.

When salespeople graduate from their initial training and hit the road, they are at first nurtured by a sales manager who attends sales calls with them, showing how the process works. Usually after that (within a week or two), the new salespeople begin to sell system sales.

Normally, the sales volume is right, and the deposits are right. The reason for the immediate success is because the new salespeople are the closest to their training as they can be.

Then, usually within a month or two, their numbers begin to decline. This is expected. The reason is simple: They begin to think for themselves and ebb away from letting the process do the thinking for them. They make certain changes because they know more and anticipate objections and start becoming creative. The more they do this, the further away they get from process. That is why the training must go in this order:

1. Dial their natural personality into a state of virtue (based on LEAD and your own observations). This must be done at the same time you are teaching the new reps Green Stage 1, demonstrative, and Green Stage 2, advantageous.
2. Once they are running sales calls (after they begin selling on-process), you must begin teaching Green Stage 3, serious (selling maturity). By instituting the knowledge needed to stay the course on process, you can curtail or even eliminate the free fall and keep them in the right selling mindset.

MANAGERS SHOULD FIX OFF-PROCESS BEHAVIORS QUICKLY BEFORE THEY BECOME HABITS

It is a **certainty** that any new salesperson will run into a number of natural distractions, things you couldn't possibly have covered when teaching your process. When these distractions come about, they will cause a great disruption in a salesperson's development if they're left unaddressed. If you're a sales manager, you have to address these issues quickly. Chief among them are new objections from prospective customers, objections that your salespeople weren't initially trained on. These newfound objections will cause a lull in sales by decreasing your new rep's efforts to demo your product and will challenge the rep's loyalty to your process. The new salesperson might decide to sell in ways that aren't in sync with your company's selling process, even going as far as to try new closes or alter your process by planning how to deal with objections (not yet even encountered) in advance. Essentially, the salesperson would then be projecting problems into existence. That's why it is vital to remain in close contact with a new rep in that first year, and even more so during the first six months, and especially in the first two.

When a new salesperson's numbers begin to decline, use the structure of the four questions below for field training. It is at this critical stage that a good sales trainer should take the time to further develop and reinforce a rep's core-belief system.

The four things a sales trainer should look for when riding along with a salesperson are:

1. What has the salesperson added to the sales presentation?
2. What has the salesperson removed from the sales presentation?
3. How well is the salesperson connecting with prospects? Logically? Emotionally?
4. Which steps in the process need concentrated effort to improve?

When a salesperson is off their game (for a week to 10 days on average), you can legitimately make the statement that they are likely to be performing off-process. As a sales trainer, don't proclaim your concerns and unnecessarily alarm the salesperson; just get in a car and join the person on a sales call. Yes, circumstances and bad leads are a fact of life, but we don't improve if we allow ourselves the luxury of **blame** when we start to falter. Your conditioned mindset (core-belief thinking) should be trained to hope you are the one responsible for low results. Accepting that responsibility is the only way you have any control to fix it.

A ride-along with a manager is crucial at this stage. Without a manager there to redirect a salesperson's efforts to finding the way back onto process, you stand a good chance of losing that salesperson through neglect. It is a critical point to understand. This is the exact place where most salespeople mentally check out, even before they realize it themselves. By you not being there to show them the way back, the path can feel bleak, and they can easily default into unconscious resignation.

A selling process has many parts, and it must be constantly revisited to keep it fresh in the minds of those who are tasked to perform it. It is expected that even a promising new salesperson will alter the company's selling process within the first two months on the road. If the process is left to be unobserved by unconcerned management, the salesperson might soon leave your company or become bad for it.

GET BACK ON TRACK AND STAY THERE

Every salesperson experiences a slump at one time or another. The key is to have a method of spotting the slump early and having the foresight to correct it quickly. One thing you can do is to video-interview every salesperson *when the person is doing well and selling frequently.*

Ask questions that are bound to spark enthusiastic answers. This video isn't formal and can be shot from your phone. It does not need to be any longer than four or five minutes on average. Ask on-camera questions like:

- How are you doing lately for sales dollar volume sold?
- How are you feeling about selling?
- Do people buy your product/service?
- How do you get people to buy your product/service?
- Describe your mindset on the ride to meet a prospect.
- Do you expect to sell?
- What is your mindset when you are presenting?
- What have you been doing lately that seems to be making a positive difference for you?
- Can you sell the leads that our company provides to you?
- What is your professional advice to others about doing the kind of work you do (selling/serving)?

Then, when the person experiences a slump, play them their video and ask, "What can this person teach you about how to get back on track? What are the changes you notice in your outlook from then to now? Do you see anything different?"

Success always comes down to a salesperson's expectation of selling or not selling. When salespeople expect to sell, they do. And when they don't, they won't. That tells you a great deal about the importance of managing a mindset. No one can get salespeople back on track better than themselves. They are the best trainers in the world when it comes to their own careers. These videos will prove priceless.

Keeping Your Company's Offer Fresh

HOW TO CONSTRUCT A KILLER SALES PRESENTATION

Don't do everything yourself, or it can take forever. If you put yourself in charge of developing a killer sales presentation, you may never get there. Bring in a professional. It's not that you can't do it; it's just that you may be better off being inspired by bringing in some new thinking to recharge your own batteries for a change. Yes, even owners and sales managers and trainers need a catalyst from time to time to give them a boost of new and inspired thinking. You just have to find the people who can help you the best. I've been involved with selling for many years; yet I reached out to an expert when the time came to change up our sales presentation. The person I selected got his start in my office. Today he is an international sales trainer, and his approach to selling was so good that sales immediately shot up when we introduced it.

Upon request, our team at info@myleadprofile.com can recommend a good number of exceptional trainers and innovative experts who can help you to develop your company's process.

However, experts can only help you if you are open-minded. John Lennon and Paul McCartney were great songwriters, but without George Martin as their producer, who knows if The Beatles would still have conquered the world? Don't try to do everything yourself;

you will come up short. You may be a renaissance person, but no one is top-notch at everything. *Maturity means **recognizing** the need for collaboration.* Go out and hire someone to deliver a sales process that can better attain your goals more quickly and intelligently.

GROW AS THE MARKETPLACE GROWS

Some people who have done their jobs for a long time—with a strict adherence to process—can at times find themselves closed to anything that sounds challenging to their well-established beliefs. Charles H. Duell, a former commissioner of the U.S. Patent Office, is often credited with saying, "Everything that can be invented has been invented." The year was 1889.

Keep open-minded, and adapt to changes in consumer buying habits and other shifts in the marketplace that play against what you think you already know. If those with a serious personality forget this, over time they'll become deficient in their serious mentality, causing a disturbance or a block to growth. Growth requires adaptation from time to time. Without allowing yourself the ability to change when needed, you will eventually find yourself out of time with contemporary thinking and falling behind. Judgment, however, tells us not to tinker with new ideas while in the middle of performing a process presentation. Those discussions are for later, back at the office in a meeting with the powers that be.

If You Were Profiled as *Serious*

If you were profiled as *serious*, you must be willing to do the following in order to advance to *influencer*:

1. Learn to shift your selling thought process away from instinct and place it completely in the hands of process. Recognize that process is stronger than instinct and will

work far more effectively in the bigger picture. Do not allow yourself the luxury of making *any* off-process moves. When that is accomplished, you will know you've made tremendous gains, so long as you keep true to that way of thinking.
2. Develop a strong core-belief system within yourself, based on sound tenets of productive selling-related thinking. Commit to the 92 Undeniable Core-Belief Statements for Selling-Mature Salespeople (see page 218).
3. Commit to a *no exceptions* rule against going off-process. Recognize that although you may lose an occasional sale by following process, you will lose your entire way if you don't. Internalize that, and commit to it.
4. Go *all in* and place yourself in the hands of a process that you might sometimes disagree with or agree with in part. Agree to follow it without making changes.

When all four goals are accomplished, move on to Green Stage 4, influencer.

Questions for Someone with a *Serious* Personality

There are three sets of questions you should ask that have been designed for the specific profiles in this book. Ask the first two sets before you hire an applicant (global and specific interview questions). And ask yourself the third set (30-day review questions) 30 days after hiring. You can access the questions and the 30-day reviews at www.myleadprofile.com.

CHAPTER 6

Green Personalities: Stages 4 and 5

GREEN STAGE 4

Personality: *Influencer*

3.2% of Green; 0.43% of all profiles

VIRTUE

Persuasive, possessing the ability to get others
to see things they didn't see before

Uncovering needs that might not be recognized by a prospect;
thus, expanding the opportunity to serve someone

TRAITS USUALLY ASSOCIATED WITH THIS PERSONALITY

Zealousness

Strong core beliefs in company, product, and value to prospects

Strong commitment to serving and improving
the lives of others through one's work

VIRTUES HELPFUL TO SELLING

Discovers a need and expands it
Expertly impacts another person's decision-making through being an exceptionally convincing presenter and honest person
Knows how to maximize opportunities
Possesses a brilliant and confident blend of process and personality
Critical thinker

DEFICIENCY (THE OPPOSITE OF THIS PERSONALITY)

Advantageous behaviors—opportunistic
Immature
Less urgent in nature
Expedient
Uncommitted to process
Lacking specific goals
Instinctual

EXCESS (THIS PERSONALITY WHEN OUT OF CONTROL)

Challenges to Selling
Manipulative; unscrupulous control of a situation or person
Psychopathic behaviors, pathological lying
Knee-jerk reaction to criticism
Hypersensitivity
Closed-minded to new learning
Stereotypical, high-pressure salesperson

WHAT YOU NEED TO FOCUS ON

Developing and discovering ways of maximizing opportunities to help a prospect. Instead of being given a need and filling it (*advantageous*/order-taking), discover a need and expand it (*influencer*/order-making). Become a great, trusted assistant buyer to your prospects and customers.

The *Influencer* Candidate

Todd's Story

Growing up, my father ruled our house. He was a gym teacher and a sports coach at my high school. He had high expectations of me, but it never seemed he could be pleased. I remember in tenth grade, when I was involved in wrestling, he drilled me every day. He made it all but certain that I was going to win, and that was that. There was a lot of pressure being applied, but I could take it.

There's one wrestling event I'll never forget. I tried my hardest, but I just couldn't pin this kid down. I was determined, but I just couldn't nail it. The ref made a bad call in the end, and it cost me the win. My father looked embarrassed that I had failed. He didn't talk to me on the ride home. At nightfall, he threw a pillow and a blanket outside and told me I was sleeping in the cold. It was devastating, but I learned that giving my father what he wanted was the only way to earn his approval.

I am an overachiever in my sales career. I have a strong will to win. Today, I have more trophies than I have space for in my office. I've learned to adapt to each of my customers and to individualize each sale. The approach has earned me top gun status at the company I work for.

It can get awkward at times. Female customers do send me cards and try to pin me down to a dancing date, which I sometimes kind of promise. Whatever it takes. I don't share that I'm married. My wife understands it's all a part of selling. I do think that sometimes customers are more favorable to me and easier to sell to when they sympathize with whatever I tell them. I'm there to win, no matter what. My trophies have proven me right in my approach. It's too bad no company ever appreciates someone like me enough.

About the *Influencer*

This is the stage where much is decided—whether you will remain a salesperson who's directed by the perceived wants of your prospects or whether you will influence those wants into something more that will benefit a prospect. Dwight D. Eisenhower, the 34th President of the United States, once said, "Leadership is the art of getting someone else to do something you want done because they want to do it." That applies to turning prospects into customers, too.

The vast majority of salespeople unnecessarily peak at Green Stage 2, advantageous. When applying the information and knowledge from the serious stage, a salesperson must make a choice: To conduct yourself either by instinct or by process. Using a blend of both is actually a default toward instinct, since process would require a full and total adherence.

If you are going to live your life with you being the one who's giving it direction, you will need a considerable amount of discipline to stay the course, especially in the most difficult times you'll face.

THE EXCESSIVE AND OUT-OF-CONTROL INFLUENCER

We'll also address the *virtuous influencer*, but first, let's begin with the other side of the same coin, the *excessive influencer*. Todd was profiled on LEAD to be an influencer, yet his selling behaviors were outlandish. He was completely out of control. Given his background, it's fairly easy to theorize what caused his need to prove he is the best at everything. He didn't feel loved by his father unless it came with a win. He was starved for some expression of love, because his father's feelings were conditioned upon how well Todd performed. It's a sad tale, as many are. It illustrates the importance of nurturing young minds with a sense of acceptance and unconditional love.

While Todd was an influencer—in that he influenced the actions of his prospects and made many of them his customers—his behavior when selling was, as noted above, completely out of control. His process was his instinct, which made his process unpredictable. His style was nontransferable, and being instinctual, it was governed only by how he felt at any given time. When he attempted a role in management and tried to show others what he did, he couldn't understand why they couldn't just sell like he did.

His maturity level was low, which was easily masked up on command, as he gave off a well-rehearsed air of intimidation and a look of menacing self-importance. Darrin McGuire, North American Vice President of Orthopaedics, Sectra, Inc., describes the dangers of self-importance in this way: "Self-importance gives people a feeling that their voice matters more than others, and people want to hear it. Self-importance is much easier to find than humility. Humility is rarely found by those who don't know the meaning of servant leadership."

Todd made many sales in his career and broke big records along the way. He was the king of the bottom line, but it came at a hidden cost. He had an office filled with recognition trophies, and he loved to be celebrated. Many companies today would look past Todd's problems, once they were discovered, and keep him employed, just to have those extra sales. He worked harder than almost everyone else, but there was so much wrong. His reckless behaviors were a cancer on his organization.

His conduct was so out of control and excessive that he would use made-up human tragedies to sympathy-sell. He straight-up lied to his prospects for pity, portraying a calculated appearance of vulnerability in order to garner sympathy and make sales. Nothing was too out of line for him. Even stolen valor: Coincidental stories of serving in the military just like his prospects, although he never actually did, were just some of the lies he told. He was so convincing that even he believed his own alternate universe, which is a testament to the power of self-talk. This, of course, is an extreme case of an out-of-control influencer in full bloom of *excessive* behaviors.

It's worth noting that influencers are rare, at only 0.43% of all profiles. If only Todd had honed his skills and learned how to sell with an honest process, he could have been a selling icon. He had a lot of natural ability, but being a natural is not the most important thing. Despite his awards, he wasn't a great salesperson; he was only a great manipulator.

Beware of the pathological liar. To the out-of-control influencer, the end **justifies** the means. Even in this extreme case, where boundaries of right and wrong are blatantly violated, excessive influencers like Todd cannot see what they do as wrong. They are pathological liars and are morally bankrupt. I guess it could be worse. With credentials like these, he could have become a serial killer, so let's just count our blessings.

Forever dissatisfied and miserable. Due to the long-term effects of unaddressed and negative foundational questions, out-of-control influencers are never satisfied with the praise they receive. They crave recognition like a heroin addict begs that high. These dissatisfied, self-consumed martyrs will forever feel underappreciated, constantly revisiting their foundational questions of unworthiness and requiring having someone close by whom they can impress. Someone who (unwittingly) takes the role of whoever first made them feel worthless. They need some enemy to prove wrong.

These unfulfilled needs are replayed in the scenarios they'll continually create—despite the strain placed on the ones they misuse for the tension they need to thrive. They'll make the owners of a company feel like they don't appreciate them the way they should. Even though they may be overpaid and recognized regularly, it's never enough to satisfy their need to prove wrong their original influencer from years ago. Except now, those feelings have been weaponized to succeed at all costs, regardless of whom it may hurt.

If these people don't grow out of the need to relive their foundational issues, they will never find any real sense of peace, no matter what they do. Whatever created that quest must eventually be addressed through *growth*, *maturity*, and *discipline*, or it will eventually devour the person obsessed by it. If people who are not interested in growth continue to show reckless and immature behaviors and are undisciplined in their need to change, keeping them on your team will prevent it from growing. Just keeping pace will be hard enough if they remain in place.

The company's responsibility. What is a company's responsibility in a case of someone like Todd? Many companies would be taken in by this kind of excessive influencer. How many companies would see only what Todd wanted them to see? You can bet he knew the right words to say to make anyone feel anything he wanted. A master manipulator has those skills sharpened and ready to use.

It's one thing for a company to hire an influencer like this, not having studied this personality and what it all means. However, it's a whole other thing to make that decision if you know what's at stake and still allow the chaos that follows. Knowingly doing so is to be willfully complicit. Trading integrity for profit, the company, too, would then be responsible for whatever happens while an out-of-control influencer is representing it. There is no virtue or integrity in any company that allows for that kind of behavior.

THE VIRTUOUS INFLUENCER

Now to discuss the virtuous side of this personality type: A *virtuous influencer* is a strong, impassioned, focused, and high-performing salesperson.

Virtuous influencers listen to the preconceived ideas of what a prospect wants, but if the prospect needs more education to realize a better benefit, they'll play the role of an assistant buyer and educator to help the prospect make a better buying decision.

Since influencers point out needs that the prospect has not considered, does this mean they are pushy? No, not at all. Not the virtuous influencers. In fact, if your approach is pushy, you are not selling; you're only forcing your will. However, while influencers are not pushy, they are not pushovers. They stand up for what a prospect needs to know, not just what the prospect wants to hear. They are advocates of helping people the *right* way and are therefore passionate about maximizing all they can do to help someone within the process of their system.

A master influencer has developed a contagious personality, one that is attractive to a prospect. This is a very important part of the influencer's success. You must always remember to give each prospect your best *you*, meaning a positive and upbeat problem-solver who cares. If you show less than your best, you're working below your ability. We all have weak moments when we let our guard down and show a less attractive side of ourselves, but the further you work up the Green stages, the less margin there is for being imprecise. To be a pro, you must place your efforts at a higher standard.

Virtuous influencers aren't counting commissions either. They aren't concerned with their own stake *when in the moment*. They are focused on the prospect. There will be plenty of time for counting chips later, and there will be plenty of chips to count. Selling is about helping. Influencers know that if they take care of a prospect, everything else falls into place. Making money will follow the right thinking. By definition, being virtuous is about showing high moral standards. It is about helping first. Don't forget: *Selling is serving, and it's how you help.*

Influencers place value on their *own* value. Since they believe in what they are selling and inherently feel it carries great value, influencers aren't known to meet prospects somewhere in the middle when it comes to price. They don't fear losing a sale if they stand firm to the best terms possible in the contracts they write. They price by process. They believe so much in the value of their offer, they know it's worth the price they are asking and believe in the terms, too. Their persistence to following process helps them to attain stronger deposits and proper finance arrangements that will work best for the companies they represent (and for customers, too). They never give away the store. True influencers will never devalue their own efforts.

Influencers understand that there is a lever between price and value. When one is thought to be high, the other is considered low. *They know that covering their entire presentation is the only way to demon-*

strate complete value. If they were to play around or let a prospect move them along and skip parts of their presentation, they know full well it will backfire in the end. They will cover all that needs to be covered despite any unwillingness of a prospect, the one who wants a quick price and tells you to nix the pitch.

Virtuous influencers are mature individuals who control their selling environment without arguing for permission to continue their presentation. They acknowledge a request to move it along, then continue covering what they had planned to cover all along. Anything short of this would show a shaky core-belief in process. The influencer has internalized that *following process is the centerpiece of demonstrating value.* In that way (and *only* that way), *objections about price are properly alleviated*, provided their presentation is well written.

Influencers understand that any action that acquiesces to a prospect's unnecessary demands will jeopardize the perceived value of what they are selling. For true influencers, that would be the ultimate betrayal of their own integrity. They work from a confident position that's honed by a well-practiced excellence.

After salespeople emerge from an advantageous cocoon and master being serious (selling maturity), they can then become influencers—yet many don't. *It takes great courage to grow a mindset that will adhere to a process without caving into instinct.* Exceptions are attractive to anyone with shaky commitment. That's where the line is drawn between the advantageous and the influencer.

An Influencer covers everything in a presentation, knowing it's there for a reason. Great sales presentations have no filler material included. Everything in a well-written presentation is important and should be covered with a prospect. I recall a story of a salesperson demonstrating our replacement windows to a couple who were both engineers. There is a stereotype that many salespeople have about engineers: They must want fact sheets, data, diagrams, charts, graphs, and metrics. While that may be true at times, this couple were most impressed when the salesperson, like a gorilla, banged a nail into a wooden board using a piece of our glass. The engineers were amazed. It's easy to forget that stereotypical consumers are people with both logic *and* emotions. If the salesperson had tried to individualize the process to fit the couple's stereotype, the salesperson probably wouldn't have made the sale. By acting as an influencer in virtue, the salesperson covered all the presentation, including using the piece of glass as a hammer.

You will never know what part of your presentation will best turn a prospect into a customer, so never skip over any of the tools that create impact. Influencers understand that. Advantageous people can, unfortunately, become more concerned with showing their own expertise in a situation. If you think you know better than the process, you will skip parts, and the parts you skip are the sales you won't make. Influencers are true believers in process. They do it all, every time.

The influencer versus the advantageous in a selling situation. Allow me to give you one more example of what an influencer does differently from an advantageous personality to maximize helping a prospect. This case study is from my industry, the replacement window business. Our company sells a high-quality replacement window called HR40. It features Heat Mirror insulating glass, krypton gas, foam-filled frames, power-strength glass, rain-wash-clean glass, and other differentiating benefits to distinguish it from competitors' offerings in the marketplace.

This window is sold mostly to people for their own residences, who will enjoy the massive decrease in energy consumption it brings. It is not ordinarily sold for purposes of investment properties, because the buyers aren't usually the ones paying the heating and cooling bills. We had an appointment, however, with a woman who wanted windows for a rental property she owned. Our system arranged it so a salesperson would meet the owner at the property to look at the work and take measurements, then travel to her residence and discuss the matter, performing a full presentation of our window there.

If I had sent an advantageous person to cover this appointment, the two would have met at the rental property, then gone to the residence as planned. When there, the topic would have been centered on satisfying the need of that rental property, likely with a lesser product we call HR20, a similar window that's less expensive and without the better energy-saving properties. After all, that's what the prospect wanted.

Instead, I sent an influencer, a person who followed the same protocols, but when getting to the residence, the influencer performed a presentation on HR40, not HR20. Why? Because it is better to go down in price than up. Price conditioning is a key element in selling. It gives comparative pricing, which makes the lower one look better in comparison. Also, after a masterful presentation, the influencer would put the windows of the prospect's own residence on the table as well. Why not do that?

If you believe in your product, your company, and your value, then everyone in every situation becomes someone you can *choose* to help. Influencers understand this thinking. It's primary to their core-beliefs about their role of problem-solving and serving a prospect. Do you see the difference? Ask yourself what stops the *advantageous* person from doing the same thing as the *influencer*, and you'll begin to understand how to become better at selling.

If You Were Profiled as an *Influencer*

If you were profiled as an *influencer*, you must be willing to do the following in order to advance and become *persistent*:

1. See prospects as people you can help—many times, even more so than they originally thought.
2. Place helping someone over a need to sell something. Recognize that you help people first, and the way you accomplish that is by selling. Be credible. Be real. Care.
3. Be prepared to overcome prospects' objections skillfully and carefully by offering corrective thinking where needed. Stand

up for what is right. Don't negotiate what shouldn't be negotiated. Value comes with a price, but ignorance comes with a cost. Help your prospects to understand the true meaning of value.

4. Go *all in* and place yourself in the hands of a process that you might sometimes disagree with or agree with in part. Agree to follow it without making changes.

When all four goals are accomplished, move on to Green Stage 5, persistent.

Questions for Someone with an *Influencer* Personality

There are three sets of questions you should ask that have been designed for the specific profiles in this book. Ask the first two sets before you hire an applicant (global and specific interview questions). And ask yourself the third set (30-day review questions) 30 days after hiring. You can access the questions and the 30-day reviews at www.myleadprofile.com.

GREEN STAGE 5

Personality: *Persistent* and with the Mindset of Emotion

2.3% of Green; 0.31% of all profiles

MINDSET EMOTIONAL COMMITMENT: BECOMING UNSTOPPABLE

VIRTUES

Achieving without any possibility of settling for less than you desire
Intensity
Fully using carefully crafted maturity and judgment to create an energy and great follow-through, as a means for achieving uncommon quality, permanence of purpose, and excellence

TRAITS USUALLY ASSOCIATED WITH THIS PERSONALITY

Accomplishment
Success
Consistency

VIRTUES HELPFUL TO SELLING

Unconscious master of all five Green stages
Master of follow-through
Consistent
Engaged
Responsive
Urgent
Proactive
Process-driven behaviors

Mature emotionally and intellectually
Disciplined, not easily discouraged
Strategic planner
Growth-oriented
Dedicated, remains hyper-focused on a course of action
despite difficulty, complications, or opposition
Open-minded to information and data
Visionary
Wisdom that comes from studying the art of selling and applying
advanced thinking in the way decisions are made
Willing to adjust plans when needed in order to stay
the course with big-picture thinking
Committed to goals, not easily discouraged
Does everything possible to persevere without compromising vision
Critical thinker

DEFICIENCY (THE OPPOSITE OF THIS PERSONALITY)
Lacking discipline, dedication, and drive
Not committed, responsive, or engaged enough
to follow through on ideas
Easily discouraged
Average
Lazy
Excuse-driven
Flighty and too impressionable to quick ideas

EXCESS (THIS PERSONALITY WHEN OUT OF CONTROL)
Challenges to Selling
Closed off from growth whenever one feels
less open to the input from others

WHAT YOU NEED TO FOCUS ON

Be completely committed to the things you do with consistency. Allow *no* non–process thinking into any selling situation whatsoever. Be vigilant about how instinct is the enemy of process and how chaos is the enemy of order. Develop new, more productive instincts by design to live by, using uncommon knowledge in whatever needs to be done, in every connection that is established, in every commitment that is made—every day, all the time, in and out of work.

Never give in, even in the face of the most brutal obstacle. Persevere and rise above.

The *Persistent* Candidate

Trevor's Story

I was not born with a silver spoon in my mouth. If ever the odds were against a person being wildly successful, that would be me. My father was not active in my life, and he had a good number of his own problems. My mother was a great lady, but she lived a simple life and had no idea about what it takes to have great accomplishments in business.

I walked out during my senior year in high school, never to return. College was out for me, and frankly, I wouldn't have wanted to go anyway.

My friend's father was a traveling salesman, and he had a pretty good library of classic motivational books. One day, I went into his makeshift home library and opened the first book I saw. It was Napoleon Hill's *Think and Grow Rich*. I was hooked. I thought, *This is my college*. There was a wealth of knowledge for the taking. I was enthralled and seduced by the positivity and empowerment in those pages.

When I was the most down on my luck, I spent my last dime on going to see a well-known speaker who focused on personal empowerment. It was a great investment. It was there that I knew I had a destiny. I know a lot of upward mobile thinkers, and I guess what separates me from the ones who struggle is the fact that I follow through on everything. I am completely disciplined in my approach. That discipline gave me the edge to become highly successful in my career.

I am retired now from my day-to-day work, but I am still, by all measures, a reasonably young guy. My advice to others: Follow through no matter what. Persistence, like follow through, is a choice. Choose it.

About the *Persistent*

Persistent is the final Green stage, because no one has ever succeeded on a grand scale without possessing that trait in spades. Certainly, people have gotten lucky and succeeded, but this isn't a book about hoping for success. It is about determining your destiny and creating your own way. Without persistence, none of the other stages will matter for very long. Persistence isn't fleeting; it is every day and all the time.

Persistent people aren't necessarily good or bad people. They understand that if you work hard at an idea and don't quit, it will eventually work. Persistent people are true believers and bigger thinkers than most. *They act beyond any limitations of negative thought, because they aren't concentrating on the consequences for failure.* They are myopic to a degree and razor-focused on what they want. This sort of thinking can lead to big achievements, both good and bad. When a persistent personality interviews for a sales position, the interviewer must be aware that *this trait is an enabler of accomplishment*, but what kind of accomplishment is the question.

Persistence doesn't determine virtue; it determines drive, perseverance, and an unusually high level of commitment. Thieves who are successful are persistent, but then again, Steve Jobs, Elon Musk, Mother Teresa, and the Dalai Lama are all examples of persistent people, too. *When virtue and persistence become interlocked, these qualities create a magnificent potential for uncommon, sustainable excellence.*

Persistent personalities are masters of impressive success. Virtuous persistence is defined as "Firm and determined continuance in a course of action that helps another person, in spite of difficulty or opposition." This is not difficult to understand but requires having an unnatural mindset to achieve, one that's trained on strict adherence to process. Truly persistent people are unusual. They are interesting people who find a way to get things done. Most candidates won't be naturally persistent, simply because of the sheer level of energy and commitment needed to get and stay there.

Persistent personalities don't give up. They are smart enough to check the soundness of their plans regularly, readjusting what needs tweaking, but not prematurely so. They will only do so if new ideas are first cleared as *in state* with the construct of their selling system and well-trained mindset. While some people hedge their bets, persistently successful people are always pushing forward and showing their commitment to their plans and ideas. They push forward and know they will win. It's not a matter of if, but when. That's why persistent people are the ones who achieve stunning greatness. They are leaders.

Rob Fried, an executive in global marketing at Bridgewater Associates, believes that persistence is the key to a long and successful career in selling. His advice is to "be pleasantly persistent with determined optimism. Gravity and laws of physics make it so that you're not persistent, you'll lose momentum."

All the greatest success stories seem to involve a very persistent protagonist as a lead character. When a person takes an idea and runs with it, driven by sheer energy, follow-through, and a commitment not to give up, it is hard not to eventually succeed. With all the cynics out there, it's easy to be talked out of a good idea. Common sense makes many ideas seem impractical and unlikely, and it often makes more logical sense not to persist. But when persistent people hear words of over-caution, they don't let it stop them. They live the tenets of proven philosophies that produce impressive success, and those philosophies live at the core of their being.

We Can and Should Be the Architects of Our Own Outcomes

Breaking away from negative early influence is hard work. When a child grows up in a household with serious problems and nonattentive early influencers or early influencers who were out of touch with the needs of their children—such as alcoholics—that child will choose one of two paths. The child will either model the behaviors of the early influencer or fight hard to avoid becoming like the early influencer.

I've seen families where the children went both ways. I've often wondered how one child could repeat the same mistakes of the negative early influencer, and yet the other sibling goes the opposite direction. Such is the case for free will, the ability to choose.

"You see things; and you say, 'Why?' But I dream things that never were; and I say, 'Why not?'" This quote by George Bernard Shaw sums it up nicely. Perspective is a choice. If we fall into negative thinking because it was our only example, it is weak-willed. This thinking operates from a default level of thought—that is, one without conscious decisions being made to counter the negative. No matter the **excuse**, it is still a choice.

We, as people, can and should be the architects of our own outcomes. It begins with a vision, which starts off as an idea. Persistent people must first find a sense of desire to become more than who they are. When people (even children) hold the ability to see beyond where they are now and can envision a better way of life, that vision (if powerful enough) can make anything happen. I can speak with some authority on this. After my father passed away unexpectedly when I was 11, my mother and older brother never seemed terribly motivated to me. They were great people but lacking in a desire to achieve much. For one reason or another, I felt differently.

The persistent among us understand the power of core-belief conviction in the words they speak and the actions they take. *You cannot fundamentally change a paradigm without a conviction in your mind and heart. You don't need to be born with privilege or be given much advantage to create great improvement for yourself, if you so choose.*

GENERATIONAL CHANGES

As with past generations (and no doubt it will be for future generations as well), today's newest working generation, the millennials, thinks differently from its predecessors. It is normal for a new generation of parents to try to right the perceived wrongs of their own childhood when raising their children. For example, baby boomers were reared in a world where a child could leave home to play with friends in the morning and not return home until it was dark, while millennials couldn't fathom the thought of that much freedom. Many baby boomers coddled their children, and with noble intentions some tried hard to make sure no child felt left out. The boomers themselves grew up in a time when it was an adult's world. Children worked to support their families, helping around the house and doing other chores. Pleasing a parent was an expectation for baby boomers, and respect was given importance in a household back then. We experienced a cultural shift, however, when the boomers had *their* children.

Since the baby boomers matured at a time when modern psychology began to recognize the hurt feeling of less celebrated children, it gave way to the infamous *participation trophy* era of the millennials' childhood. Millennials also grew up in the internet age, where everything is virtually instantaneous. If you want to buy something, you can just go online, and soon it will appear at your front door. If you want to see a movie, forget the burden of driving to a theater; just go online and watch your show. For the most part, today's world requires no waiting, and for some in the millennial culture, instant gratification is an expectation. It's a world where we can even learn at a college level by going to one of many tutorial websites.

Baby boomers made many millennial children feel special and exceptional, often before they actually had done anything special or exceptional. Parents simply trying to provide motivational self-esteem to their children may be of noble intent, but if overdone, can produce a hubris without virtue. As we are beginning to learn, being paid gratuitous compliments before an actual accomplishment breeds a feeling of entitlement. And we've begun to see that too many unearned compliments have led to other unintended negative consequences, as well.

A child who learns something too quickly and haphazardly is now more likely to feel like an expert on a topic before even scratching the surface. And when that happens, the kids don't know what they don't know. If children are challenged on what they know, they can simply find supporting documentation online to show they are correct. This is usually not a quest for knowledge. It is more commonly a search for information to prove that they are right, or that someone else is wrong, which means we are becoming hardwired to reinforce our beliefs instead of exploring them. This bias runs rampant, and confirming what we think we know is as easy as touching a few keys on a computer keyboard. This sort of closed-mindedness opens the floodgates to **blame, excuses, justifications,** and **rationalizations**.

Where does all this lead? Persistence means sticking with something. A person cannot become a master at anything if they abandon it when bored and move on to something else. Persistence demands an excellence, a *real* accomplishment, a commitment that can be helped online but requires a higher level of thinking that is produced only by learning, experiencing, and working proper disciplines with a focus. It calls for intellectual curiosity for new information, even some that might contradict what we think we already know. It requires a willingness to be challenged and an openness to reset as needed.

If your goal is to get rich quick without putting in the sweat-equity, you should rely on luck. Let me be the first one to wish you luck, as this book will have no meaning for you. If your goal is to master the skills needed to become rich, and you are willing to humble yourself enough to learn what you do not already know, you will likely find a great deal more success. And if you keep at it, you will develop the priceless skills of persistence. Regardless of what generation you belong to, *what you put into something is what you'll get out of it.*

How Motivation Plays into the Picture

Think of motivation as having three distinctions:

1. **External motivated.** Motivated by others, requiring strength and energy from others (inconsistent)

2. **Partially externally motivated and partially self-motivated.** Motivated according to how you interpret your surroundings (inconsistent)
3. **Self-motivated.** Motivated consistently by self (persistent)

The more we are self-motivated, the better we can withstand the pressures of obstacles, and the more consistently we can take the next small step. The strength to remain motivated must come from within if it's to become permanent, and motivation that is permanent becomes empowerment.

Og Mandino, author of *The Greatest Salesman in the World*, said: "I will persist until I succeed. Always will I take another step. If that is of no avail, I will take another, and yet another. In truth, one step at a time is not too difficult. . . . I know that small attempts, repeated, will complete any undertaking."

We can turn to many inspiring stories of personal triumph over difficult odds, with some of the most famous examples including Ludwig van Beethoven, Abraham Lincoln, the Wright Brothers, Helen Keller, Michael Jordan, J. K. Rowling, and Sylvester Stallone.

Then there are the stories of Christopher Gardner and Jack Andraka. Christopher Gardner overcame extremely difficult obstacles—including homelessness—to achieve great success as a businessperson and a motivational speaker. His life story was made into the much-acclaimed movie *The Pursuit of Happyness*, starring Will Smith. And Jack Andraka was the 15-year-old young man who had an idea of how to test for pancreatic cancer. His method was turned down by all but the 200th lab he approached. It was at Johns Hopkins University, where he developed a test that was 100 times more accurate and 26,000 times less expensive than the one that was already widely used, and it's estimated that Jack's persistence has saved tens of thousands of lives. Imagine all the people who dismissed a 15-year-old's crazy idea. But Jack's view was this: "You're the greatest advocate for your ideas, so always keep pushing and never give up."

The Power of Belief

It's always easier to get on board with an idea or a vision if someone has already shown you that it works. Perhaps (I joke) we can call those who need proof before taking a chance *apprehensively persistent*, a contradiction of terms.

But let's consider Mount Everest. At approximately 29,029 feet tall, it's located in the Mahlangu mountain range on the border of China and Nepal. Of course, it has been there forever, but it wasn't until May 29, 1953, when two men finally reached its apex—Edmund Hillary from New Zealand and Tenzing Norgay from Nepal. Since then, there have been more than 4,000 climbers who have also reached the top—an outstanding accomplishment for each one, indeed! Once Hillary and Norgay showed it could be done, many others followed, rapidly.

The same could be said about breaking the four-minute mile. It was widely believed that it couldn't be done and that human beings are simply not built to accomplish that kind of speed—that is, until Roger Bannister, a 25-year-old runner, did it in 1954. Since then, more than 1,400 other runners have also joined the club. Once it was proved, others did it, and did it more frequently.

What makes people believe that things are impossible and cannot be accomplished? And, conversely, what makes people attempt things that seem impossible? It's about belief.

Belief is an immensely powerful force. For some, proof propels their belief. And for the more daring, it's their belief itself that propels their effort. It's a matter of willful *persistence*. There's a certain independence that very persistent people all seem to have in common—they are going to make something happen, no matter what others say.

President Ronald Reagan had a sign on his desk that read, "IT CAN BE DONE." Reagan, similar to John F. Kennedy a score earlier, inspired a legion of politicians to follow him with his infectious belief in ideals. Both men were revered politicians. Both ran mostly positive campaigns, a rarity in politics. Kennedy's campaign touted, "We can do better!" Reagan ran a campaign ad proclaiming, "Morning in America." It is no wonder that these two American presidents are remembered fondly for their optimism. They are held as icons of their respective parties. *The empowerment of belief is the most powerful feeling in the world, with only the exception of love itself.*

Awaken yourself about belief. If there's a lesson about belief, it's this: You don't need proof to believe, and if you wait for it, you'll be in a long line with others. Somehow, I don't see Steve Jobs, Bill Gates, the Dalai Lama, Elon Musk, J. K. Rowling, Oprah Winfrey, Martin Luther King Jr., Mahatma Gandhi, Richard Branson, Amelia Earhart, or even the Beatles waiting in that line. Do you?

These persistent examples are of highly focused people who broke new ground. They didn't walk a path that had been cleared by someone else. Lots of people want to be on that path, the one that's already been cut; it's certainly easier. But those with persistent personalities had the vision to cut their own paths, and *they* are the ones you'll remember. They were bold. It isn't any wonder they all became wildly successful, too.

The Behavior of the Truly Persistent

If you are a salesperson who is assigned leads each day, and for whatever reason, you didn't receive your appointments for a particular day, what do you do? For those who look for **excuses**, they have a built-in reason why they aren't working that day. The company never gave them any appointments; they're off the hook. But is that the response of a person who is on a mission of persistence or someone looking to **justify** not being responsible for their failure?

If you are truly persistent, you'll get on the phone to your office and ask about it. Don't assume there weren't any appointments—that is, unless you didn't really want to work. Once again, successful people are active participants in their careers. Those who aren't successful have the best **justifications** for failure, and to them it's rarely because of them. Persistent people don't let things happen and merely count the chips at the end of the day. They push, drive, and follow through on anything having to do with their success. Not in talk but in action.

There's a difference between the employees who work for a company for a steady paycheck and the ones who hunger for something more. For example, during the 2020–2021 Covid-19 pandemic, how many people at various companies, having been laid off, still called their managers or owners and offered some kind of assistance in planning what would happen upon the company's return to business?

While it may not have been a requirement to do so, a truly committed and persistent person couldn't help but show interest in company affairs. *Strongly persistent people see their company as their vehicle and would be automatically drawn to making their presence known.* If you see yourself as persistent, would you do that? Would you stay in regular contact with company leaders, making sure that they were okay and that your ideas still had a place to be discussed and developed?

It doesn't require a paycheck to do that if you are persistent at a high enough level. You can bet that your employer would notice who showed concern and offered help and who remained silent in *on-vacation mode*. If that's all you want out of your present opportunity, that's fine. But it's hard to claim a virtuous interest in your company and your future and to profess that you care about growth if you tune out during a pandemic and temporarily shut down, not showing commitment. As previously mentioned, persistent people are rare—and that's why so few people make it big. This is one of many tests that show just how uncommon they are.

Your goal might not include changing the world in the same ways that Mahatma Gandhi or Elon Musk have, but there's an old saying: "If something is worth doing, it's worth doing well!" If you're going to be a marketer, why not be the best marketer of all time? If you're going to be in sales, why not be a salesperson who can one day write your memoir and inspire people who will line up to meet you? If your goals are less supercilious, why not work in a tirelessly persistent manner to prove to yourself that you are capable of greatness? Persistent people would be bored being average. What fun is in that? Who would want to work at a J.O.B. (just over broke) when you can work on a mission?

If none of these things inspires you, you should consider why. *Persistence isn't necessarily about notoriety; it's more about self-sentiment. Proving to yourself that you hold the spirit of major accomplishment in the palm of your hand is immensely powerful in building confidence.*

GET YOUR MIND SUPREMELY READY FOR SUCCESS

You can't grow a career at selling if you accept a version of reality that prevents you from achieving success. Many times, when people are new at a sales position and have not been tainted by bad habits or past history, they are fresh to the opportunity, open-minded, ready and willing. They have an *expectation of success.*

If you work in a call center as an inside salesperson, where your job is to talk to people, and you find you're not reaching anyone, never use low contacts as an **excuse**. Positive projection communicates to the universe in ways that are not fully understood by humans. The serious-minded know that they need to focus hard when making a call and they must *will* someone to answer their call. *Somehow, when we are in a supreme state of readiness for success, it happens.*

I remember working at a job hiring marketers many years ago. Whenever I lost key players, somehow, I would find new ones quickly. Yet when I was only doing "maintenance hiring," I would see a lot fewer ad responses coming in. When the need is truly real, something just happens. I noticed the difference at that time, but back then I couldn't put my finger on it. I probably thought it was coincidence.

Napoleon Hill speaks to this phenomenon in his book *Think and Grow Rich*, a true masterpiece about mindset. Some people have a hard time understanding why things happen when we most need them to. It's a bit strange, but the phenomenon is absolutely true for most successful people. Decide that you will be the party responsible for making a contact with a prospect—no one but you. *You* must be emotionally ready to make sales.

Once a manager allows the members of the team to use low contacts as a **justifiable** reason for failure, they are doomed to accepting the idea that the outcome is beyond their control and they will fail. *Where there are no expectations, there is failure.* When obstacles are accepted as reality and embraced as unavoidable, it's over. It's sometimes referred to as a "new norm," but it's only an **excuse**. You may as well just pull the plug and save yourself from a lingering death. If you run a sales organization and have any members of your team with a dire attitude, correct the attitude, or get rid of the members with the attitude. They are hurting you.

If a sales manager allows the team to **justify** not selling because the prospects weren't that interested, it will become the acceptable **excuse** that kills all future efforts, too. Great managers don't let that happen. They focus the members of the team on their own personal accountability.

Good sales managers hold weekly sales meetings to teach their staff to triumph past common objections. They don't just get upset or angry when the team fails to serve a prospect. I have three requirements for anyone working at any of my companies—to be engaged, to be responsive, and to be urgent. They are important qualities for people who are efficient. Those requirements include managers. Lazy management will kill a company vibe.

SELL BY FOLLOWING PROCESS

Sometimes managers are popular because they represent team grievances to that dastardly company. Any sales manager who plays both sides of that coin, pitting salesperson against company or company against salesperson, will not thrive for very long. It's easy to be loved for all the wrong reasons. It's far more important to be respected for all the right ones.

A sales manager must serve one purpose—to turn out salespeople with process-driven behaviors. So much so, that they should tell their salespeople the following: "You don't cover appointments to sell; you cover appointments to follow process. Concentrate *only* on following process. Selling follows process, not the other way around."

USE THE PROACTIVE MINDSET; AVOID THE REACTIVE

Your persistence and follow-through are the gateways to realizing your dreams. Brilliance without action is nothing. Creativity without action is nothing. Passion without action is meaningless. Until you decide to make something a reality, it lives as a fleeting dream, going nowhere. And the older the dream, the colder it gets. The more distance we put between dreaming up an idea and doing something to further it, the less likely it will ever get off the ground. Motivation is something that requires immediate capitalization, or it subsides. If you try to resurrect a good idea later, it will have a flat passion, which won't feel very inspired. Beatle George Harrison said, "John *was* always helpful. He said things like 'When you're writing, try and finish the song immediately, because once you leave it, it will be harder to complete.'"

If you have a vision for your company or your sales career that requires action, and you back off from doing what is necessary because you are just getting by, you are not proactive. If your company or sales career hits a point that threatens your means for survival, and you *need* to do something, you are *reactive*. Reactive behaviors put out fires and reset our efforts. *Proactive* behaviors never allow the fires to start in the first place. Proactivity is the moment a goal moves into the next level of accomplishment. The lesson is not to wait and sit back but to always move ahead with vision.

If You Were Profiled as *Persistent*

If you were profiled as *persistent*, you must be willing to do the following in order to become a *master at selling*:

1. Master the ability to captivate another person with an infectious attitude and spirit.

2. Master recognizing opportunities in every selling situation.
3. Master the skill sets pertaining to knowledge and relevant information about your specific industry and the art of selling itself.
4. Master the art of persuading others to see the things that you see.
5. Master keeping all aspects of your personality dialed into a state of virtue.

When all five goals are accomplished and are practiced with total discipline and commitment, you have what it takes to become a master at selling.

Questions for Someone with a *Persistent* Personality

There are three sets of questions you should ask that have been designed for the specific profiles in this book. Ask the first two sets before you hire an applicant (global and specific interview questions). And ask yourself the third set (30-day review questions) 30 days after hiring. You can access the questions and the 30-day reviews at www.myleadprofile.com.

Final Thoughts

Let's recap the five personality stages on the Green spectrum and recognize their importance.

First, there's Green Stage 1, demonstrative. Demonstrative is being an energy. Selling for a living requires energy. When you're electric, you're more fun, so it's natural that people will like you and enjoy your company. If you're not the bouncy type, then be the doctor-style professional, someone who commands great respect through confidence and expertise. Either way, being demonstrative is about possessing the ability to captivate.

Then there's Green Stage 2, advantageous. Being advantageous is about learning to become a technician in the field of selling. It requires some knowledge (basic skill) to recognize the opportunities that are before you. Without some training, you wouldn't know what a good demonstration of your product could produce. It requires adapting to systematic thinking (your sales process) to give your selling a lift. Being advantageous is the junior level of becoming an influencer. What's missing is the seriousness of good decision-making on a grand scale. Just knowing how to capitalize on opportunities is not nearly as impressive as discovering how to maximize each situation for a win-win between you and your customers. Being advantageous is a good place to be in the beginning of your selling career, but it's a bad place to stay. You won't last or become a great success if you do not advance into becoming an influencer (Green Stage 4). But first, you must learn selling maturity (Green Stage 3).

Green Stage 3, serious, is also referred to as *selling maturity*. It's where salespeople learn the difference between skilled thinking (on-process) and just winging it (working instinctually). Selling maturity is where a law student learns about the law, where a medical student learns about disease and treatments. It's where a salesperson studies, comprehends, and internalizes the important knowledge of a *learned wisdom*, all put together as your systematic process for selling.

In this stage, you must accept certain tenets of philosophy that, if you agree to follow and believe in, will solve a lot of problems. Life is filled with a vast majority of naysayers who would question these philosophical doctrines or add their own two cents, or only half agree, giving reasons for caveats and exceptions. Some will outright disagree with these philosophies entirely. However, I know for a fact, they work.

One tenet of philosophy is that your confidence is directly tied to your personal accountability. Therefore, *your confidence comes from the decisions you make about accepting personal accountability.*

Another tenet of philosophy states that your fulfillment in life—the feelings of happiness and joy—are tied to growth. It is a fact that if you do not grow, you remain in place. Defining fulfillment is, in structure, a model that requires movement toward purpose. Confidence and fulfillment enlarge your heart and emotionally connect you to the beautiful things in life. Your mind is the entrance to your heart. *It is through the heart that you learn to communicate in ways that are genuine and can be transferred and felt by others.* This is how we show care and concern for the people we influence. The mind needs knowledge to fulfill the mission of the heart.

After mastering Green Stage 3, serious, the information learned is then applied to the demonstrative and advantageous qualities already learned. Instead of selling only when handed an order to fill, we now discover how we can help a prospect the most. With confidence that comes from mastering selling maturity, we apply certainty to our process and learn to make our prospects feel even more comfortable with us.

Following course, mastering Green Stage 4, influencer, is the combination of advantageous (opportunism) and serious knowledge and wisdom (selling maturity). Now, we can speak with authority to prospects, without focusing on selling something but rather helping them. We now know that we best help others through maximization of our efforts, since we now believe (in our core) that what we offer has value. And that we ourselves bring tremendous benefit to our prospects.

You could never sustain at the apex of championship in anything without being at Green Stage 5, persistent. When we recognize LEAD's true meaning of the word *persistent*, we realize how unusual that quality is. Persistence is rare yes, but far from unattainable. You only need the right perspective, information, and emotionalized care and a willingness to consistently work for it until it happens.

Then, with the open eyes of awareness, persistence unlocks the door to mastering your full selling potential in virtuous ways. In doing so, you cannot extricate yourself and your everyday life from your selling life. *You are real, and the two are now one and the same.*

Index

Ability, importance of attitude vs., xxxiii
Acceptance, for preparers, 12
Accomplishments:
  beliefs and, 312
  as focus for organizations, 161
  preparers' response to, 12–13
  recognizing salespeople's, 257–258
Accountability:
  as goal for Green Stage 3, 217
  novice candidates with, 122–128
  taking, 176
Action, vision and, 317
Actionable information, 258–264
Activism, 112–114
Activist mindset, 114–116
Activist personality, people with, 109–117
  about, 109–112
  case example, 111
  connecting cause to selling for, 114–116
  goals of, 116–117
  hiring questions for, 114, 117
  selling passion of, 112–114
Adaptive behaviors:
  applying, 2, 41
  for candidates with inconsistencies, 40
  orange personalities with, 21
Advantageous personality, people with, 169–189
  about, 172–173
  advancement for, 173–178
  case example, 171–172
  fears and sales performance of, 178–180
  filling of needs by, 210
  getting caught up in details for, 244–245
  goals of, 188–189
  hiring questions for, 189
  ignoring of sales process by, 213
  inappropriate actions of, 206
  Influencer personality vs., 180–185, 299–300
  managing, 185–187
  and other Green personality profiles, 144–145
  as over-promisers, 165–166
  sales presentations by, 299
  selling potential of, 187–188
Advantageous stage:
  advancing beyond, 202–207
  advancing to, 167, 168
  other Green stages and, 146

INDEX

Aesop's fables, 70
Affordability:
   core beliefs about, 221
   perceived, 182–184
Agenda commitment, in one-call sales, 255
Agesilaus, 210
All-or-nothing philosophy, 203
Andraka, Jack, 311
Appointment tracking, 259–260
Apprehensively persistent people, 312
Aristotle, xxxvii, 233
Ash, Mary Kay, 237
Attention to detail, 231–232
Attitude:
   importance of ability vs., xx
   infectious, 317
   LEAD Personality Profile and, xxxi, xxxiii
   of "potential" candidates, 106
Authority, xxxi
Average, being, 314–315
Average gross sales, 219
Awareness:
   for adoption of Green behavior, 140
   building, with LEAD program, 205
   enlightened, 128
   for growth, 185
   of people with sensitive personality, 27

Baby boomers, 309
Balance, in selling, 139
Bannister, Roger, 312
Basic training, for new hires, 281
Bathroom close, 248
The Beatles, 285, 313
Beethoven, Ludwig van, 311
Behaviors:
   adaptive, 2, 21, 40, 41
   deficient, xxviii
   excessive, xxviii, 294
   Green, 140
   growth-orientated, 47
   nonproductive, xxvii
   obstinate, xxviii
   off-process, 282–284
   passive-aggressive, 121
   passive-resistance, 121
   proactive, 317
   process-driven, 316–317
   "professional," 154
   reactionary, 173
   reactive, 317
Belief:
   in company, 231
   openness to, 79–80, 312–313
   for people with persistent personality, 312–313
   for people with willful personality, 79–80
Bishop, Brad, 238
Blame:
   acting on changes and, 129
   for bad leads, 283
   as block to fulfillment, 42
   closed-mindedness and, 310
   for company's protocols and requirements, 113
   core-beliefs about, 231, 233
Boredom, xxxvi
Branson, Richard, 313
Bridgewater Associates, 307
Buying-signal questions, 248–249

California Gold Rush, 250
Cancellations, predicting, 264
Captivating, being, 224
Career, active participation in, 226, 313–314
Carnegie, Dale, 234–235
Cautious preparers, 16–17
Central Connecticut State University, xxiii, xxiv
Challenges, embracing, 129

Change, productive, 46, 47
Chaotic approach to overcoming
 objections, 242, 244–245
Cheating, by candidates with
 inconsistencies, 39
Choice, core-beliefs about, 308
Clarity, xxviii, xxxi, 219
Cleanliness, 236
Closed-mindedness, xxxiv, 73, 310
CloserIQ, xv
Closing sales:
 bathroom close, 248
 enhancers for, 247–249
 porch light close, 248
 quick closes, 240–241
 trial close, 234
Clothing, respectable, 222
Collaboration:
 for killer sales presentations,
  285–286
 by preparers, 13
 by soloists, 53
Comfort, 31, 270–271
Comfort zones, 274
Command of materials, 281
Commissions, 263
Commitment:
 to agenda, 255
 for candidates with
  inconsistencies, 47
 manager's 30-day assessment
  of, 33
 to providing value, 256
 to sales process, 121, 214,
  269–275
 to training, 131
Communication, 60, 237, 281
Company case (closing enhancer),
 247
Company culture:
 destruction of, 39, 140–142
 maintaining, 227, 314
 for people with persistent
  personality, 314
Company story, in one-call sales,
 255
Company's offer, for serious
 salespeople, 285–286
Complacency, 42
Confidence:
 building, 130, 217
 for novice candidates, 122–127
 in sales presentations, 212
 of willful candidates, 77–79
Confrontations, avoiding, xxxii
Confucius, 233
Connection, with product,
 232–233
Conscious competent level of
 development, 269–275, 277
Conscious incompetent level of
 development, 266–269, 277
Constancy-to-purpose approach,
 200, 230, 253
Constructive critiques, 186
Constructive dialogue,
 summarizing, 215
Contracts, 224, 232
Coping mechanisms, xxvi–xxvii,
 265–266
Core-belief thinking, xix, 195
Core-beliefs:
 commitment to, 200–201
 conviction in, 308
 developing, 216–217, 287
 of people with selling maturity,
  218–249
Counterintuitive thinking, 47,
 272, 273
Covid-19 pandemic, 314
Cowardliness, xxxviii
Creativity, xxix, 135–136
Credibility, 187, 210, 211
Critical thinking, 128–129
Criticism, xxvii
Critiques:
 of advantageous salespeople,
  185–186

Critiques (*continued*):
　assessing candidate's ability to handle, 32
　of company, 227
　constructive, 33, 186
　destructive, 186
　openness to, 188, 217
　taking responsibility in, 211
Curiosity, of others, 53
Curry, Mark, 93

Dalai Lama, 306, 313
Danaher Business System, xxiii
Danaher Corporation, xxiii
Data, for key indicator reports, 258–264
Dead sales, 225
Deal-making, off-process, 204
Deception, 216
Decision-making:
　acknowledging poor, 211
　core-beliefs about, 233
　by preparers, 16–17
　by prospects, 221
Dedication, in four Ds, 229
Defense mechanisms, xxvi–xxvii
Deficiencies:
　of activists, 109
　of advantageous salespeople, 169
　awareness of, 140
　as component in Lead Personality Profile, xxxviii
　of demonstrative salespeople, 150
　of idealists, 133
　of instinctive salespeople, 96
　of persistent salespeople, 303
　of preparers, 8
　of "professionals," 55–56
　of respectful salespeople, 83
　of sensitive salespeople, 22
　of serious salespeople, 192–193
　of soloists, 49
　of willful salespeople, 65

Deficient behaviors, xxviii
Deluzio, Mark, xvii–xxiv
Demo materials, 226
Demo rates, 218
Demonstrative approach to selling, 52
Demonstrative personality, people with, xiv, 149–168
　about, 152–153
　case examples, 151–152
　goals of, 168
　hiring questions for, 168
　and other Green personality profiles, 144–145
　successful, 160–167
　understanding, 158–160
　working with, 153–158
Demonstrative skills:
　developing, 160–161
　for "professional" salespeople, 59
Demonstrative stage, 146
Demos, basic tracking for, 261
Deposits, core-beliefs about, 222
Depression, 42
Desire, in Four Ds, 229
Destructive critiques, 186
Detail, attention to, 231–232
Determination:
　in four Ds, 229
　as goal for Green Stage 3, 216
Determined optimism, 307
Development:
　five nonnegotiable stages of, xix
　four levels of, 264–277
Device charging, core-beliefs about, 236
Dialogue, constructive, 215
Differentiation, product, 234
Directional leadership, 164–165
Disappointment, avoiding, 244
Discount coupons, 226–227
Disposition:
　of excessive demonstrative personalities, 155

LEAD Personality Profile and, xx, xxxi, xxxiv
   of "potential" candidates, 106
   potential selling ability and, xxxiii
Disrespect, 162
Dissatisfaction, 295–296
Distractions, 227–228, 282
Door-to-door selling, 250–251
Dopamine sensitivity, 53
Doubt, 180–181
Drive, in four Ds, 229
Duell, Charles H., 286

Earhart, Amelia, 313
Egotism:
   of advantageous salespeople, 184–185
   defined, 208
   dropping personal, xxviii
   of willful salespeople, 71
Eisenhower, Dwight D., 293
Electrolux, 250–251
Elevation, choosing your, 74–75
Emotion(s):
   managing, 197–198
   in sales presentations, 181, 199
Emotional buy-in, 274–275
Emotional commitment mindset, 302
Emotional intelligence (EQ), 166
Emotional senses, appealing to, 253–254
Empathy, 14
EncompassingSales.com, 162, 259
Energy flow:
   in leadership, 164–165, 168
   recharging your, 235–236
Engagement, 15, 231
Enlightened awareness, 128
Enthusiasm, demonstrating, 281
Entrepreneurial thinking, 16–18
EQ (emotional intelligence), 166
Euphoria, fulfillment vs., 43–46

Eureka, 250–251
Excellence, sustainable, 306
Excessive activists, 109, 113
Excessive advantageous personalities, 169, 185–186, 206
Excessive behaviors, xxviii, 294
   awareness of, 140
   as component in Lead Personality Profile, xxxviii
   of instinctive salespeople, 97
   with "not for one-call selling" classification, 4
   of preparers, 8–9
   of "professional" salespeople, 56
   of respectful salespeople, 83–84
   of sensitive salespeople, 22–23
   of serious salespeople, 193
   of soloists, 49
   of willful salespeople, 65
Excessive demonstrative personalities, 150, 153–158, 162–163
Excessive extroversion, xxxii–xxxiii
Excessive Green personalities:
   destruction of company culture by, 140–141
   manipulative, 141–142
   nontransferable selling styles for, 141
Excessive idealists, 134, 136–137
Excessive influencers, 293–296
Exclusivity, product, 234
Excuses:
   awareness about, 130
   as bad behavior, xxiiin*
   by candidates with inconsistencies, 37
   closed-mindedness and, 73, 310
   core-beliefs about, 231, 233
   decision to stop making, 129
   dedication to sales process without, 208

Excuses (*continued*):
  by demonstrative salespeople, 158–159
  and growth, xxvii, 125–126, 176
  growth and, 185
  by ineffective sales people, 270
  by instinctive salespeople, 100
  key decisions about, 276–285
  with marketplace growth, 286
  for nonproductive behaviors, xxvii
  for not doing things, 270
  for not following the plan, 70
  for not working, 313
  by novice candidates, 132
  personal accountability for, 127
  pitfalls of, 123–125
  by respectful salespeople, 88, 95
  to stay with what is familiar, 269
  unconscious competence and, 276
  as under-developed mental acuity, xxviii
  by willful salespeople, 80–81
Excuse-setting mindset, xxv
Expectations:
  about selling, 285
  and failure, 316
  meeting and exceeding, 229
  of success, 315
Expediency, decision-making on, 205–207
Experience, xxxvii, 202, 220
External motivation, 310–311
Extroversion:
  as coping mechanism, 12
  LEAD Personality Profile and, xx, xxxi, xxxii–xxxiii
  of novice candidates, 120–121
  of "potential" candidates, 105–106
  for soloist personalities, 53

Failure(s):
  core-beliefs about, 224
  expectations and, 316
  hiring, xxviii–xxxi
  selling process as metric for, 11
Fairness, assessing candidates', 31–32
Fear(s):
  of advantageous salespeople, 178–180, 182–184
  as deficiency, xxxviii
  growth and, xxvii, 267–268
  of price, 235
  projecting, onto prospects, 215
  of willful salespeople, 71
Feedback, from prospects, 236
Field training, 283
Fixed mindset, 198
Focus, core-beliefs about, 228
Forbes, xvi, xx
Forms, official, 214
Found interest, protecting, 178–179
Four Hs, 227
Four levels of development, 264–277
Free-fall, sales, 281–282
Fried, Rob, 307
Frustration tolerance, assessing candidate's, 30
Fulfillment:
  blocks to achieving, 42–43
  for candidates with inconsistencies, 40–46
  euphoria vs., 43–46
  growth, purpose, and, 43, 46

Gandhi, Mahatma, 313
Gardner, Christopher, 311
Gates, Bill, 313
Generational impact, 308–310
"Getting out of your own way," 75–77
Goals:
  to achieve Green Stage 3, 216–217

INDEX

to achieve influencer stage,
  286–287
to achieve persistent stage,
  300–301
for activists, 116–117
for candidates with
  inconsistencies, 47–48
for idealists, 137–138
for influencers, 300–301
for instinctive salespeople, 102
to master selling, 317–318
for novice candidates, 131–132
for people with Yellow and
  Orange personalities, 160
for "potential" candidates,
  107–108
for preparers, 19
for "professional" salespeople,
  60–61
for respectful salespeople, 94–95
sales, 237
for sensitive salespeople, 27–28
for soloists, 53–54
for willful salespeople, 81–82
GOBankingRates, 204
Gratitude, core-beliefs about, 233
The Greatest Salesman in the World
  (Mandino), 311
Green Machine Reflective
  Technology, LLC, 238
Green personalities, xx, 139–145
  advantageous, 169–189
  awareness and, 140
  demonstrative, 149–168
  destruction of company culture
    by, 140–142
  hiring candidates with traits of,
    187
  influencer, 289–301
  persistent, 302–318
  personality traits related to, 9,
    23, 50, 56, 66, 84, 97, 110
  serious (selling maturity),
    191–287

types of, 144–145
working in virtue and process
  for, 142–143
Green stages:
  about, 146–147
  adapting, for other industries, 145
  clarity and direction from, 208
  stage 1 (demonstrative
    personality), 149–168, 282
  stage 2 (advantageous
    personality), 169–189, 282
  stage 3 (serious personality),
    191–287
  stage 4 (influencer personality),
    289–301
  stage 5 (persistent personality),
    302–318
Gross amount of sales, tracking,
  261–262
Gross number of sales, tracking, 261
Gross sales, average, 219
Growth:
  for advantageous personalities,
    173
  awareness for, 185
  for candidates with
    inconsistencies, 48
  challenges for, 267–269
  and comfort zones, 274
  connecting, to purpose, 46
  defining and addressing, 271
  environments fostering, xxx
  euphoric drop and, 45
  excuses and, xxvii, 125–126
  fulfillment and, 43
  openness to, 80–81, 101, 185
Growth mindset, 198, 298
Growth-oriented behaviors, 47
Gut decisions, 17–18, 176
Gut feelings, growth and, 269 (*See
  also* Intuition)

Harrison, George, 317
Harvard Business Review, xv

Harvard Business School, xxiii, xxiv
Heath, Chip, 237n*
Helpfulness, 162–164, 225
Helping others:
    as goal, 116, 300
    sales as, 113–114
Hill, Napoleon, 305, 315
Hillary, Edmund, 312
Hiring:
    decision making about, 276–285
    failures in, xviii–xix, xxviii–xxxi
    LEAD Personality Profile Program for, 277
    of "potential" candidates, 107
    of "professional" candidates, 59–60
Hiring managers, xvi–xxi, 159
Hiring questions:
    for activists, 114, 117
    for advantageous candidates, 189
    for candidates with inconsistencies, 48
    for demonstrative candidates, 159–160, 168
    for idealists, 138
    for influencers, 301
    for instinctive candidates, 102
    for novice candidates, 132
    for persistent candidates, 318
    for "potential" candidates, 105, 108
    for "professional" candidates, 61–62
    for respectful candidates, 95
    for sensitive candidates, 31–32
    for serious candidates, 287
    for soloists, 54
    for willful candidates, 82
    (See also Six Global Interview Questions)
Hone-able, in four Hs, 227
Honest candidates with inconsistencies, 46–47

Honesty, xiii, xxxi, 206, 210–211, 227, 234
Honoring others, xiii
Hoover, 250–251
How to Win Friends and Influence People (Carnegie), 234–235
Hubris, 77–79, 237
Humility, 185, 208–209, 227
Hungry, in four Hs and, 227

IBM (International Business Machines), 224
Idealism, 135–136
Idealist personality, people with, 133–138
    about, 133–135
    case example, 135
    goals of, 137–138
    hiring questions for, 138
    personalization and individualization for, 136
    practicality for, 135–137
Ideas, sharing, 34–35, 234
Identity, connecting company and your own, 116
Immaturity, of willful candidates, 71
Impractical idealists, 136–137
Improvement, by novice candidates, 129–130
Income, potential, 219
Incompetence, 265
Inconsistencies, candidates with, 36–49
    about, 38–41
    case examples, 37–38
    fulfillment for, 41–46
    goals of, 47–48
    hiring questions for, 48
    productive change for, 46–47
Individual mindset, 220
Individualization, 38, 136
Individualized stipulations, in contracts, 232

Influence:
    core-beliefs about, 229
    energy flow as source of, 165
    of managers, 186
    openness to, 185
    responding to negative, 307–308
    sphere of, 168
    using emotionalized points for, 199
    with verbal/nonverbal messaging, 163–164
Influencer personality, people with:
    about, 289–291, 293
    case example, 292
    excessive and out-of-control, 293–296
    expanding of needs by, 210
    goals of, 300–301
    hiring questions for, 301
    openness to learning by, 206–207
    and other Green personality profiles, 144–145
    people with advantageous personality vs., 180–185, 299–300
    profit margin for, 206
    virtuous, 296–300
Influencer stage, 147
Influencers (agents of influence):
    being, 6
    generational differences in, 308–310
    on people with instinctive personalties, 100
    on people with willful personalities, 74–75
    and personality types, xvii–xxiv
Information:
    actionable, 258–264
    controlling, 235
    relevant, 318
Initial-visit pricing, 257
Inner nature, controlling, xxiv–xxvii

Innovation, core-beliefs about, 234
Insecurity, 124
Inspection, in one-call sales, 255
Instinctive personality, people with, 96–102
    about, 96–99
    case example, 99
    dangerous risks for, 100–101
    expectations of influencers by, 100
    goals of, 102
    hiring questions for, 102
    willingness to grow for, 101
Instincts, xxxvii, 224
Integrity:
    of influential salespeople, 179
    maintaining, 26
    trading, for profit, 296
Intelligence, of great salespeople, 51
Interest, creating, 223, 234–235, 238–239
International Business Machines (IBM), 224
Interviews:
    for hiring, 159, 278–281
    online, 278–281, 284–285
    during training, 284–285
Introversion, 52
Intuition:
    developing, 265–266
    and growth, 269
    new, 275
    (*See also* Gut feelings, growth and)

Job stability, assessing candidates' interest in, 32
Job-jumpers, 32
Jobs, Steve, 306, 313
Johns Hopkins University, 311
Jordan, Michael, xxviii, 311
Judgment, xxxvii
    good, xxxviii, 206, 217
    in on-process selling, 241

Judgment (*continued*):
   of sensitive salespeople, 26–27
   of serious salespeople, 218–249
   sound, 195
Justification(s):
   closed-mindedness and, 310
   core-beliefs about, 233
   cowardliness as, xxxviii
   for customer's expectations, 113
   by demonstrative salespeople, 158–159
   due to fear and laziness, xxvii
   growth and, 125–126, 176
   from Lazy Brain, 127
   for lazy pitches, 177
   for not committing to sales process, 87
   for not selling, 316
   by novice candidates, 121, 128–129
   for overpromising, 166
   personal accountability for, 122
   pitfalls of, 123–125
   for poor outcomes, 129, 130
   by preparers, 14
   protecting against, xxviii
   pseudo-superiority and, xxv
   and recognizing opportunities, 212
   as sign of selling immaturity, 214, 216
   truth in, 178
   by unsuccessful people, 313
   by weak-willed salesperson, 89

Keller, Hellen, 311
Kellogg School of Management, xxiv
Kennedy, John. F., 312–313
Key indicator reports, 258–264
King, Martin Luther, Jr., 112, 313
Kirby, 250–251
Knowledge, 61, 207, 318

Laziness, xxvii, xxviii, 71
Lazy Brain, 126–127
Lazy sales pitches, 177
LEAD Personality Profile Program, xiv, xx–xxi
   activist personalities in, 114
   beginning with, xlii–xliii
   building awareness with, 205
   characteristics and personalities in, xxxviii
   getting your, xxxiv
   for hiring, xxviii–xxxi, 277
   managers' use of, 208
   overview of, xxxi–xxxiii
   personality model in, xxxviii
   Red personalities in, 1, 2
   for selling personality types, 5
Leadership:
   directional, 164–165
   by novice candidates, 120
   by "potential" candidates, 105
Leads, core-beliefs about, 219
Lean accounting, xxiii
Lean authorities, xxiii
Lean Horizons Consulting, xxiv
Lean management, xxiii
Lean principles, xxiv
Learning:
   as challenge to change, 266–267
   core-beliefs about, 223
   discomfort in, 25
   of industry-related numbers, 218
   for influencer personalities, 206–207
   methods of, 202
   new, xxix
   openness for, xxxiv
   to sell, 2
   for sensitive personality, 27
   types of thinking for, 272–274
   willingness to learn, 33–34
Lennon, John, 285, 317
Lexico, 172

Liability, operations manuals to avoid, 26
Liars, pathological, 295
Life, foundational pillars of, 276
Lifelong learners, xiv
Lincoln, Abraham, 311
Listening, 202, 234
Logical senses, 253–254, 271–272

Management:
  of advantageous salespeople, 185–187
  of demonstrative salespeople, 157–158
  of novice candidates, 130–131
  of people with "not for OCS" classification, 6
  of "potential" candidates, 35
Managers:
  efficiency of, 316
  following of sales process by, 228
  interviews conducted by, 159
  perspective of, on hiring, xvi–xvii, xvii–xxi
  ride alongs with, 283–284
  use of performance records by, 161–162
Manager's 30-day assessment, xliii, 28–31, 33–35
Mandino, Og, 311
Manipulation, 141–142, 154
Marketplace growth, 286
Martin, George, 285
Mary Kay Cosmetics, 37
Massachusetts Institute of Technology (MIT), xxiv
Mature selling approaches, 167
  (See also Selling maturity)
Maturity, of demonstrative salespeople, 166–167
McCartney, Paul, 285
McGuire, Darrin, 294
McPheat, Sean, 196
Mediafly, xviii

Mehrabian, Albert, 163
Mental acuity, xxviii
Mental nourishment, core-beliefs about, 223
"Mention selling," 181
Mentoring, 225
Millennials, 309
Mindset:
  interview questions to determine, 30
  of persistent candidates, 302
  and personality type, xiv
  for selling, 174, 196–197
  setting, xxv–xxvii
  successful, 315–316
  (See also specific types)
Miserable, feeling, 295–296
MIT (Massachusetts Institute of Technology), xxiv
Motivation, 30, 42, 310–311
Mount Everest, 312
MTD Sales Training Specialists, 196
Musk, Elon, 306, 313
MyLeadProfile.com, xxxiv, xxxvi, xlii, xliii, 7

Natural personality, core-beliefs about, 225
Needs assessment, 161, 255
Negative self-talk, 268
Negative thinking, 127–128, 158, 308
Net dollars sold, tracking, 262
Net number of sales, tracking, 262
Net rate, tracking, 263–264
Net sales per leads issued (NSLI), 105, 218, 263
New Britain, Conn., xxiv
Nonproductive behaviors, growth and, xxvii
Nonstarter salespeople, 1–3
Nontransferable selling styles, 141

Nonverbal messaging, 163–164, 179, 236
Norgay, Tenzing, 312
Northwestern University, xxiv
Not for one-call selling classification, 4–7
Novice candidates, 118–132
   about, 118–120
   case example, 119
   classification graph for, 120–121
   disposition of, 121
   extroversion for, 120–121
   goals of, 131–132
   growth by, 125–126
   hiring questions for, 132
   immediate improvement by, 129–130
   internal blame and critical thinking by, 128–129
   leadership potential, 120
   managing, 130–131
   negative thinking and positive action for, 127–128
   personal accountability and confidence of, 122–128
NSLI rate (*see* Net sales per leads issued)

Objections:
   anticipating, xxxvi–xxxvii, 230–231
   new hires' adjustment to, 282–283
   overcoming, xxix, 173, 241, 300–301
   reverse, 184
   strategy for countering, 251–252
OCS (*see* One-call selling)
Offers, crazy, 230
Office protocols, 223
Off-process selling, 175–178, 204, 282–284, 287
Ogilvy, David, 235

One-call selling (OCS), 5–7, 104, 240, 254–258
Online video interviews, 278–281
On-process selling:
   addressing problems with, 242–243
   closing enhancers for, 247–249
   core-beliefs about, 227
   judgment in, 241
   off-process vs., 175–178
   personalized vs. individualized, 241
   for prospects who always get three prices, 245–247
   shifting to, 286–287
   staying with, 238–249
Open mindset, xxxviii, 195, 202, 209, 250–253, 286
Openness:
   to belief, 79–80
   challenges to, 16
   commitment and, 121
   as dispositional factor, xxxiii
   genuine, 160
   to growth, 80–81, 185
   to influence, 185
   to learning, xxxiv, 108, 202, 203
   to selling maturity, 185
Operations manuals, 26
Opinions:
   of advantageous salespeople, 175–176
   dropping personal, xxviii
   of managers, 230
   and willingness to lead, xxxii
Opportunism, 172
Opportunities:
   core-beliefs about, 221
   for productive change, 47
   providing prospects with unexpected, 248
   rates of, 219
   recognizing, 318
   tracking, 260

Opportunity seeking, by advantageous salespeople, 172, 179–180, 188
Optimism, determined, 307
Orange personalities, xx, 21–61
  about, 21
  candidates with inconsistencies, 36–48
  goals for, 160
  "professional," 55–61
  sensitive, 22–35
  soloist, 49–54
Orderly approach to overcoming objections, 243–245
Outcomes:
  engineering your, xxxv–xxxvii
  for persistent salespeople, 307–310
Outgoing salespeople, 51
Out-of-control influencers, 293–296
Overcompensation, 12, 154–155
Over-personalizing sales, 157
Over-practical preparers, 16
Overpromising, 155–156, 165–166, 168, 216, 265–266

Pace, of sales presentations, 238–239
Participation era, 309
Passion:
  about selling, 112–114
  of activists, 116
  for products, 234
  of virtuous influencers, 96–297
Passive-aggressive behavior, 121
Pathological liars, 295
Patience, of managers, 33
People pleasers, 166
People-oriented salespeople, xiv
People-pleasing demonstrative personality, 156
Performance:
  of advantageous salespeople, 178–180
  core-beliefs about, 228

Performance monitoring, 27
Performance records, 161–162
Persistence:
  commitment and, 200–201
  core-beliefs about, 237
  of willful salespeople, 73–74
Persistent personality, people with, 302–318
  about, 302–304, 306–307
  as architects of their own outcomes, 307–310
  behavior of, 313–317
  case example, 305
  goals of, 317–318
  hiring questions for, 318
  motivation of, 310–311
  and other Green personality profiles, 144–145
  people with willful personality vs., 72–73
  power of belief for, 312–313
Persistent stage:
  goals for advancing to, 300–301
  other Green stages and, 147
Personal accountability (*see* Accountability)
Personality types:
  classification of, xx
  and mindset, xiv
  overview of, xxi
Personalization, 136
Persuasion, 318
Plutarch, 234
Popeil, Ron, 232
Porch light close, 248
Positive action, by novice candidates, 127–128
Positive mindset, 233
Post-sale button-up, 257
Potential candidates, 103–108
  about, 103, 104
  attitude and disposition of, 106
  classification graph for, 104–107

Potential candidates (*continued*)
    considerations before hiring, 107
    extroversion for, 105–106
    goals of, 107–108
    hiring questions for, 108
    leadership qualities of, 105
Potential income, core-beliefs about, 219
Practical idealists, 136
Practicality, 135–137
Preparer personality, people with, 8–19
    ability to work for others of, 13–18
    about, 8–12
    acceptance and rejection for, 12
    accomplishments of, 12–13
    case example, 10
    goals of, 19
Preplanned processes, 135–136
Pressure selling, 4–6, 31, 162, 245
Price(s):
    ballpark, 221
    fearing, 235
    value vs., 183, 246–247, 297–298
Price conditioning, 245, 300
Pricing:
    core-beliefs about, 226–227
    initial-visit, 257
Pricing errors, 215
Proactive mindset, 317
Problem-solving skills, candidate's, 29–30
Process-driven behaviors, 316–317
Process-driven knowledge, 207
Process-driven salespeople, 142–144
Process-driven thinking, 213
Product case (closing enhancer), 247
Product differentiation, 234
Product presentation, in one-call sales, 256
Productive change, 46, 47

Professional behaviors, 154
Professional personality, people with, 55–61
    about, 55–57
    case example, 57
    goals of, 60–61
    hiring potential of, 59–60
    hiring questions for, 61–62
    as providers, 58–59
Profit, trading integrity for, 296
Prospects:
    connecting with, 222
    decision-making by, 221
    feedback from, 236
    projecting your fears onto, 215
    serving, 220
    taking advantage of, 230
Prospects who always get three prices, 245–247
Provider role, for "professional" salespeople, 58–59
Pure Food and Drug Act (1906), 250
Purpose:
    attaching selling career to, 44
    core-beliefs about, 236
    growth and, 46
The Pursuit of Happyness (film), 311

Quick closes, 240–241
Quillen, Robert, 42–43, 227n*

Rationalizations:
    by advantageous salespeople, 179
    closed-mindedness and, 310
    core-beliefs about, 233
    for failing to follow sales process, 178
    growth and, 125–126, 176
    laziness and, 87
    by people pleasers, 166
    short cutting sales process with, 176

Reactive behaviors, 173, 317
Reagan, Ronald, 312, 313
Red personalities, 1–19
   about, 1
   as nonstarter salespeople, 1–3
   not for one-call selling, 4–7
   preparer, 8–19
   types of, xx
Referrals, core-beliefs about,
   219–220
Reinventing yourself, 211–212
Rejection:
   adapting after, 61
   closing enhancers after, 247–249
   for excessively demonstrative
     salespeople, 155
   preparers' fear of, 12
Relationships:
   creating trust in, 34
   monitoring, 27
Repetition, 237
Rescission, selling based on, 222
Resolutions, core-beliefs about,
   224
Respectful personality, people with,
   83–95
   about, 83–87
   case example, 85
   goals of, 94–95
   hiring questions for, 95
   as junior demonstratives, 164
   mastery of selling process by,
     87–94
   reinvention of selling
     approaches by, 94
   respectfulness in action for,
     162–163
Responsibility:
   of company, for excessive
     influencers, 296
   deflecting, 123–124, 126, 235
   for leading, 188
   for performing on-process, 231
   taking, in critiques, 211

Responsiveness, core-beliefs about,
   231
Results, selling, 34
Reverse-objections, 184
Right, needing to be, 14–16
Risk-taking:
   by instinctive salespeople,
     100–101
   by "professional" salespeople,
     58–59
Rowling, J. K., 311, 313

Sales commissions, 263
Sales goals, core-beliefs about, 237
Sales leads, core-beliefs about, 219
Sales Management Association, xv
Sales positions, 1, 173–178
Sales potential, determining, 34
Sales presentations:
   balancing tone of, 199
   constructing, 285–286
   delivery of, 176–177, 234
   earning right to ask for order
     in, 221
   hurrying through, 214
   making up or changing parts
     of, 215
   masterful, 34
   one-call, 254–258
   shortcutting, 214, 221
   by virtuous influencers, 298–299
Sales process:
   benchmarks for, 11
   committing to, 174, 201
   constancy-to-purpose approach
     to, 200
   embracing, 48, 54, 61, 117, 132,
     138, 168, 189, 216, 287, 301
   environment for, xxix
   expediency vs. trusting, 205–207
   experience and, xxxvii
   for Green personalities, 142–143
   individualized, xxxvi
   partial offers in, 182–183

Sales process (*continued*):
   for persistent salespeople,
     316–317
   for respectful salespeople, 87–94
   revisiting, 284
   self-determination and, 205
   for sensitive salespeople, 27
   straying from, xxxv–xxxvi,
     225–226
   working only from, 213
Sales reports, 185, 235
Same-day price (closing enhancer),
   247
Sectra, Inc., 294
Self:
   being your, in sales, 185
   false sense of, 39
Self-accountability, candidates', 32
Self-awareness, 39–40, 166
Self-deception, 210
Self-determination, 196–218
Self-evaluation, 209–210
Self-governance, 196–218
Self-importance, 94
Self-interest, xxxvii
Self-motivation, 311
Self-pity, 127
Self-respect, 237
Self-reviewing, 217
Self-serving reporting, 210–211
Self-talk, to drive fulfillment, 43
Sell Blocks, tracking sales using,
   203–204
Selling:
   attaching purpose to, 44
   connecting your cause to,
     114–116
   controlling environment for, 298
   nine steps in, 254–258
   as part of human condition, 250
   passion about, 112–114
   reinventing approaches to, 94
   (See also specific types)
Selling ability, 6, 58–59

Selling challenges:
   for activist, 109
   for advantageous salespeople,
     169–170
   for candidates with
     inconsistencies, 36
   for demonstrative salespeople,
     150
   for persistent salespeople, 303
   for preparers, 8–9
   for "professional" salespeople,
     56
   for sensitive salespeople, 22–23
   for willful salespeople, 65–66
Selling maturity:
   developing, 207–213
   lacking, 207
   openness for, 185
   signs of, 213–214
   (*See also* Serious personality,
     people with)
Selling philosophy, xxix, 131, 137,
   188
Selling psychology, 252
Senior citizens, respecting, 184
Sensitive personality, people with,
   22–35
   about, 22–23, 25
   case example, 24–25
   clear thinking and judgment
     for, 26–27
   goals of, 27–28
   hiring questions for, 28–32
   manager's 30-day assessment of,
     33–35
   operations manuals for, 26
Serious personality, people with,
   191–287
   about, 191–193, 195
   case example, 194–195
   embodiment of wisdom by,
     201–202
   goals of, 286–287
   hiring questions for, 287

judgment based on core beliefs by, 218–249
keeping your company's offer fresh for, 285–286
open mindset for, 250–253
and other Green personality profiles, 144–145
self-determination and self-governance for, 196–218
transferable practices for, 253–285
Serious (selling maturity) stage:
advancing to, 188–189
advantageous stage vs., 202–207
other Green stages and, 146
Service-level agreements (SLAs), 233–234
Serving others, xiii, 217, 297
Shame, 187
Shaw, George Bernard, 308
Six Global Interview Questions, xliii, 7, 28–32, 278–281
Skepticism, of preparers, 18
SLAs (service-level agreements), 233–234
Sleep, in on-process selling, 238
Slumps, experiencing, 284–285
Smith, Will, 311
Snake oil salesmen, 250
Soloist personality, people with, 49–54
about, 49–53
case example, 51
goals of, 53–54
hiring questions for, 54
"Something is better than nothing" philosophy, 174–175, 203–204
Sparknotes.com, xxxvii
Stability, xxix
Stallone, Sylvester, 311
Stanford University, 237n*
Stereotyping, core-beliefs about, 222

Stewart, Potter, 95
Storytelling, core-beliefs about, 237
Subconscious thinking, 122
Success:
defining sales, 131–132
for demonstrative salespeople, 160–167
desire for, 216
foundational pillars of life and, 276
selling process as metric for, 11
Sweat-equity, 310
Sympathy selling, 294

Taking advantage of prospects, 230
Talent, wasting, xxviii
Teresa, Mother, 306
Terms, contract, in one-call sales, 256–257
Think and Grow Rich (Hill), 305, 315
Three-prices concept, 245–247
Tie-downs, 234
Time commitment, interview questions about, 28–29
Timeliness, core-beliefs about, 223
Timing, of sales presentations, 239–240
Tone, of sales presentations, 199
Toyota Production System, xxiii
Tracking metrics, core-beliefs about, 235
Training:
to achieve Green Stages, 282
avoiding free-fall with, 281–282
challenges to, 277–278
cost of, xv
for demonstrative salespeople, 156–157
field, 283
for new hires, 281
with ride alongs, 283–284
with video interviews, 284–285

Traits:
   of activists, 109, 110
   of advantageous salespeople, 169
   of demonstrative salespeople, 149
   of idealists, 133
   of instinctive salespeople, 96, 97
   natural, 225
   of persistent salespeople, 302
   of preparers, 8, 9
   of "professional" salespeople, 55, 56
   on respectful salespeople, 83
   on sensitive salespeople, 22, 23
   of serious salespeople, 192
   of soloists, 49, 50
   of willful salespeople, 65, 66
Transferable practices, 195, 253–285
   appealing to logical and emotional senses, 253–254
   applying four levels of development, 264–276
   delivering effective sales presentations, 254–258
   making key decisions on hiring and growth, 276–285
   using/interpreting key indicator reports, 258–264
Transparency, xiii
Trial closes, 234
Trustworthiness, 166, 211–212

Unconscious competent level of development, 275–277
Unconscious incompetent level of development, 265–266, 277

Value:
   commitment to, 256
   interpreting, 6
   price vs., 183, 246–247, 297–298
   for virtuous influencers, 297–298

Verbal messaging, 163–164
Vetting, of hires, xxviii–xxix
Video interviews, 278–281, 284–285
Virtue(s):
   of activists, 109
   of advantageous salespeople, 169
   of demonstrative salespeople, 149
   Green personalities working in, 142–143
   of idealists, 133
   of instinctive salespeople, 96
   in Lead Personality Profile, xxxviii
   with "not for one-call selling" classification, 4
   of preparers, 8
   of "professional" salespeople, 55
   of respectful salespeople, 83–84
   of sensitive salespeople, 22
   of serious salespeople, 191, 192
   of soloists, 49
   of willful salespeople, 65
   working in, 211–212
Virtue signaling, 113
Virtuous influencers, 184, 296–300
Virtuous persistence, 302–303, 306, 318
Virtuous salespeople, xliii
Virtuous selling, 143
Vision, action and, 317
Volume of dollars, tracking, 261

Watson, Tom, Sr., 24
What's in it for me (WIIFM), 234
Willful personality, people with, 65–82
   about, 65–71
   associates and influencers of, 74–75
   case example, 68
   fear, laziness, or egotism for, 71
   getting out of your own for, 75–77
   goals of, 81–82

hiring questions for, 82
hubris and confidence of, 77–79
immaturity of, 71
as junior persistent people, 73–74
openness to belief for, 79–80
openness to growth for, 80–81
persistent personality vs., 72–73
Willfulness, 80–81
Winfrey, Oprah, 313
Word, keeping your, 226
Work ethic, 58, 108
Work history, questions about, 29
Working for others, 13–18
Worldview, personality and, xxvi
Wright Brothers, 311

Yacktivists, 111–113
Yale University, xxiii
Yellow personalities, xx, 63–138
　about, 63–64
　activist, 109–117
　goals for, 60
　idealist, 133–138
　instinctive, 96–102
　novice candidates, 118–132
　"potential" candidates, 103–108
　respectful, 83–95
　willful, 65–82
Your Remodeling Guys, LLC, 93

Ziglar, Zig, xxxiii, 61, 223

About the Author

Bill Wilson is a true believer in following process. He has built his sales force and in turn his business on this belief. His passion for sharing his knowledge to benefit others has led him to become an author, inspired speaker, and coach with a wealth of business experience. Bill started his first business, a home remodeling company, in the 1980s. That business continues to thrive today due to Bill's ongoing dedication and commitment. In recent years, Bill developed a program called LEAD. This now-proven system will not only advance individuals in a selling career, but also teaches companies how to hire more effectively, train, develop, and grow their businesses. With LEAD, sales organizations have less turnover as well as a supportive workplace culture. His passion for growth has culminated into this real game-changer for selling.

Bill is also involved in the music industry. Besides his innovative work in sales, he is currently the lead vocalist for a rock band called Last Licks. You can look them up on Youtube.com. Bill presently resides in Old Saybrook, Connecticut with his wife, Jane.